Reflections in Silence

Pages from my Notebook

PRASANNA SWAROOPA

INDIA · SINGAPORE · MALAYSIA

ISBN
Paperback 979-8-89632-814-8
Hardcase 979-8-89699-532-6

Dedicated to

those who wish to

explore the realms of spirituality and life

by delving deep into their own minds,

to discover what lies beyond

mere words, concepts, and ideas,

and who are ready to challenge themselves

to carve a path that is truly their own.

———•◆•———

Acknowledgements

I hold a deep sense of appreciation for our nation's great culture, which has shaped the thoughts and lives of its people for thousands of years and will continue to do so for eternity, through the richness of its knowledge tradition.

Our culture affirms that there are numerous paths to the Truth and offers the freedom to follow one's "inner voice," allowing each person to carve out their own path on the journey to peace and contentment.

I am extremely grateful to belong to such a culture where, at its core, lies a spirit of investigation and enquiry that encourages seekers to ask questions freely in their quest for the Truth.

My deepest gratitude goes to my guru, Swami Bhoomananda Tirtha, who initiated me into this pursuit of knowledge and inducted me into the Advaita Vedanta tradition.

I wish to express my salutations and gratitude to Adi Shankaracharya, who has greatly enriched us with his compositions and commentaries on the three canonical texts of Vedanta, and for showing us the way to delve deeper into the scriptures.

I extend my gratitude to my sister, Mala Sridhar, without whose invaluable comments and observations, as well as her painstaking efforts to meticulously review and proofread the contents, this book would not have been possible.

Prasanna Swaroopa

Introduction

Beginning of a New Journey

In early 2002, I ended my career in the IT industry, having been engaged in a variety of roles and responsibilities. At that time, I had no plans and no idea how life would pan out in the coming years, nor was I very keen on knowing. There was only one thought—to open myself to the discovery of a life beyond mere employment, projects, revenues, deadlines, etc.

Somehow, a few unplanned sequences of events led me to the portals of an Ashram in Kerala. I had never imagined that I would one day embark on this journey of self-exploration.

Thus began a new phase: an opportunity to experience life in an Ashram and a journey of self-discovery. This stage enabled me to explore a very important aspect of our culture—the knowledge tradition. I was formally initiated into the Advaita Vedanta tradition and became a disciple of Swami Bhoomananda Tirtha.

At the end of 2014, after spending twelve years in the Ashram, the inner voice that brought me here also prompted my departure from there.

A Few Years in Solitude

Then, began nearly six years of living in solitude. It was the beginning of a journey entirely in the mind, delving into the spiritual pursuit. I had a deluge of questions that arose in the mind regarding the path I had been following. I began to examine all theories, concepts, terms, and approaches I had been exposed to earlier from a fresh perspective.

I challenged every idea, concept, and practice that I was exposed to—not to argue, move away from, or discard them but to understand what they meant to me. This process was a deeply revealing one.

The journey within continued to fascinate me. My explorations in the world of scriptures and within my own inner world continued in parallel.

The few scriptures I read gave me new insights. I was convinced that I had to adapt everything to my own requirements, as my journey was my own, given my personality and characteristics.

The following questions were my triggers: What do these scriptures and their messages mean to me? How do they help me attain contentment? What is their relevance to my journey? Slowly, my reading began to wane and eventually became non-existent.

I Began Making Notes

At some point in my life's journey, I started writing down some of my thoughts and experiences. These were largely born of or related to the various ideas I was exposed to. They were my understanding of the topics, or my questions and attempts to answer them.

I began capturing my thoughts on various topics relating to the spiritual journey, scriptures, the pursuit of knowledge, life in this world, practices, "spiritual" institutions, myths, and so on.

At this time, there was little inclination to share my thoughts or experiences with others. The notes I made were addressed to myself, my own mind. I questioned myself through them and attempted to write down answers that provided me insights.

Any sharing, whether in the form of discussions, a blog, or a book, came much later. I had never harboured an aspiration to write a book, but it happened later, naturally.

The notes I made over the last decade are the ones I now share in the form of this book. These notes are certainly not intended as instructions for anyone. When I originally wrote them, they were meant solely for myself.

Now, as I put it all together, I do hope that these thoughts of mine might help others pursue their own introspection in their spiritual journey.

Notes to the Reader

This book is a collection of notes that capture my thoughts and experiences at different points in time. These thoughts arose in response to situations I encountered, questions I asked, or challenges I faced in my spiritual pursuit and journey of life. Although I may have used "you," "we," or "I" in expressing my thoughts, they are addressed to my own mind.

In my notes, I have tried to capture the thoughts as they were, along with the reflections that followed, and I have not tried to fine-tune them except to work on the language in some places. In many cases, these thoughts became seeds for further questions and answers.

Some entries may seem similar, addressing the same subject. I have retained them as they are, as they emerged at different points in time and often offer a distinct perspective, even if they seem similar.

I do not claim to have addressed the questions I raised with thorough reasoning and logic, as they were not meant to convince anyone else. They came as answers for me to reflect on and then move forward.

Through the notes in this book, I am not trying to change your position or viewpoints. You may not agree with many points, for you will have your own questions and your own answers. Remember, there is no one answer to any question; it depends on who is asking, under what circumstances, and toward what end.

This book is not intended as instructions or lessons aimed at educating or guiding anyone. I am just a fellow traveller. I shall be more than happy even if a few readers feel that this "notebook" has provided them insights into their own spiritual journey.

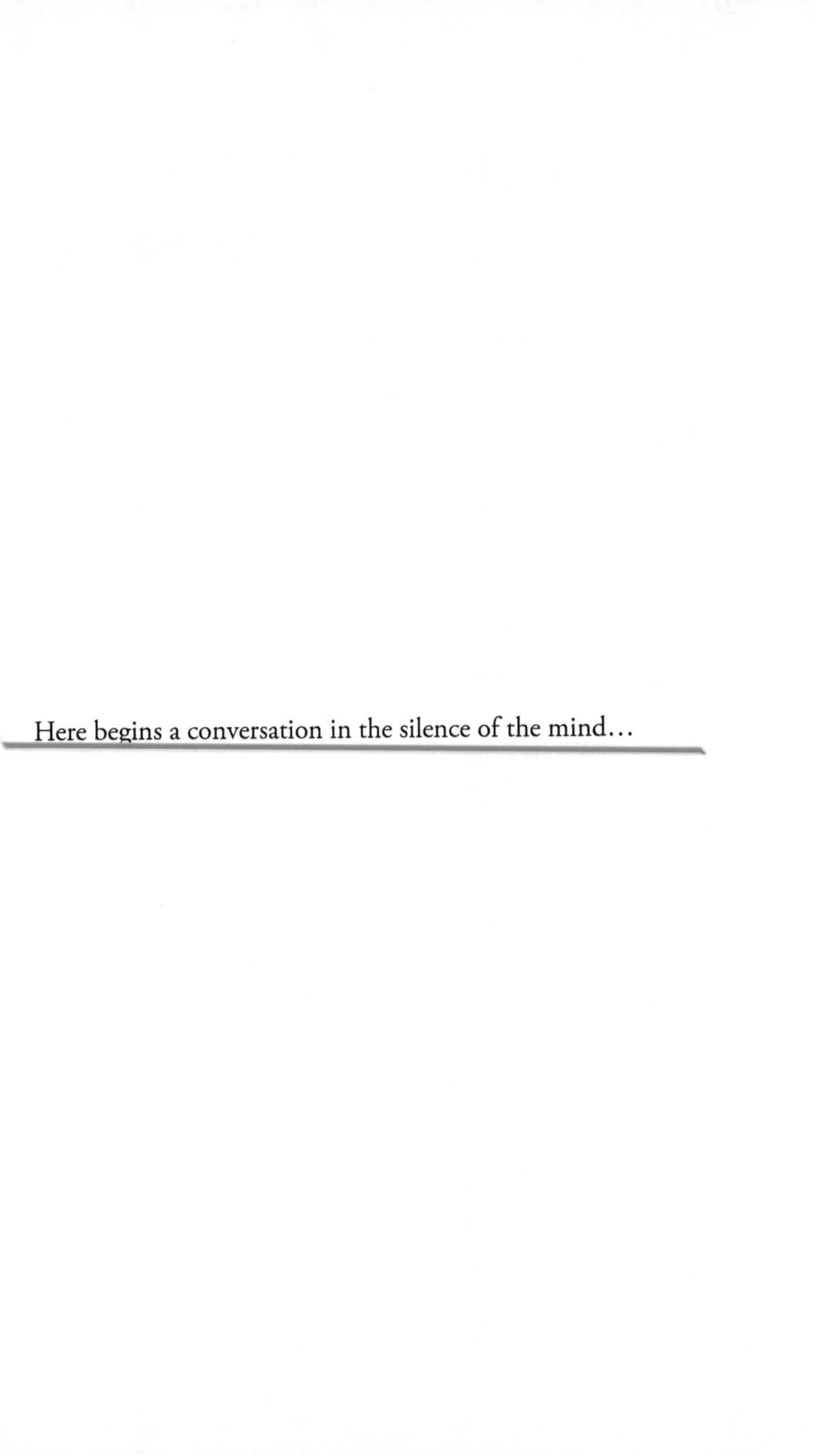

Here begins a conversation in the silence of the mind…

Do Not Seek Praise from this World

Any action you perform is merely the result of the movement of your hands and feet. Can your deeds be reduced to such a gross physical level? All creatures act at that gross level, governed by the laws of Nature. If any one entity should be recognized, it is Nature that deserves applause. Express your gratitude to Nature for it.

You claim it is your mind and intelligence, your inner faculties, that did it. But how can you take ownership of those? Think carefully. Did the ideas that surfaced in your mind truly originate from "you"? What action did you perform to create those specific ideas?

Remember, the things you call 'your ideas' simply appeared in your inner horizon without any involvement from you. You were merely a witness, like an observer of the sunrise. You happened to catch that idea, which arose from the infinite Creative Source within. And you took ownership of that. Just like that.

That Creative Source is the universal creative fountainhead of the entire cosmos. When you free yourself from your individual limitations, you allow the Creative Source to manifest freely through you. Just because a creative idea came through you, do not claim ownership of it. It belongs to the infinite Cosmic Source.

How then, O mind, can you take credit for that idea? It does not belong to you. You may rejoice in being a worthy receptacle of the creative expression. Rejoice in being the *veena* string plucked by the hands of the Creator.

Also do not desire to be the creator of the sound generated by the *veena*, for that sound too belongs to the Creator.

If you are not the creator of what happened, where is the question of seeking praise from the world for what is truly the cosmic doing?

Pity those who applaud the string and forget the Creator's hand in it. Criticism and praise of the string are meaningless, for the only thing of importance is the "cosmic" sound.

You may claim greatness as a string, but do not forget that there is also a bamboo shoot, the leaves of a tree, and the waters of a flowing stream—all instruments of the cosmos through which "music" is generated.

Submit yourself to become a true instrument in the hands of the Creator—nothing less, nothing more. Free yourself of all limitations and constrictions, and the Creative Source will shine through you, like the sun in a cloudless sky.

There is but one purpose in this cosmic wonder of nature: to free oneself of all limitations. Do not be the cloud that hides the sun. Allow the Cosmic Creator to shine unimpeded through you, and express through you. Your purpose lies in simply "being."

No effort is required; no transformation is needed. Your true nature cannot change, so what is the point of attempting to change? What can you change? Simply be, and allow the Creator to shine through you.

By expecting praise and applause from this world, we insult the Creator and Its creation. What can anyone criticize or praise? It is all from the same Creative Source. Pity those who seek things to applaud or criticize, for they miss the Creative Source in everything!

In getting distracted by seeking adulation and praise, you are missing who you truly are. Whether you see yourself as a fragment of that Creative Source or as the Creative Source itself, how can the world, which is the result of the same Creative Source within you, praise or criticise your outward words or actions?

———— •◆• ————

Do we Ever Reflect Deeply About the Idea of Prayer?

From a young age, most of us are exposed to the idea of prayer. Let us delve a little into prayer—not the concept itself, but what we pray for.

Let us take one of the earliest instances where we learn to pray with fervour before the announcement of examination results. This type of prayer intensifies just before results are announced. Yet, if we think about it, whatever was necessary for the outcome (in this case, the exam results), we have already done. So, what is the point of praying now? We rarely stop to reflect on this.

The same question can be asked in many other contexts. We can ask the question regarding anything we pray for in the physical world.

Most of our prayers relate to the material world, and this warrants serious introspection.

Some might argue, "But the Lord is the doer of everything; everything is enabled by the Lord. What is the harm or wrong in praying to the Lord? Isn't humility the focus of prayer?"

But are we truly conscious of that thought—of the Lord being the enabler of all—whenever we pray? If we were deeply clear that the Lord is everything and we have completely surrendered to that Lord, there would be no need to pray. Let us think about it.

A truly devoted mind need not pray because, having surrendered, we no longer feel the need to pray for any gain. Like a child who knows that the mother takes care of everything, we trust that the Lord knows what we need.

If we truly believe that the Lord is the doer of everything (or the enabler), then we will not be disappointed with any outcome. We will accept whatever the Lord bestows upon us, and consequently, there will be no sorrow.

Another important point is that it is almost nonsensical to pray for things in the phenomenal world.

Why? Suppose A and B pray for the same thing. How can both prayers be fulfilled? That is a key point (assuming that A and B pray with the same intensity).

Another issue is that when we pray for anything in the object-world (the world of phenomena), succeeding in our prayer would alter the course of nature, which cannot be allowed, as it would upset the equilibrium of the universe.

So, any kind of prayer related to the physical world is absurd. Everything in the object world clearly follows the principle of cause and effect—in other words, effort and the appropriate result.

Does that mean prayer is meaningless? Not at all.

What is the purpose of prayer? What does prayer achieve? What is its focus?

Prayer addresses the mind. It expands the mind, bringing it closer to its potential. When we are unselfish, prayer expands our heart. When we pray for others, it opens our hearts to compassion, kindness, and love. We can pray for developing subtler qualities of the mind, such as acceptance, poise, resilience, forbearance, and more.

When we focus our prayer (and attention) inwards, we can move towards going beyond the limitations of the mind, to strive towards "human perfection"—liberation, freedom.

When we focus our prayer in the inner core (the Self), to expand the mind to transcend its limitations, we call it meditation.

We pray for the mind, by the mind, in the mind, and through the mind. In the case of meditation, we wish to transcend the mind.

—— • ◆ • ——

What is the Human Core, Essence?

What is the core of the human being? We often think of humans as distinct from animals, defining ourselves as two-legged creatures. But are we just that—not four-legged? Is that the only identity we have?

Some might say, "No, we are different because we have 'consciousness.'" But we can never be entirely certain about that 'space' or 'dimension.'

Let us approach this question—what it means to be human—from a different perspective.

What truly makes us human is not our physiology, but what makes human interactions possible.

And what is that? Take two humans from opposite corners of the world, of any gender. When they come together—regardless of nationality, race, religion, gender, colour, or language—they connect. They do not even need to speak the same language.

Love does not need a language. It does not care who the other person is. Compassion does not need a language. It is not dependent on knowing the other's nationality. Similarly, hate, jealousy, and dislike do not need a language either. We simply feel them.

On one hand, we have our biological DNA. On the other— the side we interact with—is our values-DNA. It is the unique combination, in varying proportions, of love, peace, empathy, compassion, honesty, greed, hate, bias, and other values that makes each human unique—not our physical characteristics. And this combination keeps evolving.

This is what makes us human. And the foundation of all these values is the same. In that sense, we all share a common substratum—a cosmic substratum. This is why we are able to relate to, understand, love, and even hate each other.

This is the essence of a universal substratum or universal consciousness.

When we understand that this is what makes us human, how can we differentiate or discriminate based on religion, caste, nationality, gender, race, skin colour, or language?

Our needs are the same.

Our pains are the same.

Our sufferings are the same.

Our joys are the same.

Recognize the humanness in all.

Reflect on what truly makes us human.

Lessons for Life from the Cosmos

The Unfathomable Size of the Universe: Carl Sagan once remarked that the Earth, from a distance of six billion kilometres, appears as a "pale blue dot." The Earth's size, in the vastness of the universe, is insignificantly small. Now, reflect on our own physical presence in this infinite expanse, or our lifetime in the context of cosmic time.

Let this thought of the infinite expanse of the universe humble me, removing any ego about my own existence. Let me enquire into my own nature, which is capable of exploring the infinitude of the cosmos. What grandeur and depth must lie in the very self that investigates both the vast universe and its own inner being?

Common Ancestry: The universe is around 13.8 billion years old. The theory of evolution explains how various animal and plant species evolved, eventually leading to humans in our current form. While the evolutionary history of primates dates back 65 million years, Homo sapiens emerged around 300,000 years ago.

Let this thought that all beings on this planet share a common ancestry, elevate and enlighten me so that I may see the common origin and foundation of us all! Owing to the common source, let me awaken to the interconnectedness of all beings.

Sameness at the elemental level: Approximately 99% of our body is made up of six elements: oxygen, carbon, hydrogen, nitrogen, calcium, and phosphorus. If we examine the universe as a whole, the four major elements are hydrogen, helium, oxygen and carbon. Our body is made up of the same fundamental elements as the entire universe.

Although the inference is at the gross level, let this thought regarding the sameness of everything in this universe make me realize the sameness and equality of all beings on this planet! Let it also prompt me to explore the subtle oneness of consciousness that binds us all.

Sameness at the DNA level: All humans are 99.9% identical on a genetic level. Our closest living relatives, chimpanzees, share nearly 99% of our DNA.

Let this thought regarding the sameness of all beings help me treat all humans alike, and not discriminate on any basis.

Timeless dimension: In the context of the universe's lifespan, the idea of a decade or even a century is rather insignificant. The unit of length of time used with regard to events of the past and those that will unfold in the future are of the order of millions or billions of years. For example, the galactic collision between the Andromeda galaxy and the Milky Way galaxy (the one that includes our solar system) is expected to occur in about 4.5 billion years.

The timescales involved in all the events in the context of the universe are almost unimaginable. But, for all our actions, we expect the outcome 'in an instant', and that too always in our favour. Let this thought regarding the enormous timescales involved inspire me to be more understanding and patient regarding everything in life.

Infinite distances and the cosmic harmony: When we talk of the astronomical distances between stars, moons, planets and so on, we use the term light-year (the distance that light travels in a vacuum in one year). The sun is at a distance of about 150 million kilometres away from Earth. It is so far away that light from the sun takes about 8 minutes to reach us. Even though separated by astronomical distances, the sun, moon and this Earth we live on—being in complete harmony with each other, have facilitated life on this planet.

Let this thought of astronomical distances regarding space and the amazing contribution of the heavenly bodies in sustaining this entire universe and our own Earth, inspire me to get rid of the false pride I develop regarding my own possessions, performances, and positions. Let the thought of cosmic harmony amongst the heavenly bodies, inspire me to strive towards protecting and preserving the environment, and also inspire me to strive for peace and harmony with all fellow humans.

Birth and death: This universe was born about 13.8 billion years ago and the Earth itself was born about 4.54 billion years ago. At different points in time in the course of evolution of the Earth, many species were born and many species have also become extinct. More than 99% of all species that ever lived on Earth, are believed to have become extinct. Scientists believe that in about

7.5 billion years, our Earth will be absorbed by the Sun and all life on Earth will be extinct. Earth was born and will perish one day.

Let these thoughts about birth and death of the Earth, enlighten me about my own birth and death. Let the understanding of the impermanence of the Earth itself, wake me to the transience of everything around me.

Cause-and-effect chain: Many million years ago, volcanic activity unleashed a series of events leading to what is termed as the Permian-Triassic extinction event, killing about 90% of the species on the Earth. Later, over many more millions of years, major geological events shaped the landmasses of the world to its present form (the way we see the topological features of the Earth today). At some later point in time, the impact of an asteroid initiated and caused a major extinction, leaving small mammals as the dominant species on Earth. During the early lifetime of our Earth, certain very devastating events had taken place. These deadly events, over innumerable years, gave rise to suitable conditions for the human species to evolve and survive.

While so far, we were referring to things on a 'universe' scale, the same is true at the microcosmic level. Let me develop the right understanding towards all my actions and their outcome! Let me also recognize that I do not have the wherewithal to comprehend the cause-and-effect chain of events unleashed by my actions.

———•——•——

Are You Really Bound?
Why are You Seeking Freedom?

The path of spirituality is one that leads the seeker towards liberation, freedom. We are told (by scriptures and exponents of spiritual knowledge) "you have to be free", "you have to attain liberation", "this world is an ocean of misery", and so on.

Have we given these words any serious thought? Probably, we have simply accepted them. And now, we say, think and believe "I have to be free".

Let us reflect on this deeply. Freedom is required only for those who "are" bound. It is essential for those who "are" bound.

Consider a bird in a cage. It knows it is bound inside a cage and wants to be free from that cage. Within the cage, it is unable to fly, and flying is its essential nature. The bird thinks, "I should be free and be able to fly".

Imagine you are standing in the middle of a vast open, beautiful paddy field. Someone approaches and tells you that "you must be released from this cage where you are standing, where you are in chains." What will be your response? It is worth pondering over.

If we do not feel the sense of bondage, how can someone thrust upon us the idea that we must be liberated, freed?

But what is happening?

Scriptures (and the commentators) tell us that we must be freed, and we begin to believe that we have to be freed, even though we have not experienced bondage.

For a spiritual seeker it is important to understand what that bondage is. It is not enough to say "I am in bondage". We have to recognize what we are bound to. Only then can we be free from the bondage. We have to know who is it that is bound, and to what, in order to be free.

Just because someone told us "You must be free", we believe it, and make that our goal. We then have a new problem here.

Without understanding what bondage is and without knowing what we are bound to, have we not bound ourselves by the mere "idea" of wanting to be free, without 'really' being bound?

In the same manner, when we hear a statement like "the world is an ocean of misery", let us reflect deeply regarding the same. What is our experience?

Can there be a more dangerous set of chains than that? We are now trying to be free from the fetters that are not there. From that, we will never be free, for they do not exist.

Can we imagine this strange situation?

The path to freedom is for those who experience the bondage and feel bound. Where is the question of liberation or freedom for one who is not bound?

The important point is: when you engage with the idea of freedom, think carefully about what is bondage, and what is binding you.

Think! Are you really bound?

———•—

How can I Claim Ownership of a Thought, Idea?

Where from do thoughts arise? What triggers thoughts? What is the process of springing of thoughts? Do thoughts come from nothing? These and such other questions come to mind in the context of the notion of 'thought'.

This is not a scientific analysis. Let us just explore the subject from the point of view of our own experience.

There is no doubt regarding the fact that thoughts just *spring up* in the mind.

Of course, there are some thoughts which are a result of inference. These thoughts come up based on the data points in the brain (memory). Some thoughts arise which are a result of the processing by the cognitive function of the brain.

Let us examine another scenario. There are occasions when there arises a thought which is not a logical or reason-oriented follow-up of some information already present in the brain. It may be an astounding discovery, or an idea which is novel or an idea for a poem—which has no precedence in the mind-intelligence complex.

Where did that thought come from? How did it happen? How do I explain that thought?

I did not initiate that thought. Here is an important question. Can I claim that to be 'my thought'? How can I claim ownership of such a thought, which was not in my deliberate control? I had not initiated that thought. I did not create it.

When I tried to go back and explore the birth of that thought or the occurrence of that thought in my mind-intelligence horizon, I cannot find any reason to claim credit for that thought.

Some thought that is of "interest" to me, I now label as "idea".

I happened to be there when that thought (or idea) came. I was certainly a witness who has collected that thought when it appeared.

There are occasions when I do not 'gather' the thoughts that appear in my head, but noticed that it appeared, and before I could hold on to it, that thought disappeared.

Now I am turning my attention to 'any' thought (not just the so-called 'brilliant' thought). On closer examination, it appears that I have no control over the thoughts that arise. The thoughts just arise. Good ones, bad ones, noble ones, hateful ones— whatever kind they may be—they JUST ARISE in the mind horizon.

So, can I claim ownership of the thought? Can I claim that "that is my idea"? Can I become possessive of an idea and become attached to it?

I just happened to have had a thought that 'sounds' like a good idea. That is all. To claim copyright or patent on any idea seems a very amusing thought now!

———•◆•———

Enquire with Simple Questions

The subject of spirituality seems very complicated, with too many concepts, complex terms, ideas, frameworks, etc. Whether it is so or it has been made into one, is a question for another day. Since the Truth is indescribable, many tried to approach it in different ways and that gave rise to numerous theories, techniques, terms, vocabulary, etc.

Think about it. What is the one thing we all want in life? Everybody wishes to be happy—happy throughout life.

For that, mere concepts, ideas, etc. do not help. Because we end up being caught in figuring out those concepts, rather than addressing the key question(s) we have.

For example, there are many of us who end up spending years in understanding what 'Consciousness' or 'Self' is. Why? How does it answer our basic question of life.

What then is the solution?

Let us ask simple question(s). And lead with simple and straightforward answers.

For example, "What do I want in life? Happiness. Why? What does that word mean to me?" And so on.

Remember, to seek directions to get to a particular place (whether we use a map or not), we need to know where we are and where we want to go.

Let us allow our heart to present simple, sincere, straightforward questions and equally simple, sincere, straightforward answers. Let then the answer lead us on.

This way we define our spiritual path. In reality, we define **our own** path.

Important point to note is that the questions and answers should not include terms that are not in our simple vocabulary.

For example, "this world is an illusion" does not serve as a good answer, because it requires deeper understanding of 'the world' and also the term 'illusion'.

Another key principle in this exercise—'we shouldn't have to open a book or ask someone else for a clarification for a question or answer.' We may seek guidance, but the question and answer must be ours!

—— • ◆ • ——

The Art of Balanced Distance for Remaining Detached

Attachment and detachment have come to mean so many things that they have almost lost their true essence. These terms have become so well-defined, so sharply framed, that we rarely stop to reconsider what they really mean. It is time to re-examine.

Imagine standing just five centimetres away from a beautiful painting. Or consider walking along the slope of a hill, so close that you lose sight of its larger beauty. Or perhaps, you use a telescope to see the moon up close. Do you still see it as beautiful? Suppose you get to know a person's mind very intimately. When you step that close, does your love for them deepen or fade?

When we get too close to anything—an object, an idea, or a person—our experience changes. We stop seeing, hearing, or feeling things as we once did. For real appreciation, there must be an optimal distance between us (the observer), and what we are observing. Yet, distance is a delicate thing. Step back too far, and you risk missing the experience altogether. The challenge, then, is to find the right balance.

Attachment is when we move too close, unable to fully appreciate the beauty or essence of what we behold. Detachment, on the other hand, comes with finding the right distance, the space that allows us to observe, appreciate, and witness without losing ourselves.

The art of balanced distance lies in this careful calibration. In reality, that balanced distance from things of the world is what is "detachment".

———•———

If you are Looking for a Pill for Instant Relief Here, you may be Disappointed

Think of a typical visit to a doctor. This is how most interactions go:

We explain our ailment by describing the symptoms. The doctor has some questions, for which we provide the answers. Based on the inputs we provide, the doctor gives us the best possible advice.

Most often, we are keen to get to the point where the doctor says, "take these medicines; all will be well". We want the doctor to quickly write the prescription for the pills.

Apart from the medicines prescribed, the doctor has various other things to say. These include the following: why this may have happened; what things we should avoid; what changes we need to bring about to our routine; changes to food habits; how to prevent this situation in future; the root cause of such problems, and so on.

Do we really hear all that? Even if we hear all that, all our attention is on the pills prescribed.

Finally, we are very relieved when the doctor writes down the medicines we have to take. If some pills were not prescribed, it makes us very uncomfortable.

The "pill to pop" makes our job easier. We do not want to spend time even thinking of making changes to what we do and how we do them, or thinking about fundamental changes to life. They call for too much effort and also sometimes making changes to things we believe in.

Remember, in many cases, the pills never cure the actual problem, until and unless we adhere to all those guidelines that are to be followed.

That, was a typical scenario regarding a visit to the doctor for a bodily ailment.

Let us move to the context of the mind, and more specifically, the spiritual quest. In this case too, let us ask ourselves the question: "are we just looking for a pill?"

The situation here, in the context of the mind, is far more complex than the body. We have to be ready to put all the effort in trying to understand the mind, and also make fundamental changes to how we look at life, living and the world around us.

There is no "magic pill".

———•◆•———

I Need to Find My OWN Answers to MY Life Questions

As a human, I have had numerous questions regarding life. These questions have come up throughout my life, each depending on my state of mind at the time. Some of these questions seemed very simple and straightforward, while others were very complex or profound.

But they were all real questions.

Here are some of the kinds of questions I encountered: Why am I suffering? Why am I not happy all the time? Why was I born? Is there a God? Has anyone seen God?

The questions never ceased. The most important question of all then emerged: How do I find answers to all these questions?

Some suggested, "seek someone's guidance," "read a book," "examine the scriptures," etc.

Yes, it was a good start. But that was someone else's "answer"!

In the case of objective questions, this might have sufficed. But when it came to deeper questions like the ones above, someone else's answer did not become my answer immediately.

It might have provided an answer or comfort for that moment.

It would not become my answer unless it became an integral part of my personality, mindset, worldview, etc.

This was because all the questions I have are inter-related. Also, I already had my own explanations (whether right or wrong) regarding various things in life.

I found that answers obtained from an external source to my questions could challenge my notions/ideas in another sphere, and dislodge my understanding in another sphere.

For example, I once asked someone—"Such and such a thing has happened. I feel miserable. Why am I suffering like this? Why me? What can I do to be free from suffering?"

And I got an answer—"It is because of your karma. There is nothing you can do."

I felt I had found an answer. But, since I did not have complete faith in the theory of karma, very soon I found the suffering haunting me again.

In attempting to find an answer, I had created a new conflict in my mind. Now the suffering had become even more complex and intense. I continued to ask (a person or a book) and accepted the answers. What resulted was conflicts and more conflicts.

I realized there is only one way out.

The answer had to come from within me.

Or, if it came from someone else (or some book), it had to be tested, integrated, and assimilated into my own web of concepts, notions, ideas, etc. That called for deep reflection. Finally, whatever answer I received from the world had to become my own.

I found an easier way out! I learned to find my own answers.

———•—◆—•———

The Path is Presented to us as if it is Cast in Stone

When we begin our spiritual quest and explore the scriptures and their commentaries, the following appears to be the typical points that emerge first:

- This life is an ocean of strife and suffering that we have to cross

- The human being is ignorant, deluded and cannot cross this ocean without help

- We will have to struggle for many lives

- It is highly likely that we will not succeed in reaching our spiritual goal in this life

- We have to become free from the cycle of births and deaths

These ideas are constantly drilled into us. We are not told of the basis of these.

The interesting point is: In the beginning, we are free from all these ideas. We only know of happiness and sorrow, and we want to be free from sorrow.

But we are told that the real picture is more complex. These ideas are now etched in our minds.

The real battle now begins. Apart from dealing with the trials and tribulations in life, we are also now dealing with the complexities of the "supposed" solution.

To unravel these mysteries and find answers, we are introduced to many new terms, with which our intelligence has to come to terms with. This is the major part of the journey and perhaps in most cases, the longest one.

Why? Why should this be the case? Why are we so engrossed with this belief system? Why have we come to believe this to be the path and this to be the universal truth?

We are now trapped in these webs of ideas we have been introduced to. Freeing ourselves from this is the first step to freedom!

———•◆•———

Hearing and Witnessing Nature

During a visit to Advaita Ashrama (a centre of the Ramakrishna Math) in Mayavati (in the state of Uttarakhand), I ventured on a rather long walk through the neighbouring dense pathways.

All around me was greenery, and as if adding to the beauty, it was a hilly terrain with the majestic Himalayan range in the distance. I watched the lush green canvas of Mother Nature against the backdrop of dark, rain-bearing clouds. There were trees of different varieties, in varying shades of green. Occasionally, in the distance, breaking through the silence, I would hear monkeys moving from one tree to another. The entire scene (including the sights and sounds) was breathtaking.

I was lost in the magnanimity and grandeur of Nature.

There were no other thoughts in my mind;

No questions or doubts;

No comments;

No judgments;

No sorrow;

No joy;

No analysis of what I was witnessing;

No attempt to identify the trees;

No attempt to gauge the size of the trees;

No desire to say I should come again.

It was complete stillness.

It was—as I reflected later—just a beautiful moment of stillness, unadulterated and completely free from any qualifying thoughts.

It was a moment when I had completely surrendered to the beauty of Nature. There was none superior; there was none inferior; there was nothing beautiful; there was nothing ugly. It was just a sight!

Words, however eloquent, would not be able to convey the experience or even comprehend the fullness of the sight.

I was just listening to nature without offering my own interpretation, judgments, etc.

An 'analysis-judgment-comment-free' moment!

Timeless

What is the idea of time? Somehow our existence is quite inextricably tied to the idea of time. In an existential sense, our very being is defined in terms of time. The moment we say, "I was born, I am living and I will die," the idea of time has crept in.

This is most basic aspect of time. The moment we define time like this, rather, when we define our life in terms of birth, life, and death, we are bringing in the notion of time.

Now when we look at our life, we find that we bring in another notion of time—past, present, and future. Everything we do in life and even every thought is governed by notions of past, present and future.

This notion has imprisoned the human mind in a cage. A cage of past, present and future.

The notion of time as governed by a chronometer is the least impactful in the context of our life and living. Here the idea of a calendar is implied.

The two notions—i.e. one being the idea of 'birth-life-death' and the other being the idea of 'past-present-future'—are the ones that define the quality of life. The first one can be seen as a large cage and within that lies the second one and we are trapped inside the second one.

To be freed from these two is true freedom. Of course there are other chains that bind us. But these two are the cages.

How do we free ourselves from this cage?

When we are in the deep sleep state, time as a concept does not exist. After we come out of it (when awake), we get a feel of the duration. In the case of a dream also, time ceases. More accurately, the idea of time is not relevant. These give us an idea or a hint of what the timeless state is.

In our wakeful state too, we experience timeless moments. For example, reading a book, engaging in an activity we love, spending time with a dear one, etc.

Being free from time can be seen as freedom from the past and future, i.e. memories and expectations constantly haunting us.

The timeless state is the state of peace, poise, and a state where there is no loss of energy. A state of pure creativity.

This is Spiritual. This is Not Spiritual.

For a seeker striving to realize the "truth", what does the word 'spiritual' mean? Does the word mean anything at all?

To the true seeker, their entire life is dedicated to the goal of realizing the 'Truth' (however one defines it). The focus is on that Truth.

If that is the goal, then life revolves around thoughts, speech and action that lead one towards that goal. In this context, whatever one does—whether through action, speech, or thought—leads towards the spiritual goal.

In other words, every action, speech, or thought is 'spiritual'. How can it be otherwise?

If this is the case, what is the point in distinguishing between what is spiritual and what is not?

For a seeker, everything is spiritual.

Therefore, terms like 'spiritual', 'secular', and 'worldly' are meaningless.

Whatever we do in life, leads us to that goal. So why bother about the nature of our actions, and why should we label them 'spiritual' or 'worldly'.

By using such words, we negate the very meaning and context of life as a seeker of Truth. There is no thought, speech, or action that is not spiritual. How can it be otherwise?

The moment we label an action as 'secular', 'worldly', or 'not spiritual', that very instant we cease to be spiritual seekers and distance ourselves from the Truth of life.

Whatever we do—by way of thought, speech, and action—is naturally 'human' and therefore inherently 'spiritual'.

However, since using the term 'spiritual' implies the existence of something 'non-spiritual', it is best to drop that term completely. Let us just say 'HUMAN'.

As seekers, let us remove the words 'spiritual', 'worldly', 'secular', and 'non-spiritual' from our vocabulary!

———•▪•———

Begin With Simple Questions

In all the various quests for knowledge—be it science, spirituality, religion, or philosophy—it ultimately comes down to asking very simple questions. For example, some of the biggest discoveries in science arose from straightforward questions like 'Why does the apple fall?' or 'Is the Earth flat?'.

Similarly, in religion, we encounter questions such as 'Is there a God?' or 'Has anyone seen God?'. Why not begin our spiritual quest with our own simple questions?

For example, 'What do I want in life?' or 'What is happiness?' or "How can I be forever free from suffering?"

How Biased We Are!

Our response to any situation depends on the 'nature' of our association (attachment) with that situation or people or things involved in that situation.

Let us take a scenario to illustrate this: A marriage across community boundaries.

I am not suggesting that all of us react the same way to this situation. But there will be other situations in our life, in which we may have such or similar responses.

If it happens in a movie, we are very touched;

If it happens in another community, we are inspired by it;

If it happens in the neighbourhood, we gossip about it;

If it happens to someone at work, we appreciate it;

If it happens to someone who is just an acquaintance, we are indifferent to it;

If it happens among our close friends, we facilitate it;

If it happens to someone who seeks our advice, we guide it;

If it happens to someone in our social circle, we externally celebrate it;

If it happens to a distant relative, we support it;

If it happens in the family circle, we criticise it;

If it happens in our immediate family, we angrily condemn it;

If it happens to oneself, we intelligently rationalise it.

Same individual; same situation; different responses!

Why? Why do we act in this biased manner, even though, we claim to be rational, logical, and non-judgmental individuals?

Is this who we are?

The Consequence of Brooding

In that moment when thinking began,

An object called thought is born;

Rethink, you reinforce that thought,

And there is now an attachment taut;

Before you control that one wave,

The thought has got you for a slave;

Like in all else in this diverse world,

Behold the cyclic nature unfold;

"As we think, so we become", they say,

That single thought is fully at play;

What was a mere thought in the past,

Is more alive than the world so vast;

Where is the question of 'solitude' here,

Real now are desire, love and fear!

———————•—————

The Guru-principle Need Not be in Human Form Alone

When the enquiry into the subject of our real nature (i.e., "who am I") turns into an intense longing to know the truth, then nature manifests itself in some form to provide us the response to that enquiry. And that form is what we refer to as "guru".

In general, we expect and look for only those manifestations that are in the human form alone, and fail to see all else, and in the process lose the opportunity of finding answers to our enquiries through any other medium.

In its response to our enquiry, any animate being or even an inanimate matter could be the trigger that marks the dawn of the answer within us.

A bird, for instance, may provide the necessary guidance, and leave the scene. But we are just not open to that possibility. Because of the conditioning, we only look for a human being and that too fulfilling the various criteria that will suit our individual preferences. And to such a one we consider presenting our questions and doubts.

If we have a very deep longing for knowing the truth, it is no surprise that the guidance comes, and comes in some form from even the most unexpected quarters.

The form that provides us with the answer to our enquiry, is what we refer to as "guru". More accurately, the "guru-principle". In reality, what we call the guru-principle is nothing but a catalyst in the process of our enquiry after the truth. The answer finally comes from within; any object that fulfils the role of the guru-principle just catalyses the process of discovering the answer.

Consider the following analogy. We are looking for something in an ill-lit room. We use a torch, and the light from the torch reveals to us the objects that are there. There are two things to note here. One, the seeing is done by our eyes alone, and the torch just throws light. And two, the object that we sought is already there. The light from the torch does not produce the object we are looking for.

Similarly, in the case of Self-enquiry too, both the quest and finding the answer are done by us. The guru-principle plays the role of a catalyst, casting the necessary "light" on what we are seeking.

We are so conditioned by ideas of the "human guru" that we refuse to open ourselves to the answers from any other source. Also, what matters is the sincerity and yearning in the quest.

When does the manifestation of the guru-principle happen? When the conditions are right. What does that mean? When the atmospheric conditions reach a certain level, we have rainfall. Similarly, when our enquiry matures and the yearning deepens, the guru-principle manifests itself.

Since the answer finally appears in our mind, we may completely miss noticing the guru-principle, thinking "I found the answer".

Let us not forget that the answers to our questions will eventually come from within us. They may be guided or catalysed by the guru-principle, but the answers become real only when they arise within us.

In the text, Srimad Bhagavatam (Canto 11, Chapter 7), a mendicant reveals that he has the following twenty-four gurus—earth, air, sky, water, fire, sun, moon, dove, python, ocean, river, moth, honey-bee, elephant, honey-gatherer, deer, fish, courtesan, osprey, maiden, arrow-smith, snake, spider, and wasp.

For Those Who Feel
"I Can't Take Things on Faith"

This is with particular reference to what has been written in scriptures. Some say, "I cannot accept it just because the scriptures say it. I have a scientific bent of mind. I will accept something only if it is substantiated by reason."

In this context let me present something from the field of mathematics. It doesn't get any more "reason-oriented". It refers to a proposition (that is popularly referred to as Fermat's last theorem) that was first stated by the French mathematician Pierre de Fermat around 1637. He mentioned this in the margin of his notebook, without a proof. Since there was no proof for this, it began to be referred to as Fermat's conjecture. Subsequently, many generations of mathematicians tried to prove this proposition without any success. After about 350 years of effort, it was proved in 1994 by Andrew Wiles, a mathematician from England.

The mathematicians who came after Fermat, did not give up their effort just because they could not prove it. They continued to have faith in the words of Fermat. What was the reason they continued to strive even though so many before them failed to prove it?

Here are some key points for reflection:

- Whenever we receive any knowledge (from any source), the first response is to accept it on faith. Our entire education (in school and university) is based on this. In fact, our entire living is based on this.

- Scientific research is based on this very approach. Every researcher begins with a hypothesis or conjecture, and spends a lifetime exploring and examining it. In some cases, when no conclusion is reached, the next generation of researchers pursue it (as in the above case).

- So many things in science too were accepted to be true at a point in time. Subsequently, with new evidence the world changed its position. For example, Earth is flat; The number of chemical elements; etc.

- In life too, right from childhood, we are exposed to so many different forms of knowledge. Our first response is 'acceptance' (although in some cases, we accept it under protest). Subsequently, we may change our position. But initially, we accept it on faith.

Then why is it in some cases, we refuse to accept something on faith? It is worthwhile to examine whether our reluctance to accept is based on some prejudice.

I am certainly not suggesting that we should accept everything that comes to us blindly.

The knowledge pursuit of Vedanta involves the following three steps: listening (reading), introspection, meditation. Having heard (or read) about the truth (from the scriptures), the process of introspection helps us attain conviction in it, through reasoning. And meditation helps us realize that knowledge.

Without any doubt, our understanding and interpretation of the idea of faith must be reflected upon.

Seeking Answers in Life

We are often intrigued, puzzled, overwhelmed by questions regarding life. When we are faced with too many of these, we run here and there for answers.

We feel very satisfied, as we tell ourselves that we are asking very profound questions regarding life. We feel as if we have arrived at the haloed portals of 'spiritual arena'. We then start reading anything we come across on the subject of spirituality. Our discussions with friends revolve around meditation, mindfulness, being in the present, etc. We begin to call our vacations, 'retreats'.

What is this path that we call the 'spiritual pursuit'?

As I traverse this path, the following key aspects of this journey stand out:

- Inward Journey: The answers to questions we have regarding life lie within us. Not in outward acquisitions, activities, etc. The questions begin inside, and the solutions and their manifestations are within.

- Simple questions: Its basis lies in asking simple questions. Simple questions devoid of jargon.

- Questions from the heart: These questions are questions from the heart, and not academic questions, possibilities, etc. from the intelligence.

- Experiences: The questions and answers lie in our experience alone. The answers to life questions do not lie in lofty philosophies, sacred texts, or preceptor's instructions. The answers lie in our experiences.

- Sincerity: The foundation is established in the sincerity with which we step forward, honesty with which we ask questions to ourselves, the straightforwardness in providing answers to them, and genuineness in interpreting our experiences.

- Mind is the tool, mind is the workshop, mind is the raw material.

- Above all, the destination or the goal of this pursuit transcends the mind and its experiences.

That Limitless Ocean

I was standing on the seashore, enjoying the waves playing at my feet. What a beautiful feeling—not only the sensation on my skin but also the waves of joy created in my heart. Slowly, my thoughts went beyond the ruffled waters, as if taking a dive into the endless ocean.

The deep, vast and silent waters beneath drew my attention and beckoned me to take a plunge. I did. A dive like none I had ever taken before, a dive that went beyond imagination. I saw the ocean as a limitless expanse—a universe in itself, a space with no boundaries.

But suddenly the knowledge of geography intervened, reminding me that the ocean extended only to that piece of land which had a name, had people, and so on.

Now, the vastness and limitlessness of the ocean were gone. The ocean had a boundary.

Why do we allow the knowledge we acquired from books to interfere with our natural instinct to wonder, to be lost in imagination? Why should knowledge limit us, restrict us and constrict us?

The "highest" cannot be achieved if we do not allow the faculty of wonder to carry us beyond the limits of knowledge!

My thoughts returned to the ocean. The sight of the ocean made me feel humbled.

My salutations to Nature!

My Path is Better Than Yours

There is something unique to us humans, not that I know what it is in other species. Anything we possess, we want to feel that it is better than what the other (my neighbour) has.

This one "subconscious principle" drives humans in all endeavours. From the child one has, to the car, to the job, extending to the most obscure aspects of our lives, we want what is ours to be superior to what the neighbour has—or wish it to be so if it is not already.

One's own car appears run-down and obsolete the moment the neighbour has a better one, even if the car is in perfect condition.

The same is applicable in the spiritual or religious path.

"My path is better than yours"!

In religion, the deity I worship is more powerful than your deity. Rather, it is the most powerful deity. The scripture I follow is better than the one you follow.

The one following the path of spirituality feels it is superior to the religious path. One following the Advaita philosophy feels it is superior to the Dvaita philosophy and all other philosophies. We don't stop competing even in the higher-order pursuits of life (religion or spirituality).

One may feel Bhagavad Gita is superior to another text, and the Upanishads are superior to Bhagavad Gita, and so on.

The moment the feeling of superiority sets in, can we really get what we want in this pursuit of spirituality or religion?

The spiritual seeker feels superior to the householder; the monk feels superior to the householder and everyone else. Why?

Is this not 'competition' in the realm of spirituality? Of what use is that? Are we not reducing it to a race?

Most of the problems in humanity are the result of one religion feeling superior to another or one philosophy of spirituality feeling superior to another.

Why the clash of points of view? What are we reducing it to? It is almost like saying "my car is better than yours".

Religion or spirituality has become just another parameter to divide humanity. When will the human wake up to this travesty? "Arise, awake," said the Upanishads. Apply this 'Arise, awake' to this current problem.

With such differences or feeling of superiority, can we ever hope to achieve that which is Supreme?

⚫

A Child Playing with Toys

Have you ever observed a child when faced with many new toys, all of which the child likes? What happens then? The child picks up one; with the other hand, it picks up another. Now both the hands are occupied. It is strategy time. Depending on the size of the toys, the child somehow tries to pick up more toys.

It is fun to watch the expression on the child's face. The child wishes to pick up as many as possible. What is the child going through here? We, as adults, go through the same situation often. We want more and more, grabbing whatever we can.

But let us go back to the child. How is it that the child exhibits this behaviour? It has not yet been conditioned by life's experiences. What does it mean? Is the human being wired like that? What else could explain this behaviour?

This is how we are! With this understanding and knowing that such an attitude only leads us to trouble, we need to learn to lead a life where we are not tempted by everything around us.

The child itself provides us some hints. When the child wants another toy, while both the hands are full, it drops one or both, before attempting to pick up another.

Doesn't the child's experience with toys demonstrate that greed is an inherent nature? Recognizing our limitations and how these limitations rob us of our happiness, we need to figure out a way to lead a life of peace and happiness.

Just as we use feelings like fear and pain to keep away from danger and injury, how do we use these mental responses to world situations to work towards peace and happiness, not only for ourselves but for society and the earth?

Is this possible? I think it is. But it is not easy. However, we do not have a choice.

———— · ● · ————

I am Like the Deep Ocean

As a wondrous presence I stand,

In this creation ineffable and timeless;

Though a speck in the macrocosm am I,

I carry the whole cosmos within.

Expansive in infinite existence,

Unfragmented in my essence,

Like an ocean of this bountiful earth,

I am boundless in my subtle depth.

Rivers of trials rush into me,

I remain immovable, unruffled,

Be it holy rivers, or filthy streams,

They lose their form in my skylike Self.

Tides of joy, tsunamis of sorrow,

Are just ripples in my presence vast;

I perceive them with no difference,

For in my depths, I am the majestic calm.

———— · ● · ————

My Silent Teacher and Guide

Over the last few days, during my early morning walks, a dog has been following me. He keeps a certain distance, but like an experienced spy, he tails me doggedly. Every now and then, when I think he is gone, he appears right behind a hedge, watching me.

"Why?" I wondered.

I asked him, "Who are you? Where is your home, little fellow? Why are you following me?" Again, this morning I asked, "What do you do during the day? How do you manage your food?"

For all these questions, there was but one response: silence. He would give me a quizzical look, which seemed to say, "Don't you know?"

With his silence, he taught me this: "Don't ask me. Ask yourself. You will find all the answers."

Having returned home, I pondered. I wondered.

I realized that for every question I have, the answer lies within me. It must come from me.

What a great discovery this is! There is no searching, there is no asking. There is no teacher, there is no taught. There is just silence.

In that silence is everything. In the beginning, the question and answer were one. They were always together, and I had missed that point. I only saw the question and looked for the answer elsewhere. Now, I realize the question and answer are but one. If I look beyond the question, I will find the answer just there.

Now, like a dog eager to meet its master, I am anxious to see him tomorrow and share this insight he gave. To which, I know his response would be silence.

———•◆•———

Our Many Battlefronts

In life, when we meet and interact with others, we only see one side of them. Based on this limited perspective, we form judgments and conduct our interactions. Our vision of them is very limited. We only see them with respect to our relationship with them, and based on the history of our interactions with them, we judge and interact with them.

But we are not one-dimensional beings!

Our lives have many dimensions—both in the past and the present. Imagine each dimension as a sphere within our life. For example, our professional life is one dimension. Our life as a parent is another. Being a child, sibling, in-law, friend, etc., each represents a different dimension.

The complexity does not end there. Within each primary dimension, there are multiple sub-dimensions. At work, we may juggle various roles and responsibilities, and the same multiplicity exists in other areas of our lives.

Each dimension is like a battlefront. In this sense, we are not fighting just one battle but are engaged in many at any given time.

Take Arjuna (of the Bhagavad Gita), for example. Facing Bhishma and Drona on the battlefield was just one of the many battlefronts he was involved in.

Our lives are similar. Next time you interact with someone, remember that this individual, though engaging with you, is part of many battles, both past and present.

Here is the crucial point: While we live in multiple dimensions and face problems from each, the solutions lie in only one dimension—the INNER.

That is what makes life wonderful, beautiful, adventurous, and mysterious!

———•—◆—•———

Do not Be the Obstacle to Happiness

O Mind,

I wish for you to find peace and happiness in every moment. Yet, it seems that you are the very one standing in the way, preventing happiness from reaching you. Please, don't become the barrier to your own happiness.

I hope you discover the anchor within that reveals the treasure chest of eternal happiness inside you, allowing you to embrace and enjoy every situation you encounter. Savor the variety and diversity that life offers. All you need to do is open your arms wide and welcome everything.

May you find and experience whatever comes your way! May you find happiness and peace in every moment.

O mind! this is my heartfelt prayer.

———•—◆—•———

Why are we Looking for Answers Outside?

From time to time, we find ourselves pondering life's questions, seeking answers to make sense of our experiences. We often turn to books, consult with others, or more frequently, search online for solutions.

When we stumble upon an answer, we hastily judge its suitability, labelling it as either right or wrong. But how do we truly determine the correctness of an answer? Just because something resonates with us or fails to do so does not necessarily make it right or wrong.

We seldom allow the answers to come from within.

The right answer—the answer that is appropriate for us—lies within us.

The real challenge is whether we have the patience to look inward and seek answers from within. Instead, we often grow restless and look elsewhere for answers. This external search will never lead us to the right answers. Only the answers that come from within will be the right ones.

Even if, on certain occasions, the answer comes from an external source, it has to get adapted and completely assimilated within.

I Carry a Lantern in My Heart

You kindled in me a flame anew,

That split open a world within me.

With renewed zest, I had longed to fly,

But that flight perhaps was not to be.

Resolute, I chose another road,

The path and the end unknown to me.

I care not for the oft-beaten path;

'Freedom from maps' shall become my way.

You may deter me on this pursuit,

The way I came, I shall leave today.

You may have many more words to say,

But I have an inner voice to weigh.

You may show me a map for my quest,

But let me carve out a path that's mine.

You may talk about how to get there,

But know for sure, the journey is mine.

You may tell me how to steer the maze,

But the call at every fork is mine.

You may paint a picture of the goal,

But I shall aim for the shore that's mine.

You extend a hand for me to hold,

I know that will turn into a crutch.

You may point to your footsteps to trace,

Let me fall, and I will find my way.

You spoke, and I heard your words thus far,

But for this trip, I have my own song.

You warn me of the dark road ahead,

I carry my lantern in my heart.

Do Not Pay Attention to Milestones

Assessing progress on the spiritual path is inherently subjective and relative. Each individual experiences and perceives these ideas differently, and this perception evolves over time. This evolution itself is an indicator of progress. As seekers advance on their path, their thoughts and ideas gradually change, leading to increased clarity. These changes may be subtle and gradual, but they are always present.

This transformation also affects our understanding of our personality, our relationship with the world, and our concept of the Supreme. These ideas are in a constant state of flux.

It is challenging to pinpoint definitive indicators of progress. Each seeker must feel, experience, and introspect deeply to draw their own conclusions.

However, it is important not to become too rigid in this process. One should feel a lightness of effort. Avoid imposing strict 'assessment criteria' to gauge progress. The more rigid these criteria, the more objective we make the path, and the more we become trapped by our expectations.

Any kind of desire or expectation becomes an impediment to progress.

Let us simply enjoy the journey and not worry about the destination.

Reflect on the Fountainhead Within

Humanity often remembers and cherishes the golden words of great individuals from the past. Yet, we frequently overlook one crucial point: the words themselves are not inherently special.

It is the personality placed in a specific context, resulting in a state of mind that ultimately brought forth those words. Often, these words are part of a longer speech or writing, but over time, only one or two sentences get picked up and attain eternal status. It is that state of mind, the mental landscape from which these thoughts emerged, took shape, and transformed into words that is truly extraordinary. And it is that moment which holds true significance.

This mind is something truly mysterious. It is within this boundless realm that thoughts are born and given form, revealing the timeless nature of human expression.

———•————

The Path to Truth Lies Beyond Words

To realize the ultimate Truth, one must transcend words, concepts, frameworks, processes, and methodologies.

In Advaita Vedanta, Truth is Absolute, One, Omnipresent, Eternal, and all-pervading. It exists beyond time, space, and causation. It is beyond the body, senses, mind, intelligence, and ego.

The moment we describe Truth as "this," we turn it into an object of the mind, intelligence, and senses. In doing so, we move away from the Truth.

Using words, such as in the case of a mantra, and engaging in repetitive processes, there is a danger of becoming bound to the act itself, of becoming a slave to the process.

The moment we introduce a process, we are trapped by the process. All the attention then goes into sustaining the process. This very process introduces time, space, and causation.

Ask yourself: How do I reach that which is beyond words? How do I reach that which is beyond time? How do I transcend causality?

———•————

The Incredible Journey of the Universe Within

I wonder what drives people to follow their hearts and dive into the journey of self-discovery.

Some say it is because of all the pain and suffering in the world around us. Is it really so? Or is it because of disgust towards the material world? Or is it out of indifference towards ordinary life and mundane existence?

What is it that starts this inward journey?

Based on personal experience, here is what I feel:

This journey is triggered by the conviction that there is something beyond day-to-day existence that is more beautiful.

It is sparked by wonder, curiosity, and an urge to go beyond the ordinary and explore life to its fullest. That 'life which is fullest' lies beyond the external phenomena that we call the world.

This journey is brought about by a willingness to give oneself the opportunity to explore and discover with openness. It is facilitated by the readiness to meet anything that comes with positivity and without regret.

And this is what has kept me going on this journey all these years and allows me to stay on it with the same enthusiasm.

Living in Harmony

What is harmony, where is it to be sought?

'Tis but acceptance - the one mantra for all.

Behold and embrace the entire world as is.

Harmony is to see others as thou art,

'Tis within, being one with thy true nature.

Don't look for any harmony in your world,

And not in the objects and beings around.

Don't look for it in the accord in your ties.

Harmony is not an agreement with folks,

'Tis within, being one with thy true nature.

Harmony is not in the synchronous steps,

It's just not about having that common voice.

Harmony is not agreement in the minds,

It's not in the sharing of the same purpose,

'Tis within, being one with thy true nature.

It is not something you cause on the outside,

It's not a thing that you can will in this world.

It has nothing to do with changing your world,

It begins and ends with transforming yourself,

'Tis within, being one with thy true nature.

It cannot emanate from agitated minds,

It cannot be caused by activities around.

It's not an assurance of community life,

It's not a promise of the kinship you have,

'Tis within, being one with thy true nature.

Behold the harmony in five gross elements,

See it in the world of the rose and the bee.

Behold the fight of predator and prey,

Nature has bestowed this in every being,

'Tis within, being one with thy true nature.

Order does not assure harmony around,

Surely not the outcome of a lawful guild.

'Tis not assurance from a beautiful world,

It's assured in seeing a beautiful world,

'Tis within, being one with thy true nature.

Harmony begins with calm and poise within,

'Tis integrity of action, thoughts, and speech.

'Tis in the mind free from conflict with this world,

'Tis in the one who embraces one and all,

'Tis within, being one with thy true nature.

'Tis the vision of one in diversity,

'Tis born of the vision of one Self in all.

'Tis that which is rooted in self-seatedness,

'Tis the one substratum of co-existence,

'Tis within, being one with thy true nature.

———•◆•———

Surrender and Allow the Created Forces to Flow

In the journey of life, after being tested through time, cooked in the crucible of experiences, and matured through various situations, we find ourselves led to a particular state or activity that is occurring now. If you seek the source of this state or activity, you will find none. There is no trigger, no master, no motive, no goal, and no gain to understand. If you ponder why you are in this state or engaged in this activity, the answer comes from deep inside, echoing, "I don't know" and "I don't care."

This state or activity is driven by Nature. You are merely the medium, the channel, witnessing it all unfold as if it is beyond your control. The symptom of this activity is joy. The activity is not necessarily resulting in an output; it is simply taking place. In this laboratory of visible phenomena called the world, you are the observer, the lens, and the observed.

You may call the orchestrator of all this Nature, the Divine, or God. Upon deeper reflection, you realize that labelling it does not matter. You are simply enjoying the blossoming. In essence, you have surrendered—not interfering in the blossoming, but allowing yourself to be the instrument and medium to express. You don't even know what you are trying to express, for it doesn't matter. This surrendering to nature is the real service, if you wish to name it.

You stand in amazement of this unfolding. It is not governed by deadlines, milestones, or the nature of the output. As long as you remain a witness, an instrument, and a medium, the creative forces will continue to flow through you. They are not orchestrated or designed by you.

However, the moment you try to interfere and declare, "I want to make a difference," "I want to contribute," or "I want to bring about change," that is when you desire to be the doer. When the ego of doing comes in, the creative forces cease.

Wake up to this truth and embrace the art of allowing the creative forces to flow, unhindered.

My Next Step Knows the Way

I paused
In the middle of my journey
Wondering which way to proceed,
Hoping that someone or something
Would tell me.
I awaited a signal.

"Which road to take"
Was the question.
The guide had inputs,
My fellow passengers had views.
And doubts clouded my head.
Suddenly the road spoke:

"Take a single step.
Do not count your steps so far.
Do not worry about the next mile.
Every step knows the next.
Let the next step be your journey.
Your next step holds the map of your route,
Which you need not know,
Which you shall not know.
In not knowing is adventure.
In not knowing the map is clarity.

In your next step, you create YOUR journey.
In taking the next step is clarity."

Enquire Into the Grief
for Instant Relief from Grief

Often when we are in grief or when we are miserable, we continue to suffer. We continue to dwell upon the grief and that just enhances the suffering. We refuse to let go of the grief. After a while, the suffering refuses to let go of us.

We reiterate the point that we are suffering. We feel sorry for ourselves; we continue to think that we have been wronged, and so on. And all these thoughts reinforce the grief and suffering. It becomes a grief cycle.

And in due course of time, that thought about grief, and suffering gains sufficient ground and becomes an integral part of our memory and our personality.

If we examine it closely, most often we are constantly delving in that grief or suffering to make it stronger or rather we are making it worse.

At some level, we pity ourselves and begin to almost "enjoy the suffering". We like to think of ourselves as the victim, and relish that status. And very soon we have made this grief "real". And also, it becomes an integral part of our personality and begins to shape our thoughts, feelings, emotions, actions, etc.

What is the way out?

Go right to the beginning of the grief.

The moment we begin to feel sad or sorrowful, shift the attention from the grief. Do it deliberately. It may require effort. Begin an enquiry!

Enquire into the following: I accept what has happened, but why am I suffering? What is the cause? What triggered it? I understand the circumstances causing the grief, but why should

I suffer? Where is the suffering? Is it there all the time? At the time of suffering, if we looked at and interacted with a child, what happened to the grief? How has it vanished? Where is it now?

The moment we allow the mind to get occupied with the above kind of enquiry, we find that our mind has shifted from the grief or pain.

In fact, in that moment when the enquiry begins, we find that the pain or grief, etc. has vanished.

We may not have solved the problem. But we have dissolved the problem in that moment. We also realize the futility of the grief.

By paying attention to the grief and dwelling in it, we make it worse!

And by enquiring into the grief, the nature of the grief, the source, the transience, etc., we have refused to allow it to gain roots in the mind. Repeating this process helps to focus on the real nature of suffering.

Embracing Life: A Divine Conversation

After years of devotion to her dear Lord, she found herself in the midst of a daily conversation, earnestly asking, "What do you want me to do in life?"

Her Lord responded, "Be free like the bird in the sky; go through everything cheerfully. Live your life to its fullest and do your best in being who you are."

Intrigued and restless, she pondered over these words for nights. This was not what she expected from her beloved Lord. Why was there no mention of their relationship?

She had anticipated hearing, "Surrender to Me. Think of Me all the time. Strive to become one with Me." She mused that the instructions might be, "Read of my glories, sing to your heart's content, spread the word of your Lord."

Seeking clarity, she decided to confront her Lord. She wondered if the Lord had a different opinion of her or if she was one of the less favoured children. Summoning her Lord, she eagerly awaited the rendezvous. Somewhat dispirited, she poured out her heart.

The Lord smiled with compassion and said, "Why think of me all the time? You are here to fulfil your purpose in life. It is for each being to find that fulfilment."

The Lord continued, "Have you asked your mother what she wants? She does not want you to think of her all the time. She wants you to live life to the fullest. She wants you to find your place in this creation. That does not negate her presence. It does not change or challenge your relationship. In your fulfilment lies the crowning of the mother-child relationship. In the fulfilment of the human purpose, in the realization of humanness, lies the consummation of the divine-human unity."

She felt the tender hand of her Lord.

Her Lord said, "I will give you both joy and sorrow. I will give you success and failure. I will give you something and also take it away. Accept both, for you cannot avoid them."

Finally, she said, "Give me all the joy that you can give. Give me all the sorrow you can give. I welcome both with open arms. For the pendulum that swings, swings in both directions. If it goes to one extreme, it shall also touch the other extreme. For in its movement that includes both is time, is life."

Embracing the Infinite Within

When we see someone riding by in an ultra-expensive car and exclaim, "How rich he is!" in that moment, we make ourselves 'poor.'

When we stand on the seashore and exclaim, "What a vast expanse this is!" in that moment, we make ourselves 'finite.'

In the spiritual pursuit, we wish to realize the Supreme—the unbounded, the infinite.

The only way to get closer to that and finally unite with it is when we realize ourselves to be that infinite.

As long as we continue to see ourselves as limited, small, and finite, the realization and the subsequent union remains very distant. Unless we begin to feel the vastness within us and see ourselves as that Infinite, the realization will remain elusive.

Imagine watching the vast outside expanse through a pane in a window. But, when we step into the open, the view transforms into a completely different experience. We are one with the expanse. Imagine the scene where Julie Andrews is in the open meadows in 'The Sound of Music.'

In life, we are always seeing the world through a window. That window, framed in finiteness, makes our vision finite.

How can we attain that freedom if we constantly see the world and its phenomena through our limitations and constrictions?

The moment we say, "I want this," we are admitting a lack. It is like saying, "I lack this." How can we, who are full, lack something? The moment we say "I want" or "I lack," we make ourselves finite.

How then can the "finite" or "limited" mindset realize the Infinite identity within?

To experience true freedom, where we are completely free, we must feel that freedom—not just intellectually understand it. Feel it deep inside. 'Become' free.

This marks the beginning of our journey toward embracing the infinite within us and experiencing true freedom.

------ • ● • ------

The True Pursuit: Turning Life Inward

Why do we make life to be a pursuit? Or for that matter, anything else 'in life'—why should it be a pursuit? And when we generally say pursuit, we are referring to something external, something outgoing. More specifically, something that is an external or physical acquisition.

Right from childhood we are trained, coached, taught, and perhaps brainwashed to make life an intense pursuit to acquire, to possess, to chase. Education is also seen primarily as acquisition of information. Then comes the job—the acquisition of experience (which is building a resume of one's capabilities), wealth, and so on.

Why? Why has the pursuit of life been reduced to the physical plane alone? Is that the only purpose we can think of? Why can't the pursuit of life be inward facing? I do not mean a selfish one, but a pursuit where everything in life is achieved by a journey into the INNER REALM.

Any pursuit which allows one to express the deeper inner dimension (arts, science, or any other form) can be turned inward. If we probe carefully, even the external pursuits begin with 'inner'. We fail to recognise that. So why not make life a beautiful journey of discovering who we are and allow that discovery to yield whatever it unfolds, instead of chasing what we see in the outer phenomena?

Let the goal of life be to be goalless! Let the pursuit of life be to be purposeless! Let life be a discovery—a discovery where we are not trying to discover something, a discovery where there is nothing to be discovered.

------ ◆ ------

We Have Obscured the Sky

We are enveloped by towering concrete blocks that have sprouted all around us. When we raise our eyes to the heavens, we can't see the sky from where we stand. Even when we strain our necks to look up, the sky remains hidden from view.

In many cities, the smoke from the garbage we burn and the pollution caused by human "progress" have created a dense smog. This smog forms a thick screen, preventing us from seeing the sky.

We have also caged ourselves in the inner chambers of our homes and office complexes, where we are surrounded by walls and thus have no vision of sunlight or the sky. In our relentless pursuit of objects in this world, we have no time to look up and thus fail to be inspired by the blue sky.

That was about the outer sky, the outer expanse!

In this busy world of constant activity and progress, we have built an ego as tall as the buildings surrounding us. This ego rises above everything, obscuring our vision of the inner sky—the inner expanse.

We have built castles in the air with our desires and ambitions, which completely veil the vision of the inner sky.

We have accumulated possessions that have piled up all around us, and we have caged ourselves inside these possessions. How, then, can we see the inner sky?

We have so many dreams for the future that the walls of aspirations obscure the real inner expanse.

We need to wake up to have a vision of the inner infinite sky!

And the first step in that direction is to make a conscious effort to see and be inspired by the outer blue sky.

Here's Another Way to Understand Freedom

Seeing the flower, without thinking of what you can do with the flower,

listening to the song, without being trapped by it,

feeling the breeze, without relishing the touch,

watching the fruits on a tree, without wanting to have them,

looking at a beautiful woman, without wanting to be with her,

admiring a beautiful object, without wanting to own it,

seeing the beauty of the vast mountain range without, wanting to visit again,

that is real freedom.

Do Not Look for a Jasmine in a Rose

Do you look at a white jasmine and wish it were red? Do you look at a rainbow and wish it were square? Do you ever look at the sky and wish it were green?

Why, then, do we look at other individuals and wish they were different?

We end up wasting all our lives imagining and wishing that a jasmine was red.

Seeing the jasmine in the jasmine, the rainbow in the rainbow, and the human in the human is freedom.

Let Me be Like the Jasmine

Does the jasmine flower ever think of God? Does it pray? Does it want to be free? I do not know.

I know for sure it blooms, distributes its fragrance, lends its beauty, blooms with the rest, rejoices with the roses, dances with the chrysanthemums, smiles with the lilies, and witnesses the hibiscus that falls.

It unfolds without effort, beams with the sunshine, enjoys the rains, swings in the breeze, and finally falls unnoticed.

Let me be like the jasmine in this beautiful cosmic garden we call life.

Hell is Here and Now

Hell is caused by the mind.

Hell is in the mind.

Hell is not some imaginary place after death.

Hell is what we create, here and now.

Not being content is hell.

Complaining about everything around us is hell.

Being excessively occupied with the world of I, me, and mine is hell.

Expecting everything to be to our liking is hell.

Hell is:

Living in the past;

Always wanting to control everything;

Guilt that is not resolved through knowledge.

Constant jealousy towards others is hell.

Being in a state of constant anger is hell.

Wanting to possess everything we like is hell.

Greed for more possessions is hell.

Hell is:

Living in constant fear of this world;

Believing the world is the cause of our suffering;

Chasing after the world for happiness.

Aspiring for heaven after death is hell.

Imagining that I will go to hell after death is hell.

Recognizing all this is the first step to freedom.

Freedom from all constrictions is heaven.

Do Not Carry the Burden That is Yesterday

Yesterday is now in the past, merely a mark on the calendar, a moment gone in time. Yet, we cling to it, holding on to thoughts, events and experiences from the days gone by.

Why can't we just let it all drift away in the river of time? Why do we carry the past into the present? Why don't we create a fresh today?

The present has no place for what is past. Now is like the blossoming of a new flower, while the past has fallen away like a withered one. There is no sadness in this withering. Instead, let us look forward to and celebrate the blossoming of a beautiful now.

When you look at a flower, there is no point in thinking, "It was a bud yesterday." Behold the blossoming which is in the present alone. Let us also not think about what will happen to the flower tomorrow.

Each moment is a standalone experience, without a sign for what tomorrow will bring.

Let us embrace the present and leave yesterday behind, creating a fresh today with fresh thoughts for now.

———— • ◆ • ————

The Beauty of Recognition

Early in the morning, while I sat quietly on a chair, I saw sunlight gradually fill up my room, drenching it with light. While, because of the light, I could see all the items in the room, I realized that I failed to perceive the sunbeams that had caused it.

I marvelled at the beauty of the greenery all around, yet I failed to notice the life forces that sustained it.

Now, when my thoughts went towards the diverse and vibrant world around me, I wondered what is it that sustains the entire universe. That was the first time this question had arisen in that form.

I knew there was something that was the substratum of the universe; but what was it? I thought, "I do not need to name it, define it, or imagine a form for it. I do not even need to understand it." The recognition of it itself filled me with joy. The joy was in the following thought: The vision of the world, led me to think of something that is the foundation of the world. The vision triggered the recognition of an unknown, invisible presence.

I said to myself: "In that recognition lies beauty. And there lies the mystery and the wonder we call life."

When I acknowledged the presence of the sunbeams filling the room, seeping through the windows, I felt the beauty and wonder of the sun. How magnificent it would be to perceive the cosmic presence behind this universe and everything visible in the phenomenal world!

I told myself: "Seek to discover that presence. In that seeking lies the true beauty and purpose of life."

A Prayer for a Safe Journey

Somehow, and I do not wish to know how,

I came to travel this path.

It is my conviction, tempered over time,

That this is my journey.

A journey, I don't know how long,

But it's mine for now.

It's a path ever so beautiful,

Ever so wondrous.

There is no destination in mind,

It's a journey without milestones.

May the next firm step be the entire journey.

In that firmness may I find joy.

May the Supreme be my lighthouse.

May that Supreme show me the way.

May that Supreme bestow strength,

For a firm and decisive next step.

May I fear nothing,

May I fear no one,

May I not be deterred by hurdles,

For as they shall appear, they too shall pass.

———◆———

Importance of Human "Relationships" in Spirituality

Imagine human emotions or qualities like love, jealousy, anger, hatred, kindness, compassion, etc. All these human qualities are realized only in the presence of another human. In the absence of another, we will never fully know what being human means. We can extend this thought to any extent. The realization that we are human happens only in the presence of other humans. All these qualities are experienced in the presence of another human alone. This is a very fundamental point.

If we start questioning this, saying, "I am on a spiritual path," even there, it is only these qualities that come into play, finally. It is all in the context of another human being. When we refer to the world, it is the world consisting of others around us. It is the human relationships that are at the very core.

Take the text Bhagavad Gita, for example. Arjuna's condition, which forms the basis of the dialogue between Arjuna and Krishna, is based on human relationships.

Some who comment and speak about spirituality underplay the importance of human relationships in spiritual progress, whereas it is through these experiences that we go forward. The entire experience of spirituality, for the most part, is through the world and relationships.

Imagine all the deities in our culture. They are all human forms. Even Agni (the God of fire) is given a human form. All interactions with these deities (including rituals like worship) are modelled on human interactions.

What is devotion? It is nothing but love.

We can express our feelings to a deity or the Lord in any form. We have instances where a devotee expresses devotion to the Lord by treating the Lord as a child, as a beloved, as a master, or as a friend. Even there, we are only bringing human relationships to the forefront.

There is no doubt that the spiritual goal is to be achieved in this world, while living and interacting with the world and its objects. Human beings and relationships are an important aspect of our life and living.

The human qualities and virtues that we require in the path to that goal are cultivated, challenged, nurtured, and refined in the presence of other humans and through our relationships with them.

We often hear that human relationships are an impediment in the path to attaining the spiritual goal. This would be a hasty conclusion.

In reality, human relationships are quite essential in realizing the full potential of being a human, and also in realizing the spiritual goal.

However, a word of caution: Beware of attachment.

Our Notion of "I Know" is an Impediment to True Joy

When we hear, read, or see something, we often exclaim, "I know," "that's right," or come up with an analytical statement about it. Remember, that response of the mind is an impediment to pure joy.

Consider the following scenario: You have gone to a classical music concert. The culture of classical music is very well established in both the North and South of our country. The artist begins the concert. A few moments into the singing of the opening exposition of the melodic framework (referred to as *aalaap*), the minds of many in the audience jump up and say, "This melodic framework (*raag*) is Kalyani." Having thought of that, they look around in pride, as if expecting those around them to applaud. Some even say this aloud to the person next to them.

Note that, in that moment, they have stopped enjoying the music.

It is as if they are present at the concert only to decode it. The music concert is like a puzzle to them. It is an intellectual exercise. The moment they have decoded the piece, it is then all about making sure that the singer sticks to the notes of that *raag*. It is all about approving and blessing the singer for having sung correctly. It is not about enjoying the music. [Here, I am not referring to the conversation you have with a friend after the concert, where you may appreciate or critique the music.]

What happened is, the notion "I know" has come in and taken over the experience of listening.

Similarly, take a natural phenomenon you are looking at—a rainbow, for example. The moment you see it as knowledge, the intelligence goes on to explain that phenomenon. And you immediately bring in the knowledge of how and why it happened. Again, at that very moment, you cease to have the experience of pure joy.

I now recall an experience with a friend at the airport. It was 2 AM. We were waiting for our respective flights. From where we were seated, we could see an aircraft taxiing towards the boarding gates. Seeing that, I exclaimed in wonder, "What a wonderful sight! Just imagine this huge mass of steel carrying over a hundred people, taking off and landing." This is what my friend said: "It is all explained by Bernoulli's principle." Such an analytical explanation of what we see immediately takes away the wonder, the mystery, etc.

We are always so eager and ready to come up with a response: "I know," "you are right," "but that's not right," etc. And thus, we close the door on joy.

In every pursuit and experience in life, we limit ourselves with this "I know." You have taken on the role of a judge, and you think you must proclaim a verdict.

The most beautiful experiences are those when we allow the five sense organs to provide us with the inputs of the world, without assessing the inputs based on the expectations and impressions we carry.

* * *

Does Clarity Bring About Rigidity?

In many scenarios, there is a conviction that "I believe I am right". This conviction regarding my standpoint, makes me rigid on certain occasions.

Sometimes, I believe that this is how I am supposed to be. Take a simple example: I feel that this dress should be worn like this. There is nothing right or wrong, but this is how I have been told or conditioned. Because that notion has taken a deep seat in my mind, it has become "right", and everything else has become "wrong". In this stance—that this is how it should be—I have become rigid, mainly because I am unaccepting of every other way.

Sometimes, when I appear to be open or accepting of another's point of view, it is because I am unsure of it myself. In that scenario, I am a flexible. So, I am okay with another point of view as well.

By and large, if I am very certain about something, I become stubborn and rigid.

Is this important? In the context of the pursuit of "unconditional" happiness, it is very important.

For me, a seeker, this is a warning. This is certainly worth introspecting about.

* * *

Being at Home with Clouds
to Enjoy the Vision of Sunrise

We feel that we should have answers for everything in life. When we do not have answers, it makes us feel very uncomfortable. "I need clarity," we often say.

When we are uncertain or do not know something, it makes us restless. We also begin to feel that we are not in control. This feeling is heightened by the assumption that everyone around us is very clear about everything in life.

Often, I sit on our balcony, watching the sun rise. One day, while watching the sunrise, I had the following thoughts: The beauty of the scene, while all my attention is on the sun, lies in the clouds. The more clouds there are, dancing between me and the sun, the more beautiful the sunrise. The designs and colours I get to see are magical.

Suddenly, I saw this play of sun and clouds as analogous to knowing and ignorance in the context of life.

The more doubts I have and the more uncertain I am about things, the more beautifully the sun of knowledge shines. Life is about allowing that "ignorance" to exist. I don't have to solve every problem or have answers for every challenge that life presents.

I thought, being at home with doubts, questions, and uncertainties is what freedom is all about. Who says I must have all the answers to everything in life?

The same thought process can be extended to enjoying the mystery, wonder, and beauty of nature. Take the rainbow, for example. When you look at a rainbow, you are captivated by its beauty. You might then wonder how it got there, how it just vanishes, and so on. The questions for which we do not have immediate answers make it a mysterious appearance and enhance the beauty of our viewing experience. On the other hand, if we knew everything about the science of the rainbow and allowed these ideas to come up when we look at it, we might not enjoy the rainbow's beauty as much.

In the case of nature, the more we have unanswered questions, the more we are able to enjoy its wonder, mystery, and beauty. In fact, the word "mystery" itself means that there are things kept secret or unknown. That is why we enjoy mysteries, puzzles, and similar things.

Similarly, in life, the unknowns make it wonderful and mysterious. That is what makes life worth living. If I knew the answers to everything in life, it would not be half as much worth living.

The main point is, "I don't have to know everything!"

—————•◆•—————

If

If life is a road to freedom, why am I in bondage all the time? How can bondage lead me to freedom?

If life is a road to peace, why is my mind in a state of perpetual storm? How can unrest lead me to peace?

If life is a road to unconditioned bliss, why is my mind not cheerful? How can my cheerless mind lead me to unconditioned bliss?

If life is a road leading to fearlessness, why am I in constant fear? How can fear lead me to fearlessness?

If life is a road to freedom from anger, why is my mind intolerant of some things in the world? How can intolerance lead me to freedom from anger?

If life is a road to freedom from suffering, why is my heart clinging to objects of the world? How can clinging lead me to freedom from suffering?

If life is a road to experiencing the Infinite within, why is my mind unable to give up constrictions? How can my constricted mind lead me to the Infinite within?

If life is a road leading to Supreme Transcendence, why am I trapped in the duality of good and bad? How can duality of good and bad, lead me to the Supreme?

If life is a road to realizing the oneness of all beings, how can I have feelings like "mine and not-mine"? How can notions of mine and not-mine lead me to realizing the oneness.

—————•◆•—————

Going Beyond Time, we Transcend Conflicts

We have the following conventional ideas regarding time: "Time is money. Time is the lever that moves our lives. Time is the one resource we always want".

How to go beyond these limiting thoughts and ideas?

From experience, we know that in moments of true happiness, time vanishes. When we experience true love, we lose the notion of time. In moments of peace, time seems to disappear altogether. Whenever we find ourselves in the lap of nature, time loses its meaning.

And, meditation is a timeless experience.

Time exists when we operate in the sphere of mind and intelligence. When we go beyond the mind and intelligence, time loses its relevance and meaning.

When we operate in the realm of cause and effect, time is born. However, when we do something for its own sake and for someone we love, when we are unconcerned about personal benefits, there is no time. It is when we focus on the outcome that we introduce the notion of time.

Transcending time removes conflict. Being fully present in the moment eliminates the concept of time. Yesterday and tomorrow are conflicts; they lead to misery. True happiness is NOW!

Freedom - A Journey to the Truth Beyond Words

I read many texts (scriptures). I feel good about them. I enjoy their brilliance and delight in their beauty. Touched, inspired, and uplifted, I am drawn to the words. I feel renewed and energized, as if I have been shown a "new way".

But the important thing to note is: They have not become part of me. And soon, the effect of the brilliance of poetry wears off. What is left of the earlier inspiration are mere words in black and white.

Why? Because it was my intellect that reached out to them. It was my mind that was attracted to them. It was my emotions that connected to the poetry. But, the compulsion for inner transformation and self-discovery were not kindled.

I realize that I have to go beyond the texts. I have to go beyond the teacher. I have to go beyond the words. I have to go behind the thoughts and ideas expressed.

The inspiration to be free will wake me up. The inspiration will transform my thinking. And it will naturally propel me to freedom. The journey then shall become effortless.

For the "truth" is beyond words and is beyond the teacher and the taught.

The text was written for humanity. The words "carrying" the truth have travelled through time, space, and people. It is being conveyed through words—the words of an author unknown. An author who belonged to another time. An author with their own personal journey, whose life was different, who saw social landscapes that were different, who heard stories that we may never hear, and who saw the world and life through a different set of lenses.

To see what the author wants me to see, I need to journey with the author, and need to get into the "heart" of the author.

Holding the author's hand, tenderly, let me walk that beautiful path. For, I believe in that author. I believe that the author had seen the promised land.

To make the text personal, to make it relevant to me, and to make it matter to me, I have to dig, dig really deep. I have to discover the message that is meant for me. I have to adapt that message for my journey.

———•●•———

The Joy of the Journey is Not in the Details

Imagine a journey by road that you are about to embark upon. Before you begin the journey, you go to someone and ask, "Tell me how to get to my destination?" This person you asked, in your opinion, knows something about the route.

That person offloads all their experience, telling you about the tree to look for, the house painted pink, the cows grazing, the damaged road, the forks in the road, the huge billboards, the dilapidated house, the abandoned well, and so on, in great detail. You are also told about the stops to make, the things to carry, the breaks to take in the journey, the places to stop for fuel, etc.

Now, you start your journey, and if you spend all your time and attention looking for those signs and indications along the way, as guided by "that someone", you are not going to enjoy the journey.

Your journey will be all about the checklist and ticking off the various boxes. If you get obsessed with all those instructions, you will not enjoy the journey, the adventure, and the experience of the unknown.

But a wise counsel will tell you—start off from wherever you are, feel the road, and let each step reveal the next. Enjoy the journey. Let the road be your guide.

The same is the case with the journey to your spiritual goal!

* * *

Guru is Not an Individual

The concept of a "guru" is not that of an individual. It is not a personality. It does not belong to a tradition, or a religion. It is the river of wisdom!

It originated as a drop at the dawn of creation. As it flowed down through time, through generations, cultures, traditions, and societies, it gathered wisdom along the way, and reached us in this moment in space and time.

It is this ever-growing river of wisdom we call guru. This river is impersonal and universal. It does not belong to a race, country, or religion. It does not belong to a community, or to a tradition. It will always remain a collective wisdom, for all of humanity.

That collective wisdom we call guru is in every atom in this universe. It is in every cell in every being and it is in every experience in this universe. It is ever present in you and me!

By labelling someone or something as a guru, we are missing the universal nature of wisdom. Guru is the universal collective river of wisdom, eternally growing as a colossal river, ever-present as the Universal Consciousness.

The Peak of the Mountain of Time

The present moment is the peak on the mountain of time. Do not step back, for you will fall into the valley of the past. Then, returning to the peak will be a challenge, a steep climb.

When you step back, you see the demons of the past which trap you in yesterday. You become bound by the fetters of your sins and by your experiences in the past. They are stronger than the strongest iron chains and obstruct you from the peak, which is now.

Do not step forward, for there lies the abyss of the future. It is an imaginary world of your mind yet to be created, chiselled by the hands of time. Aspirations and anticipation for the future is a poison that kills the blossoming of the present.

On the peak alone is the eternity of the present. It is unbounded. In it, dreams of the past and aspirations of the future are replaced by the freedom of the present.

Now is the only reality in life. Human mastery and victory are at this peak, which is now. Here, you are the ruler of the universe. Here you are the ruler of time. It is only here that space, time, and causation are dissolved.

In embracing the peak is peace and contentment. In embracing the peak, you are forever free from misery. In embracing the peak, you are eternally free.

———•◆•———

I Believe, I Have What it Takes to Rise Again

I believe this is a wonderful world;

I believe this world is my home, and I belong to it;

I believe it is for me to be part of this wonder;

I believe and I shall carve out my own path;

I believe with all my heart that I shall shape my own world out there.

I believe I shall face many challenges;

I believe I shall be guided by that which has brought me here;

I believe I may not have all the answers, but

I believe the answers shall come to guide me;

I believe with all my heart that I shall shape my own world out there.

I believe I shall have conflicting thoughts;

I believe I shall hear voices from every direction;

I believe all that shall dissolve in me;

I believe the answers lie in my own silence;

I believe with all my heart that I shall shape my own world out there.

I believe what I create may not be perfect, but

I believe I shall be true to myself;

I believe through those imperfections I shall learn;

I believe in and through all that, I shall discover myself;

I believe with all my heart that I shall shape my own world out there.

I believe I shall rise and soar in the sky;

I believe I have what it takes to get myself there;

I believe I shall sometimes fall; but

I believe I have what it takes to rise up again;

I believe with all my heart that I shall shape my own world out there.

Who are Arjuna and Krishna, in the Context of Bhagavad Gita?

We seldom pay attention to who Arjuna and Krishna are, while studying the Bhagavad Gita. Is Arjuna just another warrior? Is Krishna the "all-bestowing" God? For us to apply the text to our life, it is important to understand who they are in the context of this text.

Let us begin with Arjuna. He was one of the greatest warriors of his time and there were few who could match him in archery. He played an important role in winning many battles, and his fame spread far and wide. He was an adherent of dharma, had a loving family, and his brothers, who were also mighty warriors, were fighting on his side. And now, he had come to this battle after many years of intense preparation. Despite all this, and having Krishna by his side, he was struck by severe grief in the battlefield.

Arjuna represents us—the individuals living in this world. The character of Arjuna tells us that, though we may be in possession of everything in life (resources, people, position, power, fame, etc.), even then we will face challenges in life, may experience sorrow and suffering, and also may feel helpless in various situations.

What did Arjuna do in that situation? Though his first impulse was to say, "I will not fight this war", he soon submitted to Krishna that he needed Krishna's guidance.

What are the lessons we learn from Arjuna's response to this crisis in his life? Arjuna demonstrated the following:

He recognized his helplessness, and acknowledged and accepted the condition he was in. He showed courage by expressing his weakness. He had the humility to accept that he did not know what to do, and had the humility to confess that he was confused. He wanted to find redress to his plight, and did not hesitate to seek guidance from Krishna. Importantly, he did not procrastinate, but set out immediately and sought answers from Krishna.

Arjuna's character and his response in that crisis show us the attitude we, as seekers, need to adopt in our spiritual quest.

Let us now turn our attention to Krishna. In the context of the Bhagavad Gita message, Krishna is not the "all-bestowing God".

During the battle, Krishna was just the charioteer of Arjuna's chariot, and had even told Arjuna before the war that he would not wield any weapon in this battle.

It is important to recognize that Krishna does *not* tell Arjuna, "Do not worry, I will ensure that you will win this battle. I bless you with victory and kingdom."

Arjuna does not pray to Krishna and say, "I am your devotee, please remove my grief. Please bless me with victory." In fact, Arjuna says "I am your disciple; please instruct me."

Also, Krishna does not say, "I am pleased with you, I will give you peace of mind."

In fact, Krishna reveals to Arjuna the knowledge of the Self.

It was Arjuna's responsibility to overcome his own grief through self-effort. He was to use the knowledge (of the Self) that Krishna gives to him, and become free from grief.

Krishna represents the ultimate wisdom that can bestow humans with everlasting freedom from suffering.

In fact, you can look upon Krishna as our "all-knowing" Consciousness, who is ever-present in all. Krishna himself says (Chapter 10, verse 20): "I am the Self".

In the Ocean you See the Reflection of the Expanse Within

Imagine the following scene. You walk towards a seashore, and slowly make your way to the meeting point of the ocean and land. You stop there, and face that vast expanse—the ocean.

What is the experience? What is the feeling? Not the thought; but the feeling.

An unexplainable calm dawns.

What is the reason for that sudden calm? It is because the vision of the vast ocean in front, for a moment, completely suspends all our thinking, and in that moment, we experience the vastness within. The ocean, in that moment, acts as a reflection of the expanse within.

Unfortunately, that calmness lasts only a few moments. In fact, you do not allow it to last longer than that. Why?

Because, immediately you are consumed by other thoughts like, "let me take a picture," "I should come here more often,"

"I should bring my family here," "I should come in the morning," "how beautiful" and so on.

In other words, you are distracted by other thoughts and lose the experience of that vastness. Even if you appreciate the beauty of the scene, you lose that experience. The secret lies in being free of any judgement, analysis, description, and plan. How to be free from these? Be a mute witness.

You may ask, "Do I have to visit the beach to find that calm within?" The answer is "No." Remind yourself of the key—"the expanse within." The ocean is simply a mirror. It reflects the expanse within.

Sorrow is Like the Shadow

Happiness and sorrow are entwined in our lives. Inseparable are they, like the body and its shadow. Whenever pleasures come, there follows pain. You can be sure of that. From a certain standpoint, they are almost one, like the sun and its brightness.

We never complain that the shadow is following us. When we have a light source in front, we do not see the shadow. But the shadow is still there, right behind us.

But when we are ignorant of the light, as the case when the source of light is behind us, we see the shadow.

But let us not forget that the shadow is always there. Every instance of joy in our lives has an accompanying sorrow. Without one, the other is not definable, palpable, discernible.

It is just that we are oblivious to it. Similarly, when we see only pain, we are ignoring the joy. We will never see the shadow, if we keep the light in front of us.

Where are Conflicts and where is the Resolution?

Conflicts are an inevitable part of life, appearing regularly in various forms. In many instances, conflicts can seem impossible to resolve, leading to the belief that they are a permanent aspect of existence. The question then arises: is conflict resolution merely a myth?

What is a conflict?

At its core, a conflict often emerges from a clash between multiple external options that demand attention or action. These opposing forces create an internal struggle, as decisions must be made in the face of competing priorities.

Let us take an example: A friend, whom you have not met in 15 years, is in town and you have made a commitment to meet him at 5:00 pm. Suddenly, your boss calls and demands your presence at a crucial meeting at the same time—a meeting you had requested to close an important deal. Also, your friend is to leave the city by a late evening flight.

A typical conflict, isn't it?

Yes, it also depends on how you see it.

The first response in such a situation is often panic, agitation. Then, you begin juggling things externally. You talk to people, try to shift timings, seek apologies, avoid some people, and eventually carry guilt for a long time.

This happens because you perceive the conflict as external. If both parties demand your presence in different places at the same time, no human being can resolve that. Physical limitations of time, space, and substance will always exist, and there can never be a resolution on that level.

So, where is the resolution? What does resolution look like in such cases?

First, you must realize that the conflict is internal.

The external situation cannot truly be resolved; it can only be shuffled, juggled, or managed, but not resolved. Recognizing this conflict, do not attempt to resolve it — but dissolve it. Once you acknowledge that the real conflict is inside, you can begin the process of resolution. The first step is to accept the situation. Do not resist or fight the contradiction. Simply allow it to exist.

The resolution lies in recognizing the conflict and accepting the contradiction. By accepting that no external resolution is possible, you become a witness to the conflict, and through this awareness, the conflict dissolves.

Once this acceptance comes, the next step is simple: examine the options, choose the most mutually convenient solution, and move forward without dwelling on the conflict.

In short, the resolution to conflicts happens inside.

With this recognition, you are free from agitation or disturbance in the mind. Certainly, the agitation is reduced.

Essentially, it is a striving towards CONFLICT DISSOLUTION!

Do not dismiss this as merely a play of words. Think about it.

———•◆•———

You Are the Light

The idea of any "image" is not real. Your own image of yourself varies with time and context. Others' image of you is also based on context and convenience. Be anchored in who you are.

You are an individual, a combination of integrity, intention, commitment, empathy, etc. That never changes in any sphere, context, or time. Be anchored in who you are.

Others' expectation of you will continue to vary. That is based on their worldview and convenience. They may not know what is inspiring you to do what you do. Be anchored in who you are.

The people around will question things you do. Each one expects you to do what they want. They will be critical when what you do does not align with their likes. Be anchored in who you are.

Anything significant and truly of value will take time. If your heart wants to make a difference, go after it. Do not worry about what others say. Do not be concerned about how long it takes to have an outcome. Let the outcome not be in your favour. Be anchored in who you are.

You are the light, splendour, radiance. Like the sun that shines on everything alike, you shine irrespective of what presents itself. Be anchored in who you are.

When you hear the words "Be anchored in who you are", it is natural for you to ask the question "Who am I?"

Let that one question be your compass!

———•◆•———

My Real Identity

Overwhelmed by situations, I think I am weak.
Enamoured of the status I have in society, I think I am powerful.
Looking at all my possessions, I think I am rich.
Disturbed by some disease of the body, I think I am weak.

Agitated by circumstances, I think I am sad.

Overjoyed by favourable circumstances, I think I am happy.

Taking pride in my children, I think I am a parent.

Now I realize that these are not what identifies me.

These are not what or who I am.

The world may label me as this or that.

For convenience, I may also refer to myself as this or that.

But I am above all these.

"Who am I" is the next course of investigation.

Will that be the final frontier?

—•—•—

None can Bestow Freedom Upon Me

This world of names and forms cannot bestow eternal happiness upon me. The objects of this world cannot free me from suffering.

I believe that the Truth regarding my real nature will make me free. It is that Truth that shall liberate me from suffering.

That Truth lies beyond this world of infinite names and forms. It is not in the realm of objects.

It is that Truth that I am after.

How do I attain that Truth?

I know I cannot find it in a temple. I know I cannot find it in the numerous places of worship and pilgrimage. I know the scriptures will not reveal the Truth to me. They may talk about it and give me some ideas. While the guru can give me pointers for finding the Truth, the guru cannot hand it to me on a platter.

I know I will have to find it myself. I will have to realize it myself. It is my journey.

———•◆•———

Listening is Not to Know

You say "I am listening". What does listening mean?

Are you listening to know? Or are you listening to verify what you think you know? Or, are you listening to confirm that there is another who agrees with your belief?

Listening is just listening, without motive, agenda.

If you truly wish to learn, know that listening is a deep inner process and not one associated with the faculty of hearing. It is about suspending judgement regarding what you are listening to. It is about suspending reactions like "that was easy" or "that is complex". It is about suspending even acknowledgements like "got it", "that was beautiful", "correct", etc.

Listening is not about gathering information. It is about "just listening" without opinion.

Remember, listening is only the first step towards "knowing". Introspection is the next step. And realization is the final one.

Listen as if you are watching a flower. You are looking at it, without your mind even thinking "how beautiful", or wanting to possess it, or wanting to care for it, or wanting to offer it in a shrine.

Listen without expectations, listen without attachment. Do not listen to become something, or to get something. Listening is also not about effortful attention.

———•◆•———

The Idea of the 'Actionless Self'

Imagine the scene when we are writing something.

At the physical (gross) level, we are sitting at the study table, with a table lamp shining over a sheet of paper. At the next level, we may describe the activity as writing a story, a diary, a poem, or designing a machine.

At the next level, the mind and intelligence are working on the idea at hand, developing it and processing it, according to the context. At this level, the experience of the mind and intelligence is very different depending on what we are working on—a story, poem, or design.

Now, imagine a state when we are completely engrossed in the work. In that state, we are completely oblivious to the surroundings, oblivious to the tools we are using, and oblivious to bodily experiences (including any discomfort, pain, etc.).

Going further, we are even oblivious to the nature of the work we are doing. There is no difference, at that level, between writing a poem, a story, designing a machine, or even auditing accounts.

Go a little further. At this level, there is no good or bad action. We are also free from any preference and prejudice regarding the task we are performing. In other words, we do not feel either enjoyment or displeasure. Here, there is no notion of "my favourite activity", or "I hate this job".

After we come out of that state (on conclusion of the activity), we may say, "I enjoyed it". However, we were devoid of feelings at that time. Also, at that level, our inner faculties (mind, intelligence) are in perfect harmony, and at the height of their creativity.

Think, further. This is very significant. We are free from 'ego' (pride), in that state. We are free from the notion 'I am doing it'.

This is a glimpse of the Actionless Self!

------ •◆• ------

Truth Reveals Itself

Truth reveals itself to those whose intentions are pure. This might seem like an esoteric statement, but what does it really mean? To understand such statements, it is essential to delve into the meaning of each word. Despite their simplicity, these words pose a challenge. We often assume we understand them, but do we really?

What is Truth? Truth regarding what? In this context, it relates to our true or real nature; i.e., truth regarding who we really are. This Truth will also reveal the real nature of this world and our very source—the Creator (God).

Who will reveal this truth? Not the scriptures, not a guru, not even God.

The Truth itself will reveal itself:

to the one who seeks it;

to the one who aspires to know the Truth;

to the one who is sincere, and who is committed to seeking it;

to the one who seeks to know the Truth for no other gain, but for its own sake;

to the one with a singular goal of knowing the Truth.

When the mind is free from all other wants in the quest for knowing the Truth, and when the mind has surrendered to it, Truth will reveal itself.

What does the idea of "Truth will reveal itself" mean?

When the mind is free from all other wants, when it becomes quiet, and is free from its functions and movements, then the mind returns to its true nature, which is nothing but the Self.

In reality, the mind does not become something else. The mind's real nature is always that of the Self. Due to its limitations, we fail to see that real nature. But when the limitations and constrictions are removed, what is left is the Self alone.

When we examine it carefully, we find that it is not a process of seeking; it is not a process of finding or discovery; or seeing, feeling, or experiencing.

Since we do not have a different vocabulary for dealing with the subtle Self, we use terms like knowing, realizing, perceiving, etc. But truly speaking, none of these words are appropriate, because all these words require an object to be known, realized or perceived.

Closest we can say is, the Truth reveals itself. It is when we realize that the realizer and the realized are one and the same.

* * *

In 'Letting Go' Lies True Happiness

We have heard that the path to eternal happiness is a "knowledge pursuit".

Now, we think we must know everything. We make knowledge acquisition our pursuit. The only pursuit we have heard of comes from effort. We go about putting effort in searching for it all over the world. Our effort takes us to books, discourses, guides, podcasts, blogs, etc. It is relentless effort. Consequently, we have created a world of strife that comes from effort. Effort leads to stress.

We forget to pay attention to an important fact. The knowledge we seek lies right within us. So, let us let go of the "effort" in the quest for knowledge. Make it effortless.

Knowledge pursuit is an "effortless effort".

We are exposed to practices, concepts, and techniques. We continue to pursue more of them. We think the answer lies in every other practice, concept, technique, etc., that we do not know, resulting in more effort. Let go of running after every kind of information and knowledge in the world. What we need shall come to us.

We are told that this world is full of suffering. And we accept it. We never question why we cannot be happy in this world, without wanting to change everything. We never learn to be happy in the ocean of strife. We put effort into battling the huge waves. The secret is in surrendering to the waves, letting go of the paddle. Make it an "effortless effort".

As we begin to traverse the path, and pick up crumbs of "knowledge" along the way, we feel compelled to share our experiences, believing the "knowledge" we possess to be wisdom. More effort! Allow others to find their own way; allow them to fall and allow them to figure out when to rise from the fall. Allow their mistakes to be their light. Let go of the effort to "share" information and knowledge.

Let us let go of the idea of duty, for it becomes "effort" and "bondage". Let us take up an endeavour, because it is in our nature to do it. Let it be natural. Let it be an effortless effort.

Letting go is courage. Letting go is peace. Letting go is victory.

Acceptance without resistance is happiness.

Love the Origin, the Destination, and the Journey

For any journey, you have a starting point, a destination and a journey that takes us to the destination. The starting point or origin is not just a space. It also refers to the setting or environment we have.

For the journey to be wonderful and memorable, it is important that you should be happy with the place of origin, you should love the destination and you should enjoy the journey.

And when you decide to return home, you should be happy to leave the destination and look forward to getting home, and enjoy the journey back.

This tells you the state of your mind. If you "want to run away" from a place, then the journey will not be joyful, and you will not enjoy the destination.

The same is the case with the spiritual journey. Let the origin of the journey not be a place you want to run away from. Do not take up this journey because you are not happy with where you are.

------ • ● • ------

Always Bring to Mind the Oneness of Humanity

We look at a mirror, and we believe the image that the mirror throws at us, and we act on it. When we look at the mirror, we look at the face as one. We don't see the individual components in the face and spend time addressing them. We see the face as one unit, and any act of cosmetics is carried out seeing the face as one.

Imagine going to a doctor. The doctor too looks at the body as one. No organ is completely independent, at least from the point of view of cure. That oneness of vision of the doctor is very critical for any treatment.

Let us take a few steps back… perhaps many steps back. Imagine the picture of the Earth that the astronauts have taken from outer space. Take a long look at it and instil that image well in your mind. That is the image of our collective existence.

We cannot see our individual selves; we do not see the boundaries of nations; we do not see the different races and people; we just see the Earth as one. When we use the words 'we' or 'us,' imagine that vision of the Earth, not that of the country, continent, family, community, etc.

Unless we, as humans, begin to recognize this collective identity of ours, the future of the Earth as a whole and all the creatures, including the human species, is in threat. In our assumption that we are the most important creatures on this planet, we seem to have forgotten the responsibility we have towards the upkeep of the entire ecosystem.

If we consider ourselves the most intelligent species and believe that we have certain rights over this planet, we should not forget that we also have a responsibility towards the planet and its ecosystem, and most importantly, towards the generations to come.

We have been exploring outer space and some heavenly bodies, for nearly a century now. We are beginning to even claim control over some of those regions. It is time we get our act together regarding this Earth we live on, before we populate other regions of this cosmos.

Let us begin with the first step: see this Earth as one, and recognize that we are responsible for it.

Next time we think of the Earth, let us imagine the picture of the Earth taken from outer space. Always see it as one; see humanity as one. In that oneness lies our present; in that oneness lies peace; in that oneness lies our future.

My Very First School Teacher

Gazing over my books lined on the rack,

I sensed an uncertain pat on my back;

Fond companions ever they have been,

In a delightful quest into the world unseen.

'Should I be proud of this?' I thought,

'Tis only because of the one who taught!

It was you who kindled me, none other,

For my tiny intellect, you are the mother.

I feel a twinge of pain deep in my soul,

Seldom did I hail you for your subtle role;

Eager was I to march into the future,

How did I forget you, O school teacher!

Just a few of your names, I might recall,

And your faces too aren't clear at all;

It's as if I lost the most precious treasure,

How did I forget you, O school teacher!

Words fail, my heart knows what I feel,

Now I remember you, at the altar I kneel;

Pray, these thoughts I shall always nurture,

How did I forget you, O school teacher!

I stretch my dreams and aspirations wide,

Because you held my hand in my very first stride;

With pride, I celebrate my alma mater,

How did I forget you, O school teacher!

I still hear your chalk move on the board,

Never was I proud of the marks I scored;

It was in your hands I learnt the first letter,

How did I forget you, O school teacher!

What you instilled I shall carry to my end,

I seek forgiveness, for what I cannot mend;

Though I was not your gem, O jeweller,

I remain gratefully yours, my first teacher!

Why are we so Obsessed with Wanting to Know?

How often have we heard the following: "I had a great time; it was very useful", "I had a great time; I learnt a lot", "It was wonderful working here; learnt a lot", "Enjoyed my trip with you all; a great learning experience".

Why do we assess enjoyment using returns? Everything seems to be about learning, purpose, use, takeaway. This means, if we do not learn anything, then the interaction is not fun, joy, delightful, enriching.

Consequently, when we see something—the next thought is—"I wish I could do this too", "I will learn this", etc. Anything we like, we want to be able to do it. So, we want to learn it. We are not able be a mere witness to something.

What do we mean by knowledge? The following seems to be the trend: We acquire knowledge to get a certification. We acquire knowledge to build a resume. We acquire knowledge to solve a problem in the context of the world around us (in physics, chemistry, accounts, computers, etc.). We acquire knowledge to find employment. We acquire knowledge to tell ourselves and others that "I know". We acquire knowledge to be seen as "knowledgeable".

Regarding the knowledge we are seeking, let us ask ourselves: Does this knowledge help me become human? Does this knowledge bring peace to me? Does this knowledge help me unravel the mystery of life? Does this knowledge help me reveal to me my true nature? Does this knowledge help me get closer to happiness? Does this knowledge help me put an end to seeking knowledge! Does this knowledge help me become free?

These are profound questions regarding ourselves, our problems, life, this world, etc. These questions occupy our mind, and at times, agitate our mind? Will books or certifications lead us to the answers? Very unlikely.

How, then, do we find answers to these?

To begin with, make these personal. What is "my inner tumult"? What are the questions "I have"? How sincerely "do I want to know"? How desperately "do I want to know"?

When there is intensity of seeking, the enquiry begins. The enquiry will drive our "pursuit of knowledge". It will naturally lead us to what we need to know.

Remember, it is not objective knowledge (physics, mathematics, etc.). When the intensity of the enquiry increases, the answers will come to us. May not be in the form of a book, talk or a person. But the answers will come. Let us be certain of that.

Those are the answers that will matter. They are the ones that will make a difference.

* * *

The Mind's Conception of the Human Ideal

In the beginning, the human being had only one need. The need to survive—survive under the harsh conditions. The needs were basic—staying alive, food, shelter. However, the idea of basic needs grew with time. But then those needs remained bodily, physical needs.

As time passed, we began observing natural phenomena—rain, lightning, thunder, the movements of celestial bodies, storms, and more. Patterns emerged from these observations. The most natural pattern may have been the rising and setting of the sun, which eventually extended to an understanding of the seasons and other cyclical changes in nature.

But the curious and wondering intelligence of humans did not stop there. We began inventing and discovering things to make life easier and more comfortable. Gradually, we embarked on the path of scientific invention. This path provided challenges and stimulation for human intelligence, where scientists, adventurers, and researchers thrived.

However, we soon realized that life was not only about intellectual achievement. What about the challenges for the mind and the heart? The human mind began to search for a goal beyond mere survival and intellectual triumph. What could the mind aspire to, to enrich itself? What could it seek, to bring meaning and fulfilment to life?

The mind perhaps realized that true achievement lay not in outward acquisitions. Even after acquiring everything in life, the mind continued to yearn for more. It sought something greater, loftier—something beyond the realm of external successes and acquisitions. "What is the highest thing the mind can aspire to?" became the quest.

This quest was not to be found in material achievements. It was not satisfied by riches, the conquest of nations, the most precious of jewels, or even the highest levels of fame. If external achievements could not bring true satisfaction, then what could?

We began to imagine a mind that was lofty and glorious. Naturally, the question arose: what makes the mind lofty and glorious? This profound enquiry led us to explore the nature of the mind itself—"The mind thinking about itself, exploring its own lofty state." What a mysterious, beautiful, and fulfilling challenge this became for humanity—and the human mind did not fail in this endeavour.

Where did this quest begin? Likely, in the mind itself. What characterizes the mind? What defines us as human beings? It is the qualities we exhibit—love, hate, anger, compassion, courage, generosity, greed, and so on. Yet it is the virtues we value that give us strength. These virtues are the very traits of the mind.

Thus, humans realized that reaching the pinnacle of these virtues would represent the greatest of human achievements—greatest in courage, love, generosity, compassion, forgiveness, tolerance, and strength. This was the dream, the aspiration: to become the "ideal human," the "superhuman."

And so, the conception of a new human ideal emerged. It was the ideal we aspired to emulate, the goal we dreamed of becoming.

Isn't it natural for humans to dream of being something more, something superhuman? For some, this dream gave more joy than any external achievement.

Thus, was born the idea of God. God is nothing but the human aspiration for our own potential perfection. God is the conception of a "perfect human," the imagination of what the ideal human would be. God represents our idea of perfection—the highest we can hope to achieve.

Like any other branch of knowledge or human endeavour, this too developed. In the aspiration to achieve this ideal, humans created systems that we now call "religion" and "spirituality." Various philosophies arose, with different communities conceiving this "superhuman" in diverse ways. Some of these became established religions.

The idea of "God" came into existence because of humanity's aspiration to rise higher and higher in every sphere of life. To discover the best within ourselves and attain that perfection latent in us. Being human, many of us gave this superhuman a human form. Some gave it the status of divinity, while others saw it as the greatest endeavour—the journey toward perfection.

The realization of this "perfection" or "near-perfection" is often referred to as "realization." Different systems offered different interpretations, with some calling it "God-realization" or "self-realization." The terminology is not what matters. What is important is to recognize it as the pursuit of the "potential perfection" within us.

Remember, the human virtues are the same in all of us. Regardless of where we come from, as humans, we share the same set of qualities. Externally, we may differ in gender, colour, language, and so on, but the core human qualities are universal. No human can say, "I don't know what kindness or hate is." We are all the same. More importantly, the concept of the superhuman is the same for all humans.

This is why equality and oneness are central themes in spiritual pursuit. Let us recognize that we are all equal. The potential for perfection is the same in all beings, as is the notion of "perfection" or "near-perfection" if that feels more comfortable. We, as humans, shall always remain equal. Recognizing the highest lies in acknowledging and realizing the oneness and equality of all beings. When we see equality, humility arises within us, preparing us for the highest.

Love subsumes all other qualities. Love is the foundation of all virtues. It dissolves negative traits and removes all differences. Love is the easiest path to the goal. It is the simplest way to reach that ideal.

Let us love without distinction. Let us love without discrimination. Let us love without the sense of "I and mine." In that unselfish and unconditional love, we attain the zenith of love. We become incarnations of love itself. In becoming embodiments of love, we become "superhuman"—or whatever name we choose, including "God." Love is the only true religion, if we are to have any idea of religion at all.

Transcend the Idea Called Time

We have created so many concepts in our heads that they fill our minds. On this path of spirituality, which is ultimately meant to make life simple, we have created many complex and intricate concepts, entangling ourselves in a web of our own making.

We have created a jungle of various concepts infested with demons of all shapes and sizes. In the context of the journey to realize the Self, "time" is one such notion.

The human being created the idea of time, of course, for a certain convenience. But when this notion of time enters the domain of spirituality, we are in for a surprise. Why is it so? Examine this point carefully.

When there are ideas like past and future, it gives rise to suffering. In other words, dwelling in the past or dreaming of the future, is how suffering is born. It is the Self that transcends notions of past, and future. In that sense, it is "timeless" and "eternal."

But that notion of time, which evolved as a harmless idea, has now trapped humanity in its clutches. We say, "time is money," "time is everything," "I don't have time," and so on. Every moment of our life is governed by time. Rather, we are slaves to the very time that we created. That benign entity has become a demon that devours us.

To realize the Self, one must transcend the idea of time.

———•———

Are they Your Concepts, Your Theories?

Imagine you have the following query—"why do unfavourable things happen to me?" You approach someone to find an answer to that. And you get the following response—"It is all because of your past karma".

You are quite satisfied with that answer. You had been struggling for the last couple of years trying to find out why your life is so full of problems. And this one response seems to have put your mind to rest.

You feel very relieved and a great load is off your shoulders. And life begins to feel quite peaceful again.

But after a few weeks, something happens. And you are back to square one. You think about the idea of 'karma' that you had heard about a few weeks ago. But now you are not so convinced. You have doubts.

Your negative feelings are back. You feel that life has been quite unfair to you.

Why does this happen? Just a few weeks ago when you heard that "karma" was the answer to all your problems, you were relieved. You had felt that that was the answer to your troubles. But now you are not sure about it.

Why does this happen?

You are full of your own ideas, concepts, models, theories, beliefs, convictions, doubts, etc., that you have cultivated over years, and life experiences have instilled other notions.

When earlier you were told that "your troubles were the result of karma", you accepted them because you were desperate for an answer. But soon doubts crept in and it no longer provides relief from your troubles.

The other possibility is that you soon discovered, upon deeper reflection, that the new answer you received conflicts with other ideas, theories, and your belief system. Over time, you had established a harmony among all the different ideas, theories, models, definitions, etc. When you come across another idea that does not completely dovetail into all the existing ideas, etc., you now have a potential conflict.

What do you do now?

Spend time on the new idea(s) you come across. Do not accept theories, ideas, or concepts that someone talks about, without your own assessment of them. Reflect on them well and make sure you are free from doubts, having ensured that the new idea is in harmony with your own existing system of ideas.

If the new idea is in contradiction or conflict with any other beliefs in your existing ecosystem, then that will cause more disturbance, confusion, etc. It may also begin to question some of your existing beliefs. That will give rise to more problems!

What do you do?

Think for yourself! Think, think, and think again. Devote time for understanding and introspection over any new idea till it becomes a conviction, and is deeply established in your ecosystem of beliefs. It should become part of you, and not remain a piece of information, or an intellectual point! Make that new idea your own!

———— • ⬤ • ————

Going beyond the Myths Regarding Unemployment

The dictionary defines the word "unemployed" as "not engaged in a gainful occupation." Most people interpret "occupation" as a person's profession, work, or trade. This narrow definition is where the problems begin. We fail to look at the wider interpretation of the world "occupation": "any activity that occupies a person's attention."

If we use this broader definition, then being unemployed does not seem so bad, does it? Let us now explore it further.

Why is it that people struggle to imagine a state where they are not employed? Unfortunately, for many, this state is accepted as a normal for women in certain communities and cultures even today. However, this condition is gradually changing.

But my focus here is not the gender issue; but the condition of unemployment itself.

Why are people averse or uncomfortable with the state of being unemployed? Many are even afraid of it.

In reality, it is not just the financial aspect that causes anxiety to people, though it is one of the contributors. Even those who are economically well off are unable to accept the possibility of unemployment.

However, it is rather strange that many of those who are employed continue to do so without being sure of what they are trying to achieve through employment. Most of them also realize (mostly a little late) that what they are trying to achieve (i.e. peace and contentment) is outside the domain and scope of employment.

Otherwise, after years of being employed, they would not raise questions like, "what am I doing?", "is this what life is all about?" and so on.

In general, people associate the state of being employed only with economic independence or at least economically comfortable. This too, empirically analysed, is just a mindset.

Even some of the very creative and enterprising ones cannot imagine what they would do if they were unemployed. For most, being unemployed means being inactive.

But, being unemployed definitely does not mean being inactive. Inactivity is not a state of the body. It is a state of one's mind. Physical activity begins with the mind alone.

The more important question to ask is "am I gainfully active?"

Here "gainfully" does not imply a remuneration or compensation, and "active" does not imply activity at a physical level. It is all about engaging in activities that stimulate the intelligence, intellectual capacity, creative instinct, etc. It means "not being mentally inactive."

A higher dimension of thought could be: we think of being gainfully occupied for someone else or for society or the globe at large.

This discussion is beyond the scope of those individuals who need to be employed for a compensation, to provide for themselves and others who depend on them for necessities of life.

For many, the need for compensation is non-negotiable.

Many cannot identify some area of interest to engage in (full time), "which does not bring money". They would rather be "unhappy" doing what they don't like to do or what they don't want to do, as long as they are being suitably compensated.

In fact, people in general would rather be unhappy doing what they don't like to do, for an organisation they are not happy with, for (or with) people they are not comfortable with, for salaries they are unsatisfied with, for causes they are not concerned with, for a future they are not sure of, than face the idea of being unemployed.

Based on these thoughts, let us examine and challenge some of the myths related to unemployment:

If you are unemployed, you are a loser. If you are unemployed, you are inactive. If you are unemployed, you don't know what to do with your time. If you are unemployed, you are free all the time. If you are unemployed, you have been fired. If you are unemployed, you are confused about what you want to do with your life. If you are unemployed and not looking for a job, you must have millions in the bank. If you are unemployed and not looking for a job, then you must be out of your mind. If you are unemployed, you are vegetating intellectually. If you are unemployed, you are incapable of finding a job. And the list goes on.

The important question we need to ask ourselves is: "Is the aim of employment only to bring in funds?". Many would claim that they look for job satisfaction. But even in their cases, in the final analysis, it is most often about money.

Whether it is employment or the absence of it, the assessment of one's status should be based on one's peace of mind.

------ ● ------

The Notion of Giving Back to Society

During a conversation with a friend, I was asked, "What do you do?"

"What a question!" I thought. It is perhaps a simple one, but how does someone like me—who is not employed, not self-employed, and without a specific role or designation—respond to that without seeming like I am trying to avoid the answer?

"In conventional terms, I don't do anything," I said. The next question was, "Don't you feel like giving back to society?"

Now, a day later, I am thinking and writing about it.

What does "giving back to society" mean? Giving back *what?* What have I taken? Such thoughts are arising…

Isn't "giving" a very natural process? I mean, is there a deliberate attempt or thought behind the act of giving?

Does a tree—laden with flowers, fruits, and all it has to offer, including shade—consciously think and resolve, "I must now give"?

Isn't the natural flowering and fruiting inextricably linked to giving? Doesn't the natural growth of the tree naturally result in giving? There is a harmony, a natural synchrony between the tree's fulfilment (in becoming a tree) and its act of giving.

Perhaps we should call it "taking by society (nature)" rather than "giving by the tree."

Isn't it the same for a human? Isn't motherhood a natural process of giving? Is a mother "giving back"? Motherhood, nurturing, being loved, and being nurtured—aren't these naturally *one*? Can we separate them? They are all harmoniously bound together.

What is this the result of? How does the individual experience it?

Fulfilment! When an individual is fulfilled or content, whatever follows will naturally benefit those around them.

When a plant grows to its fulfilment (maturity), what follows naturally benefits all beings—humans, creatures, and even other plants. There is no conscious effort, no deliberateness. When it happens naturally, no one is harmed, and harmony results. We call this "ecological balance" in the context of nature.

What is fulfilment in the case of a human being? It is a sense of contentment, fullness, and satisfaction—when we feel no sense of lack, when we realize that nothing in the world can bring lasting peace and happiness to the mind. There is nothing more to be done or achieved.

When fulfilment happens, what follows is the natural taking and receiving by everything and everyone around. Giving, in this case, is not a selective process—deciding *what* to give, *whom* to give to, *when* to give, *how* to give, or *how much* to give. Nature extracts and receives whatever, however much, and whenever. And there is complete harmony!

Can it be any different for humans, being such an integral part of Nature? Once true fulfilment happens, whatever follows is giving—or rather, taking and receiving—and it will be natural.

Let my endeavour be to reach that fulfilment.

Who am I to decide what to give, when to give, and how to give?

Let it be a natural evolute of the state of fulfilment.

I believe that when fulfilment happens, only giving can follow—and will follow.

———•❖•———

What is Creation and Who is the Creator?

When I am referring to the word 'creator', I am not referring to the Lord, God or any divine entity. And by 'creation', I am not referring to the universe and all that it contains. Here by 'creator' I am referring to you and I, anybody who is trying to create something. For example, an artist is a creator and the painting is the creation.

We are, all the time, up to creating something—small or big, insignificant or something valuable.

Any time we are engaged in creating something, our attention and focus are often not on the task at hand. While our hands, eyes, ears, and even part of the mind are engaged in the activity, a part of a mind is cluttered with many other thoughts.

What thoughts occupy our mind? All unrelated thoughts, at least to the task at hand.

Here are some of the thoughts that often float around in our mind: "What will people say? Will people appreciate what I have done? Will I be rewarded? I may be punished, if I fail. I will get that promotion. I might get a handsome amount of money." And so on.

When such thoughts occupy our mind, how can what we do be significant, valuable? How can it be benevolent? How can that change the course of my life, leave alone changing the future of humanity?

We just "did" something. That's all. It cannot qualify as a 'significant creation'.

But just imagine—if we did something with no other distracting thoughts—not even thoughts about why we are doing it, not wondering how we started it, not worried about when it will be completed, not anxious about whether it will ever be completed, not mindful of the response from others, not mindful of whether we will live to see it completed and so on...but only focused on giving it all that we got, all the attention of our mind, all the heartfulness we can muster.

In such a scenario, what we will end up creating will indeed be special. It will indeed be significant. Such a creation becomes greater and grander than the creator!

What a state to be in!

Unfortunately, we associate a finite dimension with the human creativity. Only the body has limits—physical limits. But from within this finite physical entity comes infinite thoughts, ideas, and possibilities. It makes the physical hand create something that has infinite reach and potential and is capable of changing the course of mankind.

From the small physical thing called the brain, comes the infinitely resourceful ideas which have the potential to alter the trajectory of the human race.

The created becomes greater and mightier than the creator.

Let us think again. The creator is not what we see as the physical individual. It is that infinite potential within that individual. If that is so, how can we say that the created is greater than the creator?

It is a never-ending seesaw of what is greater—the created or the creator!

Carve Out Your Own Path...
It is Your Responsibility

When it comes to the spiritual path, there are hundreds of texts, each talking about ways and means of attaining the "goal".

The 'goal' itself seems rather mysterious as it is also described as something that is not easily attainable, as it is not easily definable. Despite that, the different scriptures attempt to describe the goal, and to the seeker these attempts appear different.

With all that vagueness about the description of the goal, how is it that we can have a well-defined path? But the scriptures talk about their own version of the "path", with pre-requisites, techniques, obstacles, etc.

Over and above the scriptures, there are numerous commentaries each one taking a different approach to interpret the texts. Then we have the preceptors who further interpret it for the disciples, seekers, and followers. They provide guidance on what to do and what not to do, with "instructions".

While we are faced with these numerous ideas, instructions, etc., when it comes to "realizing" those concepts, the responsibility falls squarely on the shoulders of the individual seeker. No one, including the scriptures, tells the seeker how to achieve that.

Now, the seeker has to do the following:

- Interpret it for oneself (based on one's own personality and life)

- See what one needs to do and not to do

- Figure out each of the steps in the journey

If the seeker does not approach the journey with complete clarity and freedom, is the attainment of the goal possible? With chains of so many instructions, how can the goal be achieved?

It is the seeker's responsibility to figure out the nuances of the way forward. Broad terms and concepts do not help, when it comes to making sense of the activities of the mind. The seeker has to dig deeper into their own inner realm. It has to be "the individual's" own effort. None can lead the seeker to their spiritual goal.

Those Words from Many Centuries Ago

[Note: Scriptures that play an important part in our spiritual pursuit come to us from authors from centuries ago. This is addressed to those authors.]

Your words felt like the touch of a tender bud

They caressed me like the morning rays of the sun

They held me like the mother's tender embrace

Your words that were penned many centuries ago.

Your heart spoke to me from the distant past

The letters carried the vibrations through time

But I know, dear poet, they were meant for me

For they brought hope, comfort, and abundant glee.

Despatched by you, O poet unknown to me

In a language I do not claim as my own

But the waves of love from your beating heart

Now resonate with mine that is so far apart.

Your affectionate message from centuries ago

I hold in my hands, with fondness though

While the words were cast upon the lake of your heart

It has created beautiful ripples in my humble soul.

Wrapped in thoughts I send you my love

O Poet of then, who is so close to me now

I cherish this divine correspondence, my friend

I hope you feel the love of this distant soul.

Holding on to the "Notion" of Good and Bad

Somehow, all of humanity tends to believe that being good is important. "Goodness is a virtue and that is what we should pursue", is the general feeling. I am not about to challenge that belief. However, I do have a different take on the subject.

At least politically everyone favours the good, even if they actually do not live accordingly or believe it to be so.

However, if we are obsessed with the good and are constantly with the thought of doing the right, does it not naturally mean that we are becoming intolerant to the opposite, "not good", or "not right".

We become intolerant or unaccepting or uncompromising towards anything that "we believe" is "not good" or "not right". Note that we operate from the point of view of the compass we have.

Let us not forget that the idea of good or bad, right or wrong is only a "belief", a subjective assessment our mind makes based on the existing ideas we have.

So, if we make a mistake in our judgement, then there is a greater chance that we are becoming rigidly opposed to the person or situation which is not based on our belief. Over time, we tend to become more constricted in our world view, because it is constantly fed by our rigid notions of good and right. Right from childhood, we are taught to reject the bad or wrong, and we are given to labelling individuals and situations as good or bad.

What is the way out?

We need to develop the quality of acceptance of anything—good or bad and right or wrong. More importantly, we should not become intolerant of the "not good" or "not right".

The key point is: When we rigidly hold on to one view, we become intolerant of the opposite. It is so even in the case of faith or religion, or belief system. We begin to become intolerant of every other faith or religion or belief system. The same applies to our ideas, our Nation, our community, and so on.

Imagine what it does to us as individuals and consequently to the human race!

Don't Do it Because Somebody Said So

You are struggling with a challenge or a problem. You approach someone seeking guidance, or you read a book. You come across something that seems to precisely address and solve the problem you are facing.

Pause! Think again!

What you read or heard is someone else's experience, and that experience has been presented in a certain way. Going through an experience is one thing; sharing or writing about it is another. The writing or speaking can never be complete. Words and speech can only represent our experiences to a limited extent. They cannot fully justify our experiences.

Now we are trying to take those words and apply them to our lives. Wait!

There is another crucial point: what the other individual had was their experience. That experience is based on several factors, such as their personality, the circumstances and context in which the event occurred, their worldview, the people involved, their feelings and emotions at the time, the challenges they encountered before arriving at a solution, and the background or history leading up to the situation, among many other things.

All these elements are unique to each of us.

How then can we just take up someone else's experience and apply it to our lives as it is? Even in the case of fitness or dieting, what applies to one person may not apply to another. If this is true for the body, will it not also be true for the mind? Because dealing with challenges or problems of the mind is a matter of the mind itself.

So, does this mean one cannot gain anything from another's life?

No, of course we can gain from others' experiences. Let us explore in what way.

First of all, it is evidence that the problem can be addressed and resolved. If anyone can do it, I too can. That conviction is the first benefit and the most crucial.

But this does not mean that if others have not been able to solve the problem, I cannot.

Remember, there is a first for everything. (For example, Erik Weihenmayer was the first visually impaired person to climb Mount Everest.)

The other crucial point is to feel inspired. Draw inspiration from others. That goes a long way in shaping our personality and our lives. When we have role models, let us be inspired by them and their personality, rather than just trying to imitate what they do or how they live.

Often, we hear the idea of emulating what others do. This is actually not possible, for the very same reasons we have discussed above.

We can look at them and their behaviour and draw the core values they embody, then try to instil those values in ourselves.

The other key point is to examine what they did or the case studies we hear about and deeply introspect over them. Do not blindly take up what you heard or read, and do not just try to replicate them or their practices.

Introspect deeply and see how they relate to you. Get to the bottom of it, and that deep understanding will help you adapt it for yourself and internalize it.

Because we often do not introspect over these things, and we blindly take up something to adopt in our lives, we more often fail in our endeavours.

Do not simply adopt; adapt to your needs!

Do not imitate what others do. Do not be enamoured by what others do. Think deeply.

Remember, you are a different person, with a different personality, different needs, wants, desires, and aspirations. Your settings and contexts are different, as are your background, upbringing, conditioning, and thought processes. And this list goes on.

How can you then just try to imitate something just because someone said so?

Remember, it is their knowledge; it is their experience; it is from their context. It cannot, as is, apply to you.

Think! Think! Think!

Life is a Journey of the Mind

We often wonder, "What is life?" It seems like a profound question to ask. We also tend to ask this rhetorical question when faced with despair.

Here is one way to look at life: life is a series of experiences—pleasant and unpleasant, good and bad, agreeable and disagreeable. These experiences stem from situations and events that present themselves—whether comfortable or uncomfortable, easy or difficult.

Whenever we experience anything in this world, the experience belongs entirely to the mind. In other words, it is the mind that feels and interprets the experience, responding with happiness or sorrow, pleasure or pain.

While the universe and its phenomena are part of the external world, the experience itself always occurs in the inner realm of the mind. Thus, we can call the journey of life an "inner journey" or a "journey of the mind."

So, what does this mean for us? What insight does it offer about life?

We falsely believe that our happiness depends on acquiring and controlling objects of the external world. In reality, happiness comes from mastering the mind. Mastery over the mind is, in fact, the real mastery over the world.

Keep the Intelligence Away After Some Time

Intelligence is considered a key instrument at our disposal on the spiritual path. Not that, outside of this pursuit, you can set aside the intelligence and hope to succeed. What I mean is that it is often discussed and given a lot of importance. It is almost as if spirituality exists of, by, for, and through intelligence.

When you consider the mind and intelligence, the intelligence is considered superior to the mind. The Bhagavad Gita explicitly states this.

But sometimes, I wonder whether we even need intelligence at all. More precisely, I feel that trying to do too much with intelligence may not be helpful.

The moment intelligence comes into play, it starts analysing, reasoning, and understanding. And what intelligence analyses, reasons, or understands is always something other than itself. It does this so rationally and impartially because it knows it is dealing with an external entity.

Deep down, the intelligence is "rational" because it knows that it is analysing, reasoning, or cognizing "something else" (other than itself). When it examines itself, however, objectivity and rationality are compromised.

Unfortunately, we tend to accept that intelligence is superior to the mind. Qualities like *viveka* (discrimination between the permanent and transient, real and unreal) are associated with intelligence, which "intelligently" analyses everything.

Yet, in the end, what truly matters is feeling, being, or experiencing—and this is the domain of the mind. It is the experience of vastness that matters, not the knowing or understanding of it.

[*The Supreme Reality* (Brahman) is what we are alluding to when we speak of vastness, expanse, or infinitude.]

It is the experience of the oneness with the universe that is important, not the intellectual understanding of it. It is the experience of the identification with the Supreme Reality that matters, not the knowing of this identification.

Another important point: all the values required for personal transformation—love, compassion, empathy—are related to the mind.

Think!

Yes, we need the intelligence to read, study and understand the scriptures.

But the scriptures themselves state that all scriptures are a 'burden' if there is only intellectual understanding without realization. Realization refers to the living or experiencing of the knowledge in life.

Without realization, all this remains a mere intellectual pursuit.

Scriptures also state explicitly that the Supreme cannot be apprehended by the intelligence. One must go beyond the mind and intelligence to realize the Truth.

Let us not overemphasize the role of the intellect in the pursuit of knowledge.

Be Free from the Bondages of Disciplines and Routines!

What you seek is the Truth—

The Truth that is ever-existent;

The Truth that transcends space and time;

The Truth that is beyond ideas and concepts.

Why then, O Mind,

Do you seek it through regulations?

Why do you seek it through discipline?

Why do you seek it through routines?

How can you confine Truth to a "holy shrine"?

How can you structure Truth in a "sacred spot"?

How can you bind Truth to an "auspicious hour"?

How can you condense Truth in the "pages of a book"?

How can you fragment the Whole,

Into your idea of auspicious and the ominous?

How can you split that One Ever-pure,

In what you deem as pure and blemished?

How can you seek the Unbounded,

Through the strictures of a routine?

How can you seek the Unconditioned,

In the conditioned actions of a ritual?

How can you realize Truth by prostrations?

Know every action of yours to be Divine.

How can you reach the Truth through a "sacred mantra"?

Know every thought of yours to be Divine.

How can you invoke Truth through mere chants?

Know every sound in this universe to be Divine.

How can you access the Truth by lighting a lamp?

Know every atom in this universe is illumined by that Divine.

Seek Truth in freedom from limitations,

Seek Truth in freedom from qualifications,

Seek Truth in freedom from demarcations,

Seek Truth in freedom from prohibitions and injunctions.

Rise, O Mind!

Rise above the restrictions of time!

Rise above the limitations of words!

Rise above the restraints of actions!

Soar like a bird!

Go beyond the sky,

Sky is not your limit,

For, you are the Infinite, where that sky is!

Let us Not Say "I Didn't Have a Choice"

We often hear the phrase "I didn't have a choice," sometimes even coming from our own lips. But if we give it a moment's thought, we might realize that this isn't entirely true. Why?

When we say "I didn't have a choice," what we are really expressing is that the alternatives available to us seemed too difficult or too daunting to consider. The other options might have appeared more challenging, more demanding, more damaging, or involved greater struggle.

We tend to say "I didn't have a choice" when, in reality, the choices we had were simply ones we weren't comfortable making.

Isn't an Ideal Worth Striving for?

There are times in life when we do not pursue an option because we think, "It is the ideal choice, but I'd rather not go that way." This often happens in the context of self-improvement or personal change.

Why give up a pursuit or option just because it is "ideal"? Isn't that strange?

Shouldn't we be inspired or motivated to take up something precisely because it is ideal, rather than dismiss it? If we consider something as ideal, doesn't that give us a greater reason to pursue it with all our energy and enthusiasm?

What does the ideal stand for? Why did we think of it in the first place?

If the mind has conceived of it as an "ideal," it must be worth pursuing! It must be special!

What lies before us is something beyond the mundane and ordinary. Shouldn't that be reason enough to challenge ourselves to go after it? That is why we call it an "ideal."

But we choose to set it aside and label it as "ideal," almost as if it is an excuse not to strive for it. We do not want to put in the effort toward perfection or excellence. Yet, an ideal is exactly what is worth striving for.

Next time we use the term "ideal" in thought or speech, let us give serious thought to our intent in that context.

The Ego That This is "My Chosen Path"

When we take up a path—whether in religion, spirituality, or anything else—all we need to do is focus on that path.

But instead, the mind tends to dwell on paths that are not ours. We compare, overthink, and engage in discussions about how our chosen path is better than others.

Much of the public discourse centres around how one path is superior to another.

Specifically, how *my* path is better than *yours*, how *my* path is the best, how *I* am so fortunate and blessed to be on this path.

There is so much distraction. The more we follow a path simply because we believe it to be better than others, the more likely we are to someday encounter another path that appears better than ours. And when that happens, we may be tempted to try that.

So, what is the way? There is only one perspective to adopt: this is the path that will take us to our goal. We unnecessarily and incorrectly give ourselves credit, thinking we have chosen this path.

My Teachers at Every Turn

The sun that scorches, and the moon that cools,

The rains that nurture, and the harmony of nature,

The sea with its waves, and the mountain with its caves,

The volcanoes that erupt, and the rainbow that soothes—

These are my friends, guides, and preceptors forever.

The boulder that stands tall, and the river that meets the sea,

The seed so small, and the tree that gives shade,

The leaf that merrily falls, and the flower that blooms,
The lion that kills, and the vulture that soars—
These are my friends, guides, and preceptors forever.

The parents' love, and the stranger that helps,
The friend that scolds, and the mate at work,
The vendor on the road, and the doctor who cures,
The school teacher who taught, and the friend who fought—
These are my friends, guides, and preceptors forever.

The journeys I take, and the hurdles I face,
The turns I take, and the steps I miss,
The successes I got, and the failures I had,
The choices I make, and the convictions I have—
These are my friends, guides, and preceptors forever.

The questions I ask, and the mistakes I make,
The lies I tell, and the truths I uphold,
The times of sorrow, and the moments of joy,
The occasions of doubt, and sparks of clarity—
These are my friends, guides, and preceptors forever.

The traditions I inherited, and the scriptures I hold,
The conflicts I face, and the moment of silence that dawns,
The emotions I experience, and the reasoning brain,
The inner voice, and the Self above all—
These are my friends, guides, and preceptors forever.

———•◆•———

"Good and Bad" Are the Mother of all Dualities

We are largely driven by the idea of "this is good" and "this is bad." Regarding everything, we hold clear notions of good and bad. Over time, these become deeply ingrained impressions of what is good and what is bad.

On the spiritual path, where we seek to attain freedom or realize oneness with the Supreme, the idea of good and bad becomes the greatest impediment.

Why? Because these notions of good and bad create the strongest duality of all. We are so entangled in them that, throughout our lives, we continue to fan the flames of this dichotomy. This duality extends to concepts of right and wrong, which further fuel the greatest delusion (good and bad) of all. It is this delusion that guides our decisions throughout life—imagine how biased those decisions become!

It is a delusion because nothing is inherently good or bad. Good and bad are subjective, with no absolute truth to them.

We accept or reject the objects of the world—things, situations, people, etc.—based on these subjective notions of good and bad.

If we cannot be free from these pairs of opposites—good and bad—how can we hope to attain the ultimate freedom, the freedom from duality, and thereby realize the non-dual One?

How, then, can we attain a vision of equality? How can we see the Divine in both the good and the bad? How can we experience the Divine at all?

This constant acceptance and rejection undermine the understanding that it is the same Supreme Being that forms the substratum of everything.

This first pair of opposites we experience, and continue to reinforce throughout life, is the most dangerous of all. We must transcend it.

When we Come Across News Concepts and Models

When we encounter a new concept, model, or idea, what thoughts immediately flash through our minds? Often, it begins with joy; we are overwhelmed by the discovery. We feel thrilled with what we have found and are eager to share it with others. This seems like a very natural response. Many of us go through this sequence of reactions.

But often, we don't stop there. There is a tendency to map the newly discovered idea onto something we already know or relate it to other concepts we are familiar with. We feel that this new idea fits into many other contexts we have previously encountered.

And that is where we often go wrong!

This can be explained by the adage: "When all we have is a hammer, everything looks like a nail." In the sphere of spirituality, this mistake is common and quite prominent.

We have come across this often in the context of the Bhagavad Gita. We find a verse, and its message feels profound. Eager to apply it, we sometimes try to force-fit it into a context where it doesn't belong. For instance, some individuals may take a verse from the Bhagavad Gita and claim that it explains "innovation," while another verse is said to explain "human resource management."

But in doing so, several problems arise. First, we take a lofty idea and reduce it to a trivial concept. Second, we try to apply it to a context it was never meant for. Over time, as we realize it doesn't work in that context, we might wrongly conclude that the idea itself doesn't work, ignoring the fact that it wasn't intended for this situation. Lastly, repeated failures like this may lead us to conclude that the Bhagavad Gita is not a practical treatise.

So, what should we do when we come across something new?

We must get to the depths of the new concept because, with only a superficial understanding, we are bound to make the mistakes outlined above. Furthermore, we should not rush to apply it to another domain or context. And finally, we must not lose the joy of the discovery by immediately thinking of new applications. In our eagerness to find new ways to apply the idea, we may neglect to understand the full implications of the concept we have uncovered.

———•———

O Solitude—You are My Faithful Companion Forever

I thought I was but a lonely traveller,

With many things in life to discover;

Scriptures were my mates in every stride,

And my intellect was my only guide.

Everything changed for me along the way,

When I met you, without having to pray;

While my journey was still the same,

You lit it like a splendorous flame.

Your presence was a glorious light,

Made every moment cheerful and bright;

Warmth I felt in your silent words,

Was like sweet songs of cheerful birds.

I feel your company at every step,

Blessed am I for this precious help;

You, my dear, make my life complete,

I look forward to every moment I greet.

I still am a solitary traveller here,

But I feel your eternal company, my dear;

In silence I sense your hands in mine,

For me that is but the touch divine.

———•—●—•———

What is My Path?

Since this morning, a new thought has gripped me: Can a particular path give one freedom?

A given path has its own principles, disciplines, ideas, and concepts. Can a single set of these completely free me? By following this particular set of concepts, am I not getting bound again? Now, I am bound by a new set of rules, principles, and concepts. I am conditioned by these ideas because I see life, the world, and the Truth through that window (or set of windows) or lenses.

Do I really need Vedanta and its philosophies to discover the Truth?

Based on who or what I am, I need to carve out my own path. It is like saying: To get to the top of the mountain, I will have to pave my own way. Yes, it does sound counter-intuitive. But it is a journey of my mind, through my mind, and by the mind. Most importantly, it is of my mind. So, the path must be my path. I will have to pave my way through the landscape of my mind.

Walking an already traversed path may not apply to me—or rather, will not apply to me. That's because I am a different human being. Each of us is a unique individual.

All I believe in is the fact that the destination can be reached. Traversing my personal landscape is the only way. I must do it on my own terms.

In deciding there is a destination, and having the conviction that I will reach it, lies my first step.

There are no road signs, no milestones. I do see other travellers, but they too have their own journey. I am not competent to show them the way because they, too, must figure out their own path. Nor do I have to follow them; they cannot show me my path or my destination. They cannot guide me in any meaningful way. But we can be fellow travellers.

I believe that each step I take moves me forward. And I am sure I am headed in the right direction. Actually, let me correct myself—there is no right or wrong direction. Every step is in the right direction. It cannot be otherwise. I will not be lost.

I do not care how long my journey lasts. I do not care if I never reach the destination. I know that I will enjoy the journey itself. Each step, each time I move forward, is a discovery, an experience. It enriches me, makes my experience unique, and defines my journey.

I do not wish to be known as someone who has reached the destination. Perhaps I would be happier if I never reach it. As I take each step forward, let my destination shift. Let that, too, be an experience I cherish, an experience I enjoy, an experience that makes me a better person.

There is neither darkness nor light on my path. Each step carries its own light.

I do not know if I will leave footprints for others to follow. Let that not be the thought that defines my journey.

I am reminded of J. Krishnamurti's statement: "Truth is a pathless land." I am not entirely sure what he meant by those words, but I seem to have my own interpretation of what they mean.

O Lord, You are Love Itself

O Lord, the whole world searches for you. Where are you? I, too, embarked on that quest, introduced to it by others, as though I were part of a grand treasure hunt—an unsolvable puzzle, an elusive enigma.

But then, like the rising sun breaking the darkness, clarity dawned in my mind. I realized my mistake. I had been searching in a direction pointed out by others, following a path not meant for me. It was their way, not mine.

I doubted. I lacked faith, conviction. Even when I tried, my mind wandered, as if lost in a rocky terrain, as if traversing a barren desert. Then came the understanding: I cannot find you through such harsh, external paths.

If you exist, as they say you do—existing within and through all—then you are in every heart that beats, in every mind that thinks, in every being that exists, in every heart that loves.

You pervade all, O Lord. If you are present in every heart, then you can only manifest as love—nothing but love.

You are love itself. It is not merely happiness—it transcends that. It is pure, boundless love.

If you are in every heart, then you are the love that pulses within it. You are the love a beloved has for her lover. You are the love a mother carries for her child. You are the love a patriot cherishes for their nation. You are the very love that manifests this world.

How could I, O Lord, seek you by any other means? You are the love that underpins every relationship. You are even the love that exists within hatred.

How blind I have been. How lost, how ignorant. But now, I wish to find you. I wish to recognize you. I wish to embrace you, for you are love itself.

O Lord, may my heart become an embodiment of this love. May it connect with every heart that beats, for you reside in them all. Grant me the vision to see you in each heart, to recognize the love that lies beneath the layers of the blemish called hate.

O Lord, may this entire being be filled with that love, that you are, the love that every being, in essence, already is.

It is your love that colours the rainbow. It is your love that flashes in the lightning. It is your love that rumbles in the thunder. It is your love that is the warmth in the sunlight, and the coolness in the moon's glow.

O Lord, it is this love that we recognize as compassion. It is this love we call empathy, generosity, and kindness.

O Lord, fill me with this love. Let me see you in that love, for in this love alone, you and I are one.

You Are the Very Light!

Know your Self
 to be the only light of this universe;
Shine in that resplendent radiance,
 for it is your own nature;
Why wait for another day's sun,
 to bring brightness and joy?
Know, you are the very light,
 because of which the sun shines!

My Relationship with the Moon

If only I could model all relationships like the one I share with that solitary natural satellite—the moon. It is the most beautiful association.

The moon is always there. When my world becomes completely dark, my friend shows up. I see my friend.

My friend is just there, always around. There is no conversation. There is no giving, no taking.

There is just being. I am what I am, and I am where I am. The moon is what it is, and it is where it is.

Every now and then, it appears to fade away. It just *appears* to fade. But it is always there.

It is in my thoughts, in my heart. I feel the coolness of the moon. It is not cool by itself.

Despite its blemishes, it is synonymous with beauty and grace.

As with the moon, may I see the beauty in everything. In spite of the defects in them, may I see the moon in every being!

I am the Light in the Path

This spiritual path,
Is the path to enlightenment, I was told;
It is a journey,
Leading me to the Light, I heard.

But, alas!
Dense clouds of concepts, and
Rocky ideas became the obstacles;
I was stranded; rudderless I stood.

Where is the light?
When will I see sunshine?
I kept looking for a flash,
In complete darkness of my life.

Now 'twas a thunderstorm within,
Sweeping away concepts and ideas;
It was devastation like none before,
That carried hope for this lost soul.

At last, came lightning that lit the road,
That was but my own INNER VOICE;
The showers cleared it all in me,
Revealing the clear sky of my mind.

Light is not at the end of the course;

'Tis not to come from another's torch;

I am the torch bearer on my path,

And, I am the LIGHT!

Being Good as a Precondition to Being Religious. Why?

I am not entirely sure why I started thinking about this, but the thought came up, and now I find myself writing about it. I cannot recall anything specific that triggered this line of thought.

In fact, what I was really thinking about is the opposite of what I have written in the title. That is, one does not necessarily have to be a "good" person to be religious or spiritual. In other words, I can be who I am—flaws and all—and still be a devotee of God or a spiritual seeker.

At the most fundamental level, religion or spirituality is not inherently tied to being good or bad, or to concepts of right and wrong.

Why?

If we think of God as the all-compassionate creator, or as a father or mother, why would that "all-compassionate" Supreme Being discriminate between His (or Her) own children? What truly matters is the extent of devotion or love one has for God. And, in truth, even that may not matter entirely.

What I was reflecting on is the idea that being "bad" or "wicked" does not necessarily contradict being a devotee of the Lord. There are many examples of this in our tradition.

I feel the same principle applies in the knowledge tradition of spirituality. If a seeker's focus is on realizing their true Nature, they can accept their natural tendencies, even those considered defects, without issue. At the deepest level—at the level of the individual self—the seeker comes to realize that they are free from any blemishes, even if such blemishes are acknowledged.

The Illusion of Change in Others

We often remark, "So and so has changed," or "They are not the same person anymore." Both express the same sentiment.

Let us reflect on these statements. Has someone really changed? What is it that we call change?

Think of someone you know, about whom you feel this way—that the individual has changed. When you first met the person (or think of your earliest memory of them), how were they? What was their nature?

After many years of association, suddenly, we feel that a person has changed. We suddenly begin to feel this way. But can it happen all of a sudden?

More often, if we observe closely, we find that people do not change. Yet, we feel very strongly that the person has changed. Why do we feel that?

What happens is that circumstances, situations, events, and the people around them condition a person to behave in a certain way over time. The core personality, most often, remains the same.

But the individual has conditioned themselves to respond to these life situations in a certain manner. Of course, our response to life situations depends on what our core personality is.

Over the years, after being repeatedly exposed to certain kinds of life situations, we appear to have changed. But in reality, there is no fundamental change in the personality.

What has happened is that the individual has been conditioned by their life experiences to respond and behave in a certain manner. That, in turn, appears to us as change, and we say the person has changed.

Whenever we judge someone and judge them critically for what they seem to be, let us remember—they are a product of life experiences acting on their core personality.

Another person, given the same situations and life experiences, might turn out differently, and that will be based on their core personality.

What a situation makes an individual do is a matter of conjecture on our part. We can never say, "I wouldn't have done that in that situation." It is just a hope and a wish—we can never be certain.

The next time we look at someone, let us not judge them. Let us not comment on their actions, behaviour, conduct, or personality.

That individual is who they are, an evolute of nature, with many traits passed on genetically, and further conditioned by life experiences. It is almost like a cloth exposed to dye—the reaction is natural. The outcome is natural.

So, accept each person as they are, just as we rejoice in each colour for what it is!

<hr>

Listen to the Words of Your Own Heart

You muse on life and meditate on God,

In pursuit of Truth, and mind overawed.

You have days of routine with books of yore,

Alas, you lack delight in your heart's core.

Your day is ordered from dawn until night;
Prayer, study, japa, and routine tight.
You lost that smile and lustre in your eyes;
Stay quiet, and you'll hear your inner cries.

You read many books and model your life,
An idea misread may cause much strife.
You only see what you are looking for,
You think, for your voyage this is the shore.

Path of austerity made you a stone;
You call it silence and suffer alone.
You failed to rejoice in the days gone past;
Of what value is the knowledge so vast?

There are many waiting to advise you,
On Arjuna's anguish, and Krishna's clue.
Recall that warrior fought for a throne —
He had his issues, but you have your own.

"If not prayer, and not in quiet time,
To rejoice in life is a great crime."
You endure, my dear, such precepts strange;
It's time to reflect and make a big change.

With your pursuit and a regimen strong,
You are averse to a little bird's song.
In trying to see the Lord in your heart,
You fail to become the human thou art.

Arise and awake, and open your eyes wide,

Joys and sorrows, take them all in your stride.

Words and concepts are crutches by choice;

Listen to your heart; heed the inner voice.

Rejoice each moment; celebrate each day,

Welcome it all, with a smile on your face.

Glow in your eyes, and whistle of your tune,

Are signs of freedom, calm as the full moon.

Freedom from Attachment …
An Over-Simplified View?

How do I address the problem of attachment? The simple answer: detachment. But how? Let us explore this from a practical point of view.

If I am attached to only one object, the force of attachment between me and that object becomes very strong. In this context, I am only concerned with the attachment on my end. Because there are no other objects of attachment, my focus remains solely on that single object, and the force of attachment is very strong.

This intense attachment leads to fear, anger, grief, or suffering— or even a combination of these—whenever there is any threat or disturbance to my possession or association with that object.

When there are fewer objects to which I am attached, the strength of attachment naturally intensifies over time. This is because all my attention is concentrated on those few, and the emotional force increases as a result.

So, how can I take the first step towards detachment? The answer is to dilute the attachment. How do I dilute it? It is simple and logical: increase your association with more objects. In this way, the attention and attachment are no longer centred on one object. By spreading it thin, I have other things to fall back on, which lessens the emotional intensity tied to any single attachment.

But here is a deeper extension of this idea: When I increase my association with multiple objects without bias, reservation, or discrimination, my heart opens up to connect with many. It associates with them through love, and not just attachment.

However, does this process completely remove the pain and suffering caused by attachment? No, not entirely.

To transcend this, I must extend my attachment to the One entity that is Supreme—the source and substratum of all. This is the One which is ever-present in everything and everyone. By directing my association to the Universal Presence, the Universal Consciousness, I am lifted above the limitations of worldly attachment.

In essence, attachment to the Infinite Consciousness becomes 'no attachment' at all.

——•◆•◆•——

Alas, I Am Still Searching for You!

I see this beautiful world around me, that's You.

I experience this wonderful variety everywhere, that's You.

I am bathed every moment in nature's bounty, that's You.

But alas, believing You to be invisible, I am still searching for You!

I am unable to fall in love with a flower, that's You.

I fail to enjoy the sight of a beautiful tree, that's You.

I am unable to delight in the rising sun, that's You.

But alas, believing You to be formless, I am still searching for You!

I stand with my back to the rainbow, that's You.

I miss the beauty and cooling rays of the moon, that's You.

I fail to see the wonderful expanse of the sea, that's You.

But alas, believing You to be transcendental, I am still searching for You!

I receive all the love I get from those around, that's You.

I also am the recipient of hatred from some, that's You.

I enjoy the company of friends and relations, that's You.

But alas, believing You to be attributeless, I am still searching for You!

I received an abundance of pleasures and pains, from You.

I got my share of problems, and they were resolved by You.

I thought I was very successful in life, but it was because of You.

But alas, believing You to be unfathomable, I am still searching for You!

Each moment, I am living this wonderful life, that's You.

Most secure in the lap of Mother Nature, that's You.

Most comforted in the company of all beings, that's You.

But alas, believing You to be formless, I am still searching for You!

In my wakeful state, I enjoy the silence, that's You.

In my dream state, I delight in the fantasies, that's You.

In my sleep state, I am in my quietest form, that's You.

But alas, believing You to be beyond these, I am still searching for You!

I came across an indigent beggar, that's You.

I lost my bag with its contents to a thief, that's You.

I saw a little girl selling balloons, that's You.

But alas, believing You to be attainable only through meditation, I am still searching for You!

I fail to love all the beings around, that's You.

I fail to be compassionate towards all, that's You.

I fail to feel the oneness in all, that's You.

But alas, failing to see You, I am seeking to reach You by contemplating upon You!

Is It Really Patience or my Unrecognized Limitation?

Whenever we think, "I am being patient," it is often in the context of another person. We feel that we are being patient with them—their behavioural quirks, eccentricities, etc.—and begin to see ourselves as virtuous for doing so.

But by feeling this way, are we not judging the other as the one who needs to be attended to patiently? Are we not viewing them as someone with a limitation, thus elevating ourselves to a position of virtue by being patient?

There is something important to note here. In such a scenario, are we really sure that the patience we perceive as a virtue is truly so? Or is it merely a 'constriction' within us, masquerading as virtue?

Why? Because by saying we are being patient, we have assumed that the problem lies with the other person. At least in our own minds, we are reinforcing the belief that we are being patient with "the problem of the other."

Consider another example—when we think we are being forgiving. We believe we are forgiving the other, or that the other needs forgiving. In doing so, we have already judged the other's actions as something that requires forgiveness.

In other words, whenever we think we have acted virtuously, we are, in effect, 'elevating' ourselves. Unknown to us, we may actually be lowering the other. Even if we look at it physically, we can be on a higher level either by rising ourselves or by lowering the other.

Instead of trying to understand the other person and reflecting on our own limitations or our non-acceptance of them as they are, we continue under the delusion that we are virtuous.

How dangerous is this assumption?

In fact, we are reinforcing our own weakness—a completely misplaced understanding of our own constriction.

I am not suggesting that patience is not a virtue, nor that this applies in every situation. But we must be cautious before drawing conclusions about our own virtuousness!

We need to be watchful when we associate virtue with our thoughts, speech, or actions. Are we truly being virtuous? The best place to examine this is at the level of thought, rather than basing it solely on our actions. Often, we operate within the framework of "the end justifies the means," but here, just because we have acted in a certain way does not necessarily mean our intent is virtuous.

Someone may say, "You are so virtuous." But deep down, **we know.**

What is Freedom? Here is a Point of View

Freedom is interpreted in many different ways. What is it, in reality? Is there an absolute definition?

As we progress through the journey called life, the definition of freedom seems to change depending on the phase, context, and setting.

Let us take a simple view and reflect on it in the context of the world we live in, surrounded by others—whether directly or indirectly part of our lives. We must understand freedom within this backdrop, where we interact with people and the world around us. In this setting, freedom takes on a particular significance.

True freedom is not about being able to do whatever we want, when and how we want to do it.

Real freedom lies in allowing others to be who they are and do what they do, without being disturbed or agitated by it.

It means being free from comparison, independent of the world around us.

This is the greater freedom.

During the morning today, I came across a man walking his dog. I see him almost every day. Today, as I passed him, I overheard him say to his dog, "Don't walk like a cat, walk like a tiger."

This simple moment made me reflect on how often we project our own expectations onto others—just like the man wanted his dog to behave like a tiger. True freedom is letting others be themselves, free of our judgments or expectations.

Discrimination Between Human Beings is Nonsensical

Let us examine the notion of discrimination from the point of view of a spiritual seeker. Here, I am not using the term discrimination to mean the ability to distinguish between right and wrong or real and unreal.

As a seeker of spiritual truth, we are looking at a deeper question: "Who am I?" This is a fundamental question for any seeker. While everyone seems to like talking about it, I sometimes feel it has almost become a fashion statement, with people frequently quoting Ramana Maharshi and other great thinkers. But in practice, there is discrimination at various levels in the society.

But does it even make sense to discuss this? I wonder. Because when we do, we may inadvertently violate the very fundamental principle of spiritual truth.

For instance, the idea of a man-woman distinction (or any other gender distinction) applies only at the level of the body. It is only when I mistakenly identify the 'I' with the body that statements like "I am a man" or "I am a woman" become relevant. In fact, even at the level of the mind, such distinctions do not apply.

When we look at the world, is the experience of life any different for a man or a woman? All emotions—joy, sorrow, love, hatred, jealousy, compassion, courage, weakness—are universal, regardless of gender.

The distinction of man and woman is purely physiological and serves a functional purpose created by nature, primarily for procreation and the continuation of the human species. How, then, can we justify any form of discrimination between humans based on gender?

When I say "I," I am not referring to the body. Nor am I referring to the mind, intelligence, ego, or any other attribute. Similarly, statements like "I am rich," "I am a manager," "I am an artist," or "I belong to this caste" are equally meaningless.

At the level of the "I," all these identifications and differences are irrelevant, inapplicable, and nonsensical. Even if we do not fully realize the Supreme Truth, simply understanding this idea should dissolve any basis for discrimination based on the body, status, race, community, or any other external attribute.

The "I" is nothing but a pointer to the true identity, the Self. At the level of the Self, distinctions such as man, woman, tall, short, or any other attribute do not apply.

Can I not extend this line of thought and elevate my perspective to dissolve any distinctions between humans based on wealth, skin colour, language, profession, nationality, race, community, or tribe? All these differences are only at the physical level, and they do not hold when we recognize our true identity as the Self.

The Wonder That is The Universe Within

We behold the tranquil sunrise, its golden rays gently waking the world. We witness the vast, breathtaking expanse of the open sea, stretching endlessly before us. We are stunned by the miraculous birth of a calf, a new life entering the world. We are mesmerized by the delicate unfolding of a blooming rose, each petal revealing its hidden beauty.

While these wonders seem to take place in the outer world, in reality, these phenomena are unfolding within us.

They captivate us because these seemingly external phenomena echo something profound within our own inner landscape.

149

These experiences arise from within, springing forth from an infinitude that resides deep inside.

The vast, external universe pales in comparison to the boundless space within each of us—a realm of infinite depth, beauty, mystery and wonder.

------◆------

Clouds of Ego in the Path of Light

In our pursuit of knowledge, we are often plagued by anxious thoughts: "*I have to know. I want to know everything. There is so much to know, but so little time. Everyone else seems to know, and I don't. I feel as though I have wasted my life on unnecessary things. I should have started this journey earlier.*"

These feelings are not uncommon. We may find ourselves thinking: "*I should have known this by now. I can explain this better than others. I know what I need to know, so why am I struggling to understand even this simple thing? When will I finally know? Why is it that I am unable to grasp this?*"

These thoughts are distractions, mere clouds that obscure the light of knowledge. They prevent the light from revealing itself, keeping us from truly understanding, knowing, realizing the truth. The ego, in its many subtle forms, obstructs this light, clouding our vision and distorting the truth.

We often believe that our journey is about accumulating knowledge. But the truth is, it is not about striving to know more—it is about allowing knowledge to reveal itself, unobstructed. True knowing is simply a revelation, an uncovering of what is already present.

That is why Truth is often described as knowledge itself—it is not something to be attained, but something to be unveiled, realized once we clear away the clouds of ego and other distractions that block the light from shining through.

——•◆•——

Bhagavad Gita is Not a Book of Values and Virtues

The Bhagavad Gita is not a book of edicts. It is not a list of do's and don'ts.

It is not a set of instructions on how to become a good person. Instead, it reveals the secret to going beyond the concepts of good and bad.

It is not a book on dharma or righteousness. Rather, it shows the way to transcend right and wrong.

Though set as a dialogue in a battlefield, it is not a book about war. Nor is it a management handbook or a manual on administration.

The Bhagavad Gita reveals the truth of our real nature. It guides an individual towards the realization of one's true identity. It discusses the Self and the paths to realizing the Self, offering guidance to seekers striving for freedom from limitations, while still living and interacting with this world.

It is not a book on renunciation. It is a book about embracing the entire world without reservation.

It is not a set of beliefs. It is a guide for seekers, based on study, introspection through reason, and direct experience through meditation.

——•◆•——

O Mind, Embrace the Silence

In the silence of nature lies the cosmic symphony;
In the silence of lightning lies thunder;
In the silence of the night lies daylight;
In the silence of the ocean lie the waves.

In the silence of vision lies beauty;
In the silence of words lies wisdom;
In the silence of action lies excellence;
In the silence of thoughts lies joy.

In the silence of the mind is eternal bliss;
In the silence of the intellect lies creativity;
In the silence of the heart lies love;
In the silence of desires lies contentment.

In the silence of hatred lies compassion;
In the silence of the moment lies experience;
In the silence of our being is life;
In the silence of life lies death.

Silence is Love;
Silence is Peace;
Silence is Bliss;
Silence is Fullness.

Silence is Contentment;
Silence is the Self;
Silence is the Divine.

How Do You Respond to a "No"?

How often do you hear a "no" to something you offered, proposed, or said? And how do you react to that "no"? We often hear people say, "he/she doesn't like hearing a 'no' from anyone." But how do you personally respond to a 'no'? You may not immediately react or lash out at the other person, but something starts happening in your head. Let us try to understand what that is.

In every situation where you hear a 'no,' what's your internal response?

You asked: *Can we talk now?*
The response: *No, I will call you later.*
You conclude: *He doesn't like me. He's avoiding me.*

You asked: *Can I serve you some curry?*
The response: *No, I will take some rice.*
You conclude: *He doesn't like curry.*

You asked: *Can we meet on Sunday?*
The response: *No, I have made other plans.*
You conclude: *He's disrespecting me.*

The next time you hear a "no" and find yourself jumping to conclusions, pause and reflect. Why did your mind respond that way? What led you to think like that? And were those conclusions really justified, especially since nothing like that was actually said?

Also, these thoughts are not fleeting—sometimes they may linger for a long time, influencing how you feel and act.

—•—

Grace is Our Inner State of Surrender and Acceptance

When things go our way, we often say, "It is by God's grace." These words roll off our tongues almost instinctively, like a customary "thank you" after a favourable event.

But have we ever paused to truly reflect on what grace is? Whose grace are we acknowledging? And why do we believe that we are the recipients of grace? Is grace something that is bestowed upon us by some external force (someone or something)?

The answer lies within. If I am the object of grace, then grace depends on me. It is not another who bestows grace upon me—there is no "other" at all. It is only I, and I alone, who embody grace. Grace, therefore, is not some distant blessing; it is a quality within me, a state of mind.

Grace is the state in which I surrender myself to the flow of life, accepting whatever happens, whatever comes, and whatever goes. Every moment then becomes an expression of grace.

Grace is the counterpart of humility. It is the companion of surrender and the essence of acceptance. To open oneself to whatever life brings is to live in grace.

Grace does not pick and choose. Grace is in being non-selective about only the "good", and not seeking that which is favourable. Grace is the willingness to submit oneself fully to the workings of nature.

Grace is my humility, my ever-present receptivity, my surrender. In grace, I do not seek grace. In grace, there is no "other" to bestow it upon me. In grace, I do not pray for it, for in true grace, the one who bestows grace ceases to exist as a separate entity.

In true grace, I open myself to everything around me, recognizing the grace in every atom, in every situation, in every moment. Grace is ever-present, manifesting all the time, in all things. In true grace, there is only grace—no division between the object of grace and the bestower.

'Thoughts'—They Are an Eternal Dance

Worries, vision, insights, and plans,

Hopes, desires, ideas, and views,

In myriad forms and diverse hues,

They are part of a sublime dance.

They are all experiences of my life;

In essence, thoughts are what they are.

Like waves in the ocean of my mind,

Surfing them is the game I call 'life'.

They are all rainbows of my soul;

Sentience is the light by which they glow.

With the shower of vitality within me,

It's a display of the cosmic dance.

In rhythm with the beats of my heart,

In tune with the music of my world,

In harmony with my innate nature,

They engage in this surreal dance.

Guests they are at the door of my mind;

I welcome them with an open heart.

I do not join them when they depart,

For I know they are in a ceaseless dance.

Uninvited, these thoughts arrive,

Unbridled, they all sing and dance,

Free in the sky of my vast being,

Unaffected, I simply smile and watch.

I do not react to this ethereal ball,

Nor do I capture it for a future recall.

I am just a stage for this divine waltz;

In being a witness alone, is infinite joy.

———•◆•———

Idea Generation Requires the Right Environment

I looked into the dictionary. It says an idea is 'any conception existing in the mind as a result of mental understanding, awareness, or activity.' Yes, that too (the idea) is a thought. But how do we get an idea? How do we solve problems? Who or what solves the problem in us?

Let us explore how this happens from a layman's point of view—not the way a neuroscientist or brain scientist would examine it. Take the case of a scientist or researcher. How does problem-solving take place? The researcher has an area (or more areas) of competence and a lot of acquired knowledge about a particular subject. From existing knowledge, how does the researcher come up with something new?

Here, I am not referring to information already discovered by mankind, which is part of the logical deduction process, where there are not many possible conclusions from the existing knowledge. In that case, the mind (or intelligence) will eliminate all the possibilities that are factually incorrect.

For example, if I take two elements—carbon and oxygen—they can combine in only so many possible ways. There are defined sets of possibilities. This seems rather simplistic. So, let us move away from this kind of a problem, where science defines the solution through a deduction process.

In other cases, where the answer is not known to mankind or where it involves a novel deduction or conclusion, how does it happen? The individual may have a lot of knowledge in various areas, but how does the answer come? Where does it come from?

More importantly, as we may have observed from our own experience, it is not a conscious process. The emergence of an idea is not a logical process. We may, in hindsight, give it a logical explanation, but when the idea arises, it is neither conscious nor wilful.

Scientists, musicians, and creative people often say that they came up with an idea at the most unexpected times—while in the bathtub, for example. It seems as though, at the subconscious level, different pieces of knowledge come together, leading to a solution or idea. But what makes this happen? How does it occur at the level of the subconscious mind?

What role do I play in facilitating this process of subconscious discovery? From my observations, it appears that such discoveries often happen unexpectedly, usually when we are not actively working on the problem. They seem to emerge in a calm state of mind, free from external pressures or the threat of looming circumstances. There is no fear involved, and the mind is often rested or distanced from the issue at hand. The process unfolds effortlessly, without deliberation, and seems to occur when we are least expecting it.

What does this indicate? Even though the individual may be an expert in a particular area, the solution to the problem often comes through a subconscious process. What lies within our control is creating an environment that fosters these conditions, then allowing the magic of nature to unfold.

O Mind, Realize the All-pervading Cosmic Presence!

Have you looked up

to see the bright blue sky?

Have you savoured

the sight of the starry night sky?

Have you paid attention

to the busy army of ants?

Have you observed

a honeybee hovering over the plants?

Have you noticed

the noisy flock in a tree at twilight?

Have you wondered

where they go when it is sunlight?

Have you marvelled

at the river cutting through rough terrains?

Have you admired

the initial drops of rain caressing the plains?

Have you wondered

how a seed gives rise to an entire tree?

Have you been puzzled

that a mango seed never yields a pea?

Have you been stunned

by the rainbow painting the horizon blue?

Have you been enthralled

seeing the molten lava, the volcanoes spew?

Have you been moved

watching an animal giving birth to its hatchling?

Have you been baffled

by a beast chasing its prey before the killing?

Have you been captivated

watching a bird feeding its chick?

Have you felt compassion at the same time

seeing the struggling worm in its beak?

Fooled by the seeming stark contrast,

do you wonder why nature is cruel and blind?

O Mind, goodness and evil are but concepts;

Are they not just products of the limited mind?

Do you see only what the eyes show,

or do your thoughts go beyond your sensory vision?

Does your heart leap in ceaseless wonder

and feel the Cosmic Presence that is beyond reason?

The Cosmic, all-pervading presence

transcends good and bad, wrong and right;

Transcends cruelty and compassion, virtue and sin,

transcends beauty and ugliness, darkness and light.

The Universal Presence is a glorious symphony

of all pairs of opposites that make the world herein;

O Mind! Going beyond all limiting notions

realize that glorious oneness in your Self within.

Journey Full of Signboards Becomes an Arduous Journey

Imagine yourself on a long journey, driving through a beautiful countryside. The roads are full of signboards—speed limits, warnings for sharp turns, landslide alerts, and various other instructions and warning signs. What kind of journey would that be? You find yourself so caught up making sure you do not miss any signs that you can barely enjoy the scenery. Now, imagine you also have a companion in the car, constantly offering advice and adding some more warnings.

Would you enjoy such a journey? Probably not. Most of us would feel better off without such a stressful experience.

Now, think of the spiritual path as a journey like this, full of instructions and road signs. Many of these signs are in a language you may not fully understand—representing concepts and teachings that need to be deciphered. The path turns into one where you are always busy trying to figure out what each sign means. By the time you have understood one signboard, you have already missed several others. Then, just like in your road trip, there are fellow travellers chiming in with their own opinions, advice, and warnings about which routes to take. Everyone seems to have a different opinion on the right way to go.

In the end, the destination feels unreachable. More importantly, this long journey has been reduced to a 'treasure hunt'—you are solving puzzles the entire time rather than moving forward.

What can we learn from this? The lesson is simple—take the journey alone. Keep it simple. Do not over-plan, do not turn it into a long and burdensome trek. Travel light, without the weight of too many signboards, advice, or distractions. Do not have any expectations from the destination. Focus on the essence of the journey itself, rather than the clutter around it.

And finally, perhaps the most profound thought: sometimes, no journey itself is the greatest journey.

— • —

The Journey is More Beautiful Than the Destination

In the spiritual journey, we often encounter doubts like: "Am I progressing?" "Am I moving forward or stagnating?" "Am I on the right path?" These questions surface from time to time. However, the most crucial realization in this journey is to understand and believe that the journey is more beautiful than the destination.

Let us consider a simple example: the process of taking a bath. Why do we bathe? To become clean, pure, or whatever your perspective may be. You start the bath, pour water, scrub yourself, and repeat this sequence of actions. Isn't the process itself enjoyable? The refreshing sensation of water, the feeling of renewal—it is an experience in itself.

Now, once you complete the process, dry yourself, and step out of the bathroom, impurities begin to accumulate again. You may start to sweat, and soon enough, you are no longer as clean as you were just moments before.

Isn't the process of the bath more enjoyable than the completion of it? The journey of cleansing, the refreshing flow of water, offers more joy than simply being "done" with the bath. Similarly, in the spiritual path, it is the journey—its learning, its experiences, its unfolding—that is far more fulfilling than any final destination.

⸻ ◆ ⸻

Inner Freedom: My Two Wings for Soaring Beyond

Viveka is the mind-born wing on my left,

To judge the eternal from the transient.

Vairagya is the stable one on the right,

To detach me from the diverse world so bright.

With my two wings, I soar in the worldly sky.

Tranquil I am, though many troubles I face,

Unfazed am I by failures in my life.

I embrace all, without a bias of my own,

Free forever, not bound to anything here.

With my two wings, I soar in the worldly sky.

Identity is not in fortune and fame,

'Tis not in the many positions I hold.

It is not governed by the roles I play,

Also not defined by the things I create.

With my two wings, I soar in the worldly sky.

Mere labels are what the world thrusts upon me;

They appear and vanish like a lightning flash.

My real nature is in my deepest core;

Delighting in that, I am untouched by the world.

With my two wings, I soar in the worldly sky.

My plumage takes me beyond neglect and praise;

With them, I reach the space of eternal peace.

They take me beyond the clouds into the light,

To find the creative source that's within me.

With my two wings, I soar in the worldly sky.

[**viveka:** The faculty of discriminating the real from the unreal, or the permanent from the transient. **vairagya:** Detachment to objects of the world.]

The Pursuit of Equilibrium in Human Life

Imagine pouring a jug of water onto the floor. The water flows in all directions, influenced by the surface's contours, until it eventually settles and reaches a state of equilibrium. And then there is no more flowing.

In nature, this concept of balance is universal. Plants and other beings reach a point of physical growth, where they achieve a stable height and mass. Their equilibrium is mainly on the physical front.

But for human beings, growth is not limited to the physical. It involves the mind as well, and the state of the mind largely determines the quality of life. This raises an important question: What does equilibrium look like for a human?

In our day-to-day lives, we find joy or pleasure when we acquire something or engage with things that are favourable or agreeable. Each time we attain something desirable, we feel happy. Our entire lives can become consumed by the constant pursuit of happiness. There seems to be no end to this cycle. We always want more, and this pursuit of "more" becomes an endless journey. Even when we reach the age of 70 or 80, the desire for more often remains, leaving us asking: When does this pursuit of more finally end?

Like in the case of water, what, then, is the state of equilibrium for a human being? This is a question each of us must investigate. On the physical level, there is no end to wanting more—whether it is material possessions, experiences, or achievements. But in the inner world, equilibrium is reached when we arrive at a state of contentment or satisfaction. This is the moment when the endless wanting and avoiding come to a halt.

True equilibrium for a human is found in this contentment, a state often referred to by names such as moksha or liberation. It is the point where we are no longer driven by the desire for more, where the need to seek or avoid fades away. Achieving this inner equilibrium gives meaning and purpose to human life.

In the final analysis, it is not external accumulation that brings lasting fulfilment, but the inner journey towards peace and contentment that defines our true state of equilibrium.

———•◆•———

Are We Truly Happy, or Just Saying So?

In everyday conversations, we use the word "happy" in a wide range of contexts, from small day-to-day transactions, to different phases of our lives, or for that matter for the entire life itself. We use this simple word to express our feelings in a wide range of situations.

To illustrate the point, let us examine some expressions, where we convey our feelings and emotions by using the word "happy". Consider how we casually use the word "happy" in the following contexts: "I am very happy to meet you," "I am happy we are going on holiday," "I am so happy we could have lunch yesterday," "I am happy I finally got some quiet time," "From age 22 to 36 was a very happy phase of my life," or "We have been happily married for 20 years." We also say things like "I am happy with my team," "I am happy I finally got the promotion after years of hard work," or "We had a baby, and we are very happy."

Whether referring to a fleeting moment or a stretch of 20 years, the same word captures it all.

It is incredible how liberally we use "happy" to express everything from short-term excitement (in day-to-day interactions) to long-term contentment (relating to phases of life).

Some may substitute words like glad, delighted, ecstatic, pleased, elated, thrilled, jolly, or joyous. They might even intensify the expression with adverbs like extremely, exceedingly, immensely, or hugely. But despite the varied vocabulary, all these words seem to be used as synonyms for the same basic idea: happiness.

At first glance, one might ask, "So what?" However, there is a deeper issue here. Are we constrained by the language we use? Or are we limited in our ability to conceptualize and describe our true feelings? Perhaps it is a combination of both.

Language is essential not only for communication with others but also for how we think and process our emotions. Even in our minds, we often use language to define our emotions. It is only the emotions themselves that don't need words to be felt.

Now, let us turn back to the feeling of happiness. Reflecting on a phase of life—say, the first ten years of your career—if you have no major complaints, you might say it was a "happy time." But does the absence of complaints really equate to happiness? Perhaps those years were filled with both good and bad experiences, and the good ones stood out more in your memory. Is that enough to call it happiness?

This brings up the question of understanding happiness itself. We often equate "no complaints" with "happiness," but is that an accurate interpretation?

In the case of "happiness" it may not matter much because we are expressing something which is a positive experience which is favourable to us, and we do not often think about it again apart from having a good memory of it.

On the flip side, if we experience more challenges than rewards during a period, we may conclude it was a "miserable time." But are we being fair in labelling it that way?

We tend to let negative memories dominate our perception of entire phases of our lives. Does this skewed recollection lead us to draw incorrect conclusions? And when we make faulty diagnoses about our experiences, are we ever truly equipped to solve the problems we face? In the end, the cumulative effect of these misjudgements may leave us feeling more miserable than we truly are.

Could it be that our cultures and languages limit our ability to express the full complexity of our experiences? Although we often think of human progress as advancing, are we losing the linguistic tools necessary to articulate our inner world? As our lives become more complex, do we need to extend our vocabulary to better capture the nuances of modern life?

In an era of rapid change and increasing complexity, it may be time to rethink how we define and describe our huge range of experiences.

In Separation, There is Union

Is a tree shedding its leaves, or are the leaves breaking free? When a leaf falls from its parent tree, it often appears as though the leaf is trying to liberate itself. Our school textbooks taught us that "trees shed leaves," and further explained how this phenomenon is linked to the growth of the tree.

In reality, the falling of leaves is not about separation—it is about growth. Neither the tree nor nature mourns this so-called separation.

If anything, nature rejoices. The falling leaves signal the arrival of a new season. Where we see separation, nature sees union—the union of the leaf with the earth.

As autumn approaches, marking a time of full maturity, the falling of leaves symbolizes not loss, but a deeper union. This process of separation is a pathway to a greater, more expansive connection.

Similarly, in life, we often mourn separation. Yet, if we learn to look more deeply, we can also learn to rejoice in it. Just as a parent watches a child grow and eventually leave the nest, there is a certain joy in that separation.

When a leaf is separated from the tree, it still carries with it the essence and identity of the tree. However, it also carries a greater identity—one that is linked to the earth, the sky, and the cycle of life.

In recognizing this larger identity, the leaf finds its true fulfilment. Its attachment to the tree was but a temporary association. In its growth, maturity, ripening, falling and drying, we see separation, but for the leaf it is fulfilment.

The leaf does not fall to fulfil a purpose. It never had one. It may become food for another, a home for a creature, or nutrient for the soil. But it did not fall with these intentions in mind. It did not fall to seek out a purpose, create one, or fulfil one. To fall was simply in its nature. The act of disengaging from the tree was part of its inherent being. Even the place where it lands is not predetermined.

Whether the leaf disengages on its own or is forced, where and how it falls remains unknown. It may land gently on the ground, or it could become entangled in a branch below. Perhaps a breeze will carry it further, or a bird might pluck it.

A human may cook it, or some other creature might eat it. The leaf does not choose, it does not lament, and it doesn't rejoice. For the leaf is always joyous, always "green". It remains a leaf in the book of life.

May I, too, be like that leaf—free. The leaf does not fall to seek its own identity, nor does it need to know where it will land. Likewise, may I be free to fall, at anytime, anywhere, into the embrace of nature and the arms of time. Without seeking my own identity, for I know that I am part of the whole. And more than that—I am the whole.

***

The Voyage Through the Sea of Life

Waking up, as if from an eternal sleep,
I found myself in a passage called life,
Adrift was I in the endless open sea,
I sail forth, without a harbour in mind.

I do not know which shore I came from,
I have no thoughts of a coast to sail to,
Allowing waves of the moment to carry me,
I sail forth, without a harbour in mind.

I don't know who put me on this journey,
I don't wish to find out how I got here,
I don't dwell on the purpose for my cruise,
I sail forth, without a harbour in mind.

The sea greets with outstretched arms,
The limitless waters lift my soul sky-high,
I feel the warm embrace of cold waters,
I sail forth, without a harbour in mind.

All the directions eagerly hail me to come,
I don't have a map that guides my boat,
But ushered by the compass of my heart,
I sail forth, without a harbour in mind.

I surrender to the elated tidal waves,
Under the care of the lively aquatic winds,
And carried by the buoyant foamy waters,
I sail forth, without a harbour in mind.

I hear silence in the sounds of the surf,
I see the entire cosmos in a drop of water,
I feel stillness in the dance of the waves,
I sail forth, without a harbour in mind.

For in this cruise is the joy of discovery,
Here lies the adventure of the unknown,
With no goal, I feel the ecstasy of freedom,
I sail forth, without a harbour in mind.

Wherever I am, is my destination now,
Here, I discover the next step somehow,
Arms wide, I welcome the coming stride,
I sail forth, without a harbour in mind.

Any doubts of purpose can sink my boat,
Strides of conviction keep my life afloat,
Every move is always in the right course,
I sail forth, without a harbour in mind.

I am not looking for a beacon to guide,
Each step brings with it its own light,
Carefree, I look forward to a new find,
I sail forth, without a harbour in mind.

I don't wish for others to show me the way,
For they too have their own path to stay,
My passage unfolds like an endearing maze,
I sail forth, without a harbour in mind.

I am on a trail with no milestones to see,
Each stride of chance is a way ahead for me,
In every direction is a road to explore,
I sail forth, without a harbour in mind.

I do not care how long my journey lasts,
The moment is the key and the effect it casts,
Not the voyage, but the instance that is life,
I sail forth, without a harbour in mind.

Let me cherish the tryst with each moment,
Let me enjoy every instant for itself,
Let me savour the drift without fear,
Let me sail, without a harbour in mind.

It dawned in me like the morning sun,
The voyage of life is in my mind-ocean,
In here are the storms and tidal waves,
With the mind quietened, I sail, I sail!

To Seek God, do not Chase Ideas in the World... Be Still

From childhood, we are presented with various ideas of the divine. Each concept differs from the other, and as a result, we are left confused about how to interpret the idea of God.

There comes a time when we spend more effort trying to comprehend the concept of God than actually seeking, finding, realizing, or becoming one with God.

What, then, is the answer?

Let us wipe the slate clean. Let us free ourselves from every idea of God we hold. If God is our origin, then believe that we know it naturally—that God is part of us.

The problem is that we mistakenly think God is alien to us. But in our deepest core, we already have the answer.

We simply spend so much time chasing every idea we have heard of—every method, technique, philosophy—that we lose conviction in any of them.

Start with a clean slate. Forget all bookish ideas of purity, and be your true self. It does not matter what acts you have committed in the past, what good or bad words you've uttered, or what good or bad thoughts you've had. What matters is the pure heart, free from hidden motives or expectations.

In that empty state—your clean slate—enquire deeply, and you will find the answers. Be your natural self. Be true to yourself. Do not look elsewhere. In the quiet or silence of your heart, you will find your God. Your discovery will be your revelation.

Allow the silence to reveal your God. Allow God to manifest in the stillness of your heart.

Preconceived ideas prevent that manifestation. When you are filled with preconceived notions, you expect God to match a certain description.

In fact, even if God were to present Himself or Herself, you might not connect with that presence because it would not match the image you have constructed.

Even in the spiritual pursuit, seekers can become trapped in the web of terms used to describe the Supreme or the Self—words like formless, eternal, omnipresent, and infinite.

Those concepts begin to drive your thinking, each one conflicting with the other, and each one giving birth to techniques and approaches that constantly shift your perspective.

This only leads to confusion, not conviction. The formless notion conflicts with the idea of form, and the indescribable clashes with the notion of the divine with form.

The only answer is to let go of all known ideas and dive deep into your silence, free from all disturbances. There, you will find YOUR answer.

------ • ◆ • ------

What Does the Term 'Spirituality' Mean?

The term "spirituality" has been used by different people in different contexts to mean different things. As a result, one does not always know what is being referred to when the term 'spiritual' is used.

When someone says, "everything is spiritual," what does it mean? I continue to wonder. It has a tone of being profound. But it has become superfluous, almost meaningless.

Has the meaning been diluted? Perhaps it has. It is almost like the word 'happy.' It is used in so many contexts that you cannot make out what it really means.

Also, people seem to like the term so much that they drop it into their conversations often, leaving you wondering what it even means.

It seems to convey a sense of control, a sense of achievement, or the notion of pursuing something beyond the mundane. People seem to derive some solace from using this term.

Is it wishful thinking, a desire to explore the spiritual path?

Not that there is anything wrong with using the term—just that we need to be clear about what we mean or intend to convey when we use it.

I almost do not use the term anymore.

------ • ◆ • ------

An Experiment in Being Still and Quiet Amid the Distractions

Here is something I often do and enjoy. Try it out; it is interesting and revealing. You might have already experienced it.

You are in a hilly region. One morning, you are sitting at the edge of a cliff, looking at the vast mountain range in front of you. The expanse is very striking and captivating. In the initial moments, the vastness makes the mind still. The mind is quiet. There is no other thought. It is a very blissful experience.

But the mind is not able to hold that stillness for long. It wants change.

After those initial few minutes, the mind notices a moving object in the distance. A tiny speck of colour grabs your attention. That tiny thing is now moving, and you begin to follow it.

The stillness that your mind was experiencing is gone. Now, you are following that coloured speck, which may be a person, a vehicle, an animal, etc.

Even if there isn't much movement, you search for something to focus on. You may finally fix your attention on something yellow and moving, and then you follow it.

The mind, almost compulsively, looks for moving objects.

Why is the mind unable to stay with the expanse, without focussing on something specific? Why is it unable to stay still without seeking some object to fix its attention on?

Let us learn to stay with the stillness in that expanse.

You do not need a mountain range for this experiment. Take, for example, a flower in a flower pot at home. Look at it. After that first moment, you are no longer just looking at it. You are admiring it, wanting to share it, planning for a larger pot, or taking a picture, and so on.

Learn to stay with the stillness, without wanting to do anything with the object.

Now take yourself to a crowded spot and try to keep the mind still in that setting.

If the mind cannot stay still while perceiving the objects of the world, how will it remain still when you close your eyes during meditation? It will be flooded with thoughts of objects and movements that the mind creates—overwhelmingly more wondrous than the visible world. You can say goodbye to stilling the mind during meditation.

Let us practice staying still in any setting.

—— • ◉ • ——

Should I Fear Attachment, or Should I Embrace It Naturally?

The scriptures repeatedly warn us of the problems of attachment, urging us to cultivate detachment in order to achieve the goal of everlasting peace.

But should I fear attachment? Why should I?

I am neither attached nor unattached. Does that seem like a state to be in?

Consider the flower. Initially, it is attached to the plant, and there is a process of give and take between the two.

But then, is the flower truly attached? Through its detachment, does it not bestow joy? Does it not spread its fragrance, decorate the altar, adorn a maiden's hair, or get offered in devotion at the Lord's feet?

In its detachment lies its complete and wholesome giving; in its detachment lies its unconditional sharing and love. In its detachment lies its freedom from discrimination as to who receives its gifts. In its detachment lies the complete absence of bias.

With that detachment, the flower easily falls from the tree, shedding itself naturally without pain. With that detachment, it allows itself to be discarded from the altar, even if it is with disdain.

Think about it. The flower is both attached and detached. Or, can we say the flower is neither attached nor detached?

Does the flower not bloom again? Does it not distribute its joy, fragrance, and beauty, unconditionally, to all?

What is detachment? What is attachment?

Is it not a natural state of the mind that truly matters? Does attachment or detachment come about as a result of deliberate action?

Can I consciously decide in each of my interactions: "Now, I should not get attached" or "Now, I should not get detached"?

Let me bloom like a flower, naturally, and fall like a flower, naturally.

What is the force of gravity? Is it not a form of attachment? And what is it that holds the universe in harmony, in equilibrium? Why, then, should we fear attachment?

Do We Need to Realize The Oneness to Live in Peace?

According to Advaita Vedanta, "Everything is Brahman"—the Ultimate Reality—and nothing exists apart from it.

The aim of the seeker on this path is to realize that the individual Self and the Universal Self (Brahman) are, in essence, one and the same.

However, this raises an important question that I invite you to reflect upon: Is it truly necessary to reach this realization of oneness in order to live a peaceful and contented life in this world?

The simple answer is no. You do not need to fully grasp or embody the philosophy of Advaita Vedanta to experience peace and happiness in your interactions with the diverse and multifaceted world around you. It is not essential to understand the non-dual nature of existence to find inner calm.

In fact, it might be the reverse—attaining a sense of peace and contentment is often a prerequisite to realizing the deeper truths of Advaita.

What is critical to lead a life of peace, contentment and freedom is to gain clarity of our real nature. Our real nature is that of the Self, which is distinct from the body, the mind, the intellect, and the ego.

If a person is able to disentangle the Self from these external and transient elements (as it truly is), peace and contentment will naturally follow.

And yes, I believe this level of peace and clarity can be achieved.

In essence, the path to peace and contentment begins not with the lofty goal of non-dual realization but with the practical wisdom of understanding who we truly are. As this understanding deepens, the realization of oneness may naturally follow.

The Invisible Chains We Create in Our Lives

I often hear people use the phrase "chains of worldly existence" or "bonds of worldly existence." I wonder why they use this phrase, with such a negative tone, to refer to life in this world.

Particularly when spirituality is mentioned, it is strange that people use this phrase to describe life.

Some say, "Who has succeeded in breaking free from the chains of worldly existence and suffering?" This is often said as an excuse for not doing anything about their suffering.

It is disappointing when people deeply engaged in spiritual pursuits use this phrase. By repeating it, they start to believe in it. The imaginary chains become real, and they find themselves bound by these illusory fetters.

For some, this phrase also conveys their belief that life is inherently full of suffering and that nothing can be done about it, as if human beings are destined to suffer.

How many such notions do we live with? More importantly, how many imaginary notions do we make real?

In reality, these are the "real chains of bondage."

This World is YOUR Altar

Worship,
Was the instruction when young!
The child in me obeyed;
The youth in me rebelled;
The man in me reasoned;
And now, the heart soars.

YOU are,
But my inner voice;
Sculpted by my mind;
Animated by my breath;
Enthroned in my heart;
And illumined by my love.

You, who are my very life,
The very pulse of this creation,
How can I enshrine YOU
In a temple of mortar?

How can I trap sunbeams

In a golden cage?

This beautiful world is YOUR altar;

My life is the lamp,

My actions are the bells,

My waves of joy are the incense,

The tears of my sorrow are the holy water,

My living is YOUR worship.

For our inseparable oneness,

Like that of the flower and its fragrance,

How can worship be an act?

How can the flame worship the brilliance in it?

To that cosmic wonder of existence,

I bow down in humble acknowledgement!

———•◆•———

Where Do We Find Role Models?

We have become so conditioned to judging everyone we come across in life. Whether it is someone in our personal circle or a public figure, we spare no words of criticism. Think of any personality—we are ready with a list of faults, criticizing their words and actions.

Even if a person has just one fault, or commits a single mistake, we often condemn their entire character. We dismiss everything about them, saying, "Not acceptable." It is as if they are condemned for life, with no hope for redemption.

In doing so, we have condemned humanity as a whole. We are left with no one who qualifies as a role model.

There are two key points to consider here: (1) We have appointed ourselves as judges, and our verdict is final; (2) There seems to be no one left who fits the bill of a role model. What a sad situation!

In other words, we have adopted an overly critical view of the world around us. This perspective suggests that the entire world is devoid of virtue. It paints a gloomy picture, where everything appears negative, and we see only flaws in everything and everyone.

But if we do not see role models or people who inspire us, how do we motivate ourselves to navigate tough and challenging situations?

The only recourse, some might say, is to place our faith in God. Yet even there, people often have reservations. So, what is the way out?

We must remember that we, as humans, all have our faults. No one is above them. But we should also possess the ability to overcome our weaknesses.

We may dislike certain qualities in a person, but that is no reason to condemn them entirely. If we continue to reject everyone because of a single flaw, we will be left with no one to emulate in this world.

—•●•—

Love is the Foundation for Liberation

Scriptures constantly reinforce, "Through knowledge alone, liberation is attained." So much emphasis is placed on knowledge. However, the underlying virtue that supports this knowledge is love.

Knowledge must be converted into practice, and in practice, it takes the fundamental form of love. From that fountainhead of love, all other virtues arise.

What is this knowledge? It is the knowledge of the Self—the true nature of every being. The same Self resides in all. The one way to realize that Self in everyone is to "look upon every being as one would look upon oneself."

We need to cultivate a love for a life of righteousness (dharma), a love for peace and happiness, a love for all beings, and a love for nature.

What is equal vision or equanimity? It is nothing but a state of loving-kindness toward all.

When we reflect on the idea of equanimity or equal vision towards all beings, it naturally translates into love for all. There is no other way to embody the principle of "seeing the same Self in all beings."

Love is the foundation! It is through love alone that liberation is attained.

━━•◆•━━

Why we must Reflect on Taking, Receiving, and Wanting

There is much discussion about 'giving'—charity and generosity—but hardly any about receiving or taking. Occasionally, parents remind their children to 'say thank you,' but that is the extent of the conversation.

How often do we really think about receiving or taking? How deeply do we understand the concept of receiving? Another layer to this discussion is the idea of wanting—wishing to possess something. Do we ever pause to regulate or moderate that desire? Why not?

From a young age, we are always on the receiving end. But why don't we stop to think about it? Why don't we learn to regulate our acts of receiving, taking, or even buying? By not moderating these actions or the thoughts behind them, we are continually cultivating greed.

Our unchecked habit of taking from nature is what has led to the natural disasters we now face. What thought drives our taking, receiving, and buying? It is the desire to have, to possess.

As humans, we need to learn how to moderate our receiving and taking, and even the thoughts that lead us to these actions. This idea is not just about avoiding greed.

If we observe nature, animals and plants only take what they need—no more, no less. So why do we, as intelligent beings, take more than necessary? Why should we? Shouldn't our intelligence guide us to act with more restraint and mindfulness?

———•—•———

Is it Happiness that We are Looking For?

What is the one thing we, as human beings, are looking for? Happiness. Is it really so? I believe we are not actually looking for happiness. Let us see why.

The simpler answer is—we do not know what happiness is. So, how can we be looking for something we do not understand? Suppose you are searching for a person in a crowd—you need to know what that person looks like. Can you search for someone you have no idea about?

Now, imagine there is a basket of fruit on the table, and you are given the chance to be the first to pick up an apple. But you have no idea what an apple looks like. How can you pick one? How is this different from the earlier example of searching for a person?

Probably not different. But, if you were not the first person to pick a fruit, you would probably attempt to pick an 'apple' based on what others are choosing. This is often how we go through life.

Have we ever thought about what that feeling or state of mind we call happiness really is?

Suppose happiness is the most natural or default state we are born with—in other words, our "factory setting" was 'happy.'

But then, what happened to us? This isn't hard to understand. As we go through life, we experience disappointment, failure, obstacles, setbacks, defeats, blows, calamities, and more. The list keeps growing. Over time, we add to the list of things we don't want to face.

We encounter people, events, and situations that give us feelings we are uncomfortable with. These situations that evoke uncomfortable feelings are clearly registered in our memory. We dislike these feelings, and we label them as 'sadness.'

This becomes a well-defined and catalogued list.

So, what do we seek? We search for a state that balances out these unpleasant experiences. In other words, we are looking for ways to avoid the feelings we label as sadness.

Think about it!

More than searching for happiness, we are constantly looking for a state of sadness-avoidance or rejection-of-unpleasantness. Clearly, this state is short-lived because it isn't our natural state.

The first step is to explore what our natural state of being is. Let us avoid calling it happiness.

Because, when we think of happiness, we are often unsure of what it really means. Or we have definitions shaped by all the things we wish to avoid in life.

We think that avoiding sadness will lead us to happiness. If one path leads to sadness, then the opposite path must lead to happiness, right?

Think! What is happiness really? Or start afresh!

Reflect on what our state of mind would have been before all those negative forces occupied it—before life's experiences sullied our mind.

———— • ● • ————

My Inner Voice or the Whispers of My Ego

'You are wrong', said a voice;

Looking around, I realized,

It was my own inner voice.

I took pride;

Pride in my sense of righteousness,

Or so I thought;

I felt I was a good human,

With my inner voice being my guide

I began to listen,

I listened more intensely,

I looked for that cry within,

185

That was my divine companion;
Or so I thought;
Whatever I heard was gospel to me;
The last word;
The final verdict on my mind's call.

Thus, guided was I,
By the murmur within,
That showed me the light for the ill-lit path;
Or showed the mind to my own face;
I took it to be the hand of God,
That guided this blinded heart;
It was grace, I thought,
For I had a moral compass within.

At the next crossroads, Alas!
When faced with a crisis, not large,
I listened, and listened,
With stillness of mind;
I acted on that advice,
From the friend unseen;
Once again, I thought
That was the inner voice.

But I now hear another voice;
That seemed louder than the thunder in my heart;
This 'seemed' humbler than the last.
I listened, intrigued,

I realized the blunder at last.

What was the inner voice I thought,

'Twas the ego,

Masquerading as nobility in my heart!

———•—◆—•———

What Really Makes Great People?
Key Questions to Ask Ourselves

We often look at great men and women from history or even in present times, marvelling at their achievements, fame, and success. They are celebrated with adoration and fanfare.

But what do we really see? We focus on their external accomplishments: the awards they've won, the wealth they've accumulated, or the recognition they've earned. However, we rarely pause to ask ourselves deeper questions about their essence.

What truly makes them who they are? What drives their spirit of endeavour? Who are they beyond the public eye? What is the unseen force that makes them persevere, pushing through challenges where others falter?

We often overlook the core of what shapes their greatness. Take, for instance, a successful lawyer. We may focus on their oratory skills, the number of cases they have won, or the controversies they have been part of. But these outward signs don't tell us the full story. They didn't become great because of public opinion or popular controversies. There may be those who seek fame through controversy, but those aren't the people we admire for true greatness.

True greatness, integrity, and humility don't come from external achievements alone. So, where do these qualities stem from? What internal strengths shape these individuals, enabling them to rise above the ordinary and make a lasting impact?

We seldom ask ourselves these key questions. But by learning to do so, we can begin to decode what truly sets these people apart. It is not just about what they do; it is about who they are at their core. We must shift our attention from the surface and seek to understand the deeper values and principles that make greatness possible.

———•———

'Blessings'—What Does it Mean?

"It's all because of His blessings."—This is an expression we are very familiar with. It is a sentiment that often comes to mind and to our lips. Similarly, we say, "It's all His grace."

But what are we really trying to express?

Think about it. Very often, we find that it is just an expression at the level of the lips. It doesn't come from the heart; rather, it comes more from the head, as that seems like the most appropriate thing to say in the moment. Let us go beyond this surface level.

In this discussion, we are not using the word 'blessing' to mean 'approval.' Instead, we are exploring its deeper meaning.

Let us dig a little deeper.

When we say, "It's all His blessings," we are acknowledging someone or something as the 'bestower or giver of blessings or grace.' But does it really happen because someone is 'giving'?

What we are actually doing in this expression is positioning our mind to be a receptacle or receiver. There doesn't have to be a physical giver or bestower.

By saying 'blessing' or 'grace,' we are essentially saying, "I am a receptacle." That is the feeling we are manifesting. Without this feeling of being a receptacle, there cannot be any bestowing. Furthermore, when we say, "I am a receptacle," there is no underlying sense of "please give."

In fact, even at a physical level, if I do not make myself a receiver, there cannot be a giver. This fundamental law cannot be violated.

The feeling of "I am a receptacle," in essence, makes us humble. In the sphere of acquiring knowledge, it is equivalent to saying, "I don't know," which also makes us humble and prepares us to become a receptacle, ready to receive. In that state of "I don't know," we receive from everything and everyone around us. At that point, it doesn't matter whether there is a teacher or a text directly imparting knowledge. Everything—every encounter, every thought—becomes a source of learning.

In this state of readiness to receive, born from the feeling of "I don't know," we open ourselves to knowledge from all directions. This is the essence of the famous statement from Rig Veda, "Let noble thoughts come to us from every side."

The same principle applies to grace or blessings. When we experience the feeling of grace or blessings, all the following emotions come together:

I am opening my entire being.

I surrender to the laws of nature.

I cultivate humility.

I accept and receive whatever comes my way.

I welcome everything with gratitude.

This is what the feeling of grace or blessings truly is.

However, the important thing to remember is that there is no sense of "please give" here. There is no need to imagine a giver bestowing grace or blessings. Without these feelings of openness, humility, and gratitude, no one and nothing can give anything to us.

It is simply a matter of self-assertion and receptivity.

———— • ■ • ————

Love is Nothing but True Beingness

When we feel a deep sense of love for another person, what's our real state? Have you ever wondered? When you truly feel love toward another, examine that state of mind; examine that feeling.

Actually, it is the most natural state of being. And in the real sense, that feeling is devoid of 'another.' Although we imagine that love is for the other, in reality, that feeling is independent of the other person.

There is no 'other' in love. If there is, then it is merely attraction or attachment.

That 'love'—where the 'other' is not there—is true love, and that's our true identity. It gives us a glimpse of our true nature.

That's the real state of our being! It is undirected love, like a multidirectional wave filling our entire being. In that moment, we come in touch with our true self!

———— • ■ • ————

Do Not be Fooled by the Term 'Knowledge Pursuit'

Many refer to spirituality as a knowledge pursuit. The problem with this notion is that, over time, for many, this has been reduced to a 'pursuit of knowledge.'

This reduces spirituality to a pursuit of intelligence, and by the intelligent; and sadly, so 'for the intelligent.' The word "intelligence" here is used in the general parlance, not in reference to wisdom (spiritual).

Hence, the idea of 'I have to know' becomes important, and all the attention shifts to 'knowing.'

But life is an experience—love, compassion, faith, hate, jealousy, greed, etc.—and all of these have a place in it.

Knowledge, too, is important and subsumed in many aspects of our life. Even the most fundamental notion of 'I AM' is an experience (though some refer to it as knowledge).

Thinking that the Self can be realized as 'knowledge' misleads us. We study more, listen to different perspectives, attend various retreats, and learn different approaches to realizing the truth.

In reality, the Self is beyond the mind and intelligence. Therefore, intelligence cannot take us there. What do we do then?

We gain knowledge of things and phenomena in the world through the senses, and also through inference.

The realization of the Self is neither perceived through the senses nor through reason and inference.

It is realized through direct perception, independent of the senses, where the knowable is no different from the knower. It is intuitive knowledge of the Self.

—◆—

If you are Committed to Seeking the Truth

Let the Faith be in the Scriptures;

Let the love be for the Knowledge of the Self;

Let the gratitude be to the Guru;

Let the goal be Freedom;

Let the devotion be to the Truth;

Let the identification be with the Reality;

Let the playing field be this World.

------•------

The Mighty Ocean is a Great Teacher

Since we are an integral part of nature, it comes to us as no surprise that there are so many elements in nature that are constantly speaking to us—provided we are willing to listen. For a seeker who wishes to uncover the mysteries of life, the ocean is a great teacher.

As seekers, we are constantly engaged with the following questions: What is my real nature or identity? What is the nature of the Supreme? What is my real purpose in life? What is the relationship between the individual and the Creator? How to live in this complex world? ...

Here are some of the lessons that we can learn from the 'ocean.'

Ocean of life: Life—the period between birth and death—is compared to an arduous journey on the ocean. And the spiritual pursuit is meant to help us cross this ocean of worldliness.

Life is transient: Life is unsteady like a wave on the ocean—it is there one moment, and in the next, it is not.

Ever-changing life: In life, we pass through different stages—infancy, childhood, youth, and so on. These stages in life, the accumulation of wealth, the relationships, and the human body itself are all transient like the waves on the ocean that are continually changing. There is no permanence.

Boat of Knowledge: We use a boat to cross an ocean. In the same manner, to cross the ocean of worldliness, we need the boat called the knowledge of the Self, the knowledge of our real identity.

Our real identity: The waves appearing on the surface of the ocean are no different from the ocean. Similarly, know the Self to be no different from Brahman (the Supreme Reality), in which the entire universe appears. Knowing this, be free from suffering.

All human beings are the same: There are many waves on the surface of the ocean. Each wave is different from the other in shape, size, capacity, etc. But in essence, all the waves are but 'water' and are no different from the ocean. Any difference or separation is only perception. In the same manner, the separation and difference between any two individuals is only apparent. In reality, they both are one and the same—the One Brahman. Any difference is only perceived out of ignorance.

Everything is Brahman: Just as the waves, tides, currents, whirlpools, tsunamis, etc. are all in essence but water, in the same manner, everything we see in the universe is the Supreme Brahman.

Oneness with the Supreme: Every drop in the ocean, in essence, is nothing but the ocean. One may say the drop is nothing but the ocean, or the ocean is the same as the drop. In the same manner, the individual Self is the same as the Universal Self. The individual and the cosmic are one and the same.

The One Supreme manifests as many: The same ocean, in different places on the surface of the earth, appears differently, as blue and green colours, shallow crystal-clear waters, not so clean waters in some places, and so on. In the same manner, the same Supreme manifests differently as different beings. In essence, they are but the very same, the one Supreme.

The inner calm: Even when the waters of the various rivers are constantly rushing into the ocean from all sides, in its depths, the ocean is unshaken and calm. In the same manner, even when challenges and situations of the world confront us all the time, in our depths, we are unshaken and calm. Realize that tranquillity!

Full and complete: The ocean is still and full of water on all sides. It continues to remain ever-still, even when the waters of the various rivers flow into it. In the same manner, even while remaining active in the world among the variety of sense objects, interactions, and activities, the one in whom the various kinds of desires arise and dissolve without causing any longing, attains peace and freedom.

Infinite Potential: In its depths, the ocean is unfathomable, unsurpassable, and steady. Like the ocean, our inner expanse too is boundless, infinite. In reality, we are complete, unshakeable, fearless!

Unattached in the world: When the waters of the rivers flow into the ocean, it remains changeless, without overflowing. In the same manner, even when the diversity of attractive objects of the world come at us, we are unaffected, not swayed by the temptations of variety.

All-embracing personality: The ocean is ever-welcoming of the numerous rivers that flow into it. While externally displaying a dance of waves, in its depths, the ocean is calm. We are like the ocean—poised and ever-ready to meet the various challenges of the world. While externally responding to the world situations, know that in the depths (in our real nature), we are calm, tranquil.

Purpose in life: Rivers, originating from snowy mountains, flow through various terrains, and through all their flow, they know that they have to merge with their very source—the ocean. In the same manner, the seeker courses through life with the aim of realizing the oneness with its source—Brahman, the Supreme Reality.

One goal for all: The rivers, in different shapes and sizes, flow through rocky terrains, villages, fields, and hilly regions, ultimately to merge with the very source—the ocean. In the same manner, for each individual (pursuing whatever occupation, activity, or responsibility), the goal is the same—to realize the oneness with the Supreme.

In conclusion: The reality of our nature and how we can lead a life of peace can be understood from every aspect of the all-pervading, wonderful nature. For, in essence, what we call the microcosm and the macrocosm are verily one and the same.

Will I, the Hibiscus Bud, Blossom?

A hibiscus bud looking like a tiny bulb,

In the lower regions of a lush green shrub,

I live in the corner of a vacant bed,

My identity lies beyond the colour red.

In the dance of creation in the form of seasons,

We are a mystery that is beyond reasons;

Like any artefact of the cosmic creator,

It is mine to live and merge with nature.

Here I have buds and flowers of my kind,
That with great precision He has designed;
All that shrouded inside a tiny seed,
Dexterity of The Lord is amazing indeed.

Fed by sun, earth, rain, and air, around,
With a divine alliance, we are bound,
In an inextricable bond we all unite,
I feel a sublime union with the infinite.

Some long for the Lord's temple altar,
While others dream of garland and glamour;
Decorating a wreath some may be joyous,
In simply being I shall fulfil my purpose.

Don't know if I have beauty and fragrance,
Or whether I present a lotus-like elegance,
Not sure if I have the purity or the shine,
To be at the Lord's feet or in a holy shrine.

Any day I may decay and fall from the tree,
Or snatched by a storm I may tumble free;
Ripped by elements or an unnatural scheme
I will still fall into the hands of the Supreme.

In a colony of beautiful dense bushes,
Among buds and flowers of varied sizes,
To all I express my feelings of gratitude,
I am one who must find fruition in solitude.

I don't aspire to become a bigger flower,

Neither do I wish to change my colour,

But I do hope that I naturally blossom,

Before I wither, or lose my rhythm.

Veiled by Clouds of Untruth

There are days when the sun is veiled by a thin film of clouds, and we can see the full circular shape of the sun. But once those clouds move away, we cannot look at the sun because of the glare. Similar is the truth. Often in life, we are not able to face the truth. It is okay when it is veiled by some clouds of untruth.

Embracing Humanity is the Real Pursuit of the Divine

We often think that by focusing on thoughts of God, we will elevate ourselves. Believing this, we engage mentally, verbally, or physically in activities that remind us of the Divine.

We convince ourselves that, "I should only do this; engaging in anything else is not good," and live our lives by these self-imposed restrictions.

However, by clinging to the idea of holy activities, sacred readings, and such, we become intolerant of other aspects of life. We shy away from worldly engagements—whether with things, people, or events—labelling them as "bad" or believing, "I shouldn't be involved with so-and-so."

The problem is: by constantly thinking of and filling our days with only these so-called spiritual activities, we forget how to be human.

Moreover, we become unwilling to accept many things and people as they are because they conflict with our rigid "dos and don'ts." This leads to suffering in isolation.

What we truly need is to embrace our humanity and live as humans. Only by practicing humanness can we become "humans" and stay grounded in our humanness. Realizing the full potential of our humanity is, in fact, realizing the Divine.

We forget that being human is an expression of the Divine within us. Anything else only distances us from the path to realizing the Divine.

Double Standards and the Illusion of Superiority

When someone from another religion adopts certain Hindu practices or reads Hindu scriptures, Hindus often feel immense pride and are quick to welcome them. Their hearts swell with joy.

However, if a Hindu shows interest in another religion or reads its scriptures, the reaction from fellow Hindus is often critical. Why?

This reaction is not exclusive to Hindus; people from any religious background tend to behave similarly.

Why this double standard?

The root lies in a misplaced sense of superiority—"what we have is greater than anything else."

It can work the other way too. When we see a friend embrace a different religion, philosophy, or practice, we might even feel a hint of curiosity and believe that there is something special about the other, that one is missing.

What is needed, however, is conviction and faith in our own practices.

We must understand that all religions are simply different paths aimed at elevating ourselves toward a higher good, a greater ideal. Each religion or philosophy is a path, not the only path.

Anyone who begins comparing religions, or spiritual philosophies has entirely missed the point.

———•—●—•———

Fear is Imaginary

Fear has no true presence. It is merely the mind's imaginary projection of unfavourable future possibilities onto present circumstances.

———•—●—•———

"The earth is One Family"— The Right Perspective

This statement (*vasudhaiva kutumbakam* in Sanskrit) from the scriptures is familiar to many and often used. Let us examine the true purport of this aphoristic phrase.

Some use it in the context of culture or values. Some believe that the people of this land, for ages, held this mindset of "the earth is one family," suggesting our ancestors lived by this ethical code. Others propose that this maxim should serve as a guiding principle for humanity today.

It is indeed beneficial for humanity to be governed by such principles. The statement itself seems simple and pleasant, offering an inspiring idea. However, it is a common mistake to examine it in isolation and draw conclusions without understanding the context in which it was made.

This phrase is often used in speeches and debates, causing its impact to diminish, with people rarely seeking to understand its deeper meaning.

The statement is part of a verse (in Sanskrit) that translates as: "'This is my relative,' 'this is not'—such is the reckoning of those who are small-minded; but for the broad-minded, the entire earth is a family."

This seems like a straightforward idea. One thing that is very clear from the verse is that the phrase "the earth is one family" is not a standalone principle. It is conditional, i.e., "the entire earth is one family for one who is broad-minded."

The term broad-minded here should not be interpreted in its everyday sense. It applies to one who is forever established in the Eternal, All-pervading and Full Brahman (the Supreme Reality). This mindset comes from realizing the Self and the unity of all creation.

The vision of "the earth is one family" belongs to one who, "possessing a universal vision, renouncing attachment to worldly objects, and being well-established in the Self, moves about in this world liberated, free from all anxieties and afflictions."

The verse appears in the Upanishads, which present the loftiest knowledge, revealing to us our true nature—the Self.

It refers to the mindset of those who have realized the oneness of the entire universe. I am not suggesting that we should refrain from speaking about this concept. On the contrary, whenever we encounter this idea, let it prompt us to ask: "How can I attain that state of mind where the entire earth becomes one family?" The answer to this lies in the teachings of the Upanishads.

* * *

Every Action is Successful

When we perform any action, we use the notion of success or failure to assess it. Often, this idea of success or failure is based on whether the outcome is favourable or unfavourable to us.

Something could be favourable for the performer but unfavourable for another. So, success or failure is not absolute. Also, the same outcome could be favourable today and unfavourable on another day. It depends on the context.

But there is another way to look at this. Every action follows the laws of nature, and the outcome or the fruit of action depends on those laws. Nature never fails us. There is always a cause for the effect, and the effect has a reason for what it is.

Isn't that reason enough to conclude that every action is successful?

In Sanskrit, the outcome or fruit of action is referred to as *'phala'* (literally, 'fruit'). The word for successful is *'saphala'*, and that literally means 'accompanied by fruit'.

Etymologically interpreting it, every action or work is successful. This is something worth deeply introspecting over.

* * *

O Mind, You Live Life only through Conflicts

To enable physical movement,

You have to overcome the force of inertia;

To experience the pleasure of swimming,

You have to resist the forces that try to drown you;

To enable the body to ascend,

You have to subdue the pull of gravity;

To experience true happiness,

You must swim across the ocean of sorrow;

To experience the glory of victory,

You pass through the tunnel of conflicts;

To strengthen the bonds of love,

You mature through the thorns and swords of differences;

To feel the freedom of true liberation,

You need to break the fetters of bondage;

To experience the ecstasy of great heights of success,

You need to conquer the gravity of failure;

To enjoy the strength of values,

You must endure the agony of contradictions;

To enjoy the comfort of relationships,

You must mature through frictions in interactions;

To become a better human,

You have to be tested in the crucible of challenges;

O Mind, what is life without discord!

In conflicts lies concealed the real harmony of life!

It is All About Sustaining Those Minor Doses of Detachment

Detachment arises in the mind more often than we care to believe. It is just that we are not aware or sensitive to its presence.

Whenever there is anything unfavourable, or when there is sadness or even when we commit a mistake, we often think about it. During that process of reflection, we may have the following thoughts or something similar: "What can I do about it? I could have done better. Anyway, it is done, I cannot change it. Let me be more careful next time. It was not in my control. The way it came, it will also pass. That is all this is about. A fleeting response in my mind. Nothing more." With this kind of reflection, we often get rid of feelings of grief, guilt, anger, etc.

After such reflection, the mind feels quieter and a sense of indifference dawns. This feeling of indifference is nothing but detachment (referred to as *vairagya*, in Sanskrit). It can also be seen as a sense of "moving away," "not wanting," or letting go.

But the problem is that this feeling does not last. It is very short-lived, because it often does not arise as a very intense thought.

Primarily, during such instances of grief, mistakes, or wrongdoing, the sense of detachment or dispassion that arises comes from the conscious act of reflection or analysis. It is in this situation that the intelligence comes into play, raising many questions in our mind, and thus detachment arises.

But we are not able to sustain it. Intelligence soon quietens, and the mind or the emotional aspect of the personality takes over, and we are back to our usual ways.

If only we were able to sustain or retain that state of detachment.

Spiritual knowledge and practices are all about cultivating and sustaining that detachment.

The moment the difficult situation or the unfavourable conditions pass, intelligence gives up its deliberate act, and detachment seems to subside.

The important point to understand is this: We know what detachment is. We often experience it. We know it is the answer to many of the situations that arise. Let us recognize that detachment is the key to facing the challenges of the world with poise.

Thus, spiritual pursuit is all about: How does one retain the state of detachment which appears in small bursts throughout the day?

Our Mind Aggravates the Misery, Even if it is the Body that is Unwell

One of the problems we struggle with in life is illness, from common colds to the flu to chronic ailments. Every one of these agitates us. We often feel that a common cold is better than diarrhoea, diarrhoea is better than a kidney stone, and a kidney stone is better than a brain tumour, and so on.

Think about it carefully. Is this line of thinking really helpful? When something hurts—even if it is just a toenail—we desperately want the pain to go away. In reality, we do a lot of thinking when we are sick, especially when lying down and trying to rest.

But by dwelling on the ailment, we reinforce and multiply the suffering. Each time we feel sorry for ourselves, we intensify the negative feeling, increasing the intensity of the suffering.

No, I am not saying we do not feel pain or discomfort; that pain is a natural phenomenon, and we have no choice in that matter.

But do we need to feel miserable about it? Here, we have a choice! Let us see how.

Let us start from the very beginning. Because of a symptom, we identify a condition (ailment). We go to a doctor and begin treatment. The first point here is that the body has a way of telling us there is a problem. That communication comes to us through pain or some other symptom.

So, let us recognize and acknowledge it. We have no option but to accept it and seek the treatment it requires.

Let us go beyond this. Take, for example, the case of a common cold, fever, and headache. Imagine yourself lying in bed, struggling with a blocked nose. It is not a pleasant feeling; in fact, you feel very miserable. By the third or fourth day, you exclaim, "I would rather be dead than go through this. I cannot eat, drink, talk, read, or even look at my phone."

Think back to the last time you faced such a situation. Do you remember the experience? The pain? The misery?

Of course not! You remember the occasion; you remember feeling miserable and that you could not do anything useful. That's all. You do not remember the pain, misery, or discomfort.

Pain, misery, or discomfort is not part of memory!

Pain, discomfort, or suffering is only felt NOW, in this moment. In the very next moment, it becomes part of history, and you cannot recall the pain later. Whatever your experience is, it is present only in this moment.

You experience the pain, itching, burning sensation, shivering, ache, spasm, discomfort, or nausea—only in this moment.

Like any experience—happiness, sorrow, jealousy, greed—pain is also experienced only in this moment.

The pain or discomfort we experience from a cold, flu, or diarrhoea is no different from the pain of a kidney stone, arthritis, or spondylitis. It is only experienced in that moment.

The pain experienced from a kidney stone and that from spondylitis are essentially the same, though they may vary in intensity. The nature of pain, shivering, ache, spasm, or itching may vary—but the discomfort is the same, in that it is experienced in the moment, and all such sensations share the common attribute of being unpleasant. You do not enjoy it. That's all.

But we do feel miserable! And the misery lasts, often extending into times when we are not even experiencing the pain, ache, etc. Why, then, do we feel miserable?

It is because we view illness or disease on a timeline, adding a time dimension to the problem. We go beyond the moment.

We feel more misery when we introduce the time dimension!

We think: "It's been six days since I got the flu, and there's no sign of it going away," or "How long will I have to suffer this pain?" or "When will I be free from pain?" or "How am I going to live with this for two more months of treatment?" or "Oh God, I have to endure this for the rest of my life."

While ailing, the mind races ahead in time, constantly thinking about the future. Worries and fears about the future grip our minds. More than the actual pain or discomfort, the mind's misery becomes more troubling. Pain or discomfort from the ailment becomes "suffering" in the mind, and the overall torment increases.

When we bring in the 'time' dimension, we spoil all the moments surrounding the moment of pain. Remember, pain is only present in that one moment.

But we bring thoughts outside of those moments, aggravating our misery.

Think carefully. When you have pain, discomfort, or ache, does it exist every moment, continuously, forever? Probably not!

But by introducing the time dimension, we aggravate the situation.

I am not suggesting that this is possible in all situations. Some conditions have severe pain or discomfort. Let us not forget, however, that even in such cases, some people can still bring a smile to their faces.

Imagine the visually impaired Erik Weihenmayer becoming the first blind person to reach the summit of Mount Everest!

How did he overcome that physical disability to achieve something that is quite difficult even for those who are healthy and endowed with vision?

———•◆•———

Others' Wellbeing as a Guiding Principle in My Spiritual Pursuit

In any human pursuit, such as spirituality or religion, what is the object of the pursuit? Quite often, the way it is presented—or the way it is understood—makes it seem like a very selfish pursuit.

That is, one follows this path to achieve peace, happiness, joy, contentment, etc., solely for oneself.

Or, it is said that when you attain the goal in your pursuit, you will naturally act for others' welfare, from the state of realization of the Truth.

But how many of us truly reach that peak? Thus, the pursuit remains largely self-centred.

As I reflected on this, it appears to me that others' wellbeing should be an ongoing concern or outcome as I progress on the path. Perhaps it should be an essential component and even a means to attain the goal.

Does the thought of others not draw us out of our narrow definition of who or what we are? Does it not enrich our hearts? Does it not inspire us to move further?

Without the thought of others' wellbeing, any human pursuit seems incomplete!

Shouldn't the spiritual pursuit begin with the thought of others? When we have a thought, say something, or perform an action, should we not have others' welfare in mind?

How else do I move towards the thought of the ever-present Self? How do I progress toward the idea of the universal Self if I remain locked within my own thoughts? How else can I see the same Self present in every being?

Does the thought of others' welfare not bring about the expansion of my mind, which is the cornerstone of spiritual pursuit? This expansion of mind is what helps me realize the all-expansive Self.

I must say that this orientation has made a profound difference in my own thinking and pursuit, though I confess that I have a long way to go.

I believe that thoughts regarding the wellbeing of others should be a key principle at the beginning of any spiritual pursuit!

In Karma Yoga, we talk of detachment from action and its outcome. What better way to achieve that than by offering the action and its outcome in service to others, or doing it with others' welfare in mind?

Wouldn't this be a practical way to cultivate detachment?

———•◆•———

The Inward Journey of Infinite Dimensions

For a long time, I have wondered: *How vast is our universe?* Of course, today people ask another question: *How many universes are there?* Terms like "multiverse" are now commonly discussed. For now, let me stay with one universe, as that's how I have thought of it—as one universe.

Let us begin with a simple fact: we are residing on this Earth. We can also easily see that Earth is contained *somewhere*, as part of the solar system, which in turn is part of a galaxy, and so on. The galaxy, further, is part of something bigger. I am not sure what term is used to describe that.

As we continue outward, it becomes clear that each physical entity must be contained in something larger. Basically, if we think of any physical object, that object has to be contained within something. So, no matter how far we go and claim, "This is the edge of the universe," it cannot be; because that edge would be contained in something else. It never ends. It is almost like reaching the last number in the number system.

Is space actually infinite? Where lies the 'edge of the universe'?

The word *space* has a few meanings. Today, the common meaning is how the various space agencies of different countries use it.

But, let us look at the dictionary definition of *space*: "the unlimited or incalculably great three-dimensional realm or expanse in which all material objects are located and all events occur." Note, the dictionary says *unlimited*.

I often wonder: this is perhaps the only concept that is truly unlimited. Everything else we can imagine in the universe is finite.

The more I think of it—*space being infinite*—it is such a wonderful, exhilarating, stimulating, thrilling idea. Almost difficult to imagine!

Mysterious! I cannot shake the thought: *What lies beyond this so-called space of the universe?* Where is that infinite space contained?

There is no limit to the imaginative power of the mind. I continue to enjoy this mental journey to the "edge of the universe." It excites me today as much as it did many years ago.

At some point, though, the mind reaches the limit of this imaginative journey. It is beyond human comprehension.

What does infinitude mean in the context of space? Is the human brain capable of grasping this complexity? Where does it exist? The obvious answer seems to be "everywhere." That means there is no place where the universe does not exist. If it did not exist in some place, then infinity would be disproved.

Is it possible that the universe, as we understand it, is finite in terms of its millions or billions of galaxies? Even if that is so, it must still be contained within *something*. And that journey continues—the idea of *container-contained*—and it cannot but be infinite.

Let me pause that journey for the moment!

Over time, my thoughts shifted to what we refer to as *Supreme Reality* (in the context of the spiritual pursuit of Vedanta philosophy).

In Vedanta, we understand the Supreme Reality (termed *Brahman*) to be infinite, unbounded, all-pervading, etc. In fact, the scriptures use the analogy of *space* to describe the unbounded, all-pervading Supreme. Remember, though, that analogy is limited.

But when it comes to the Supreme Reality, if we think only in terms of physical space, we will get nowhere.

We must go beyond the physical understanding of infinitude to relate to that Supreme. According to Advaita Vedanta, the Individual Self and the Supreme Reality (Brahman) are one and the same.

How, then, should we try to understand the idea of infinitude when it comes to OUR REAL NATURE? This is why the Self and the Supreme are described as unfathomable, indescribable, imperceivable to the senses, and so on.

How fascinating is this challenge before humanity!

Longing for the Sky: A Flight Beyond the Senses

Scaling the vast horizon with my *sight*,

My heart soars and takes a wondrous flight.

Blessed with wings like the eagles that fly,

I desire to reach out and touch the sky.

I feel the *touch* of falling soft snow,
Fields revel as ice to rivers flow.
Like vapor rising, when waters rarefy,
I desire to reach out and touch the sky.

I *listen* to the roars of thunder loud,
Rains and winds clear many a nimbus cloud.
A rainbow tells me not to question "why?"
I desire to reach out and touch the sky.

I *taste* raindrops as they caress the earth,
In those streams, flora rejoices in mirth.
To me, the drops bring a message from high,
I desire to reach out and touch the sky.

I *smell* the scent of roses and jasmine white,
As they smile with glee at the beaming light.
The rays from the sun reach my inner eye,
I desire to reach out and touch the sky.

Then comes a message from the hoary past,
That speaks of the inner expanse so vast.
An endless inner realm that beats the eye,
I desire to reach out and touch *that* sky.

Rest, O senses! Stop scanning outer space,
The inward flight is the one I embrace.
Inner light! Be the one to testify,
I wish to dive and touch that inner sky.

The Secret and Power of Being a Witness

Recently, I have been reflecting on the frequently used term, "witness." The more I think about it, the more absorbed I become in it, feeling it holds the key to many secrets in the context of spiritual pursuit.

In the spiritual path, many have been guided to examine their breath when sitting for meditation. What is happening then? We are often instructed, "observe your breath." But what is observing? We are simply watching the inhaling and exhaling. Aren't we witnessing the process?

So, what happens when we are the witness? We become a 'spectator,' not an instrument or participant in the process. Breathing is an involuntary act of the human body. Even at this very moment, you are breathing without consciously engaging in the act.

During meditation, the question to examine is: are we merely witnessing the breath as it flows, or have we unintentionally modified its rhythm? Sometimes we become involved without realizing it. And when that happens, it disrupts the practice of meditation.

When we are the witness, what happens? We are just observing, and our attention shifts away from other thoughts. We slowly begin to follow the rhythm and become engrossed in it. This practice helps us distance ourselves from the clutter in our minds.

There is another similar practice where we are encouraged to observe body sensations or feel different parts of the body. Next time you try it, notice what else is happening—what thoughts and feelings pass through your mind.

Now, let us extend this idea of "being a witness" from these physical points to something subtler. Suppose we are hurt by something someone said. When that feeling of hurt arises, we often feel immersed in it, as if our whole being is engulfed by the pain. It almost becomes a physical experience. Yet, pain or suffering, in this context, is not a physical experience.

Instead of becoming absorbed in the pain or suffering, try being the witness to it.

How can we transition from experiencing pain to witnessing it? Next time you feel hurt or distressed, pause for a moment and ask yourself a few questions: Why am I feeling hurt? Where is this hurt? Where is it residing? When did it start?

Gradually, you will find yourself examining the pain or suffering as a witness. This shift happens because you have made the pain an object of experience and are now enquiring into it.

Then what happens? The intensity of the pain or suffering diminishes. It does not hurt as much anymore because you have created distance from it.

It is similar to a situation when a friend shares a painful experience with you. Your friend may be in deep anguish, and the narration may be very detailed, yet you are not suffering because you are merely a witness.

Try to see if you can become the witness to your own pain and suffering.

Moving from experiencing pain to becoming its witness—here lies the answer to many of our problems. Is it possible? Certainly. Life offers countless opportunities to practice this. Begin with small instances.

This does not apply only to pain and suffering. We should learn to witness joy, peace, and other emotions as well.

What is one major advantage of this approach? When we become the witness, we gain insights into what causes pain, joy, and misery. This understanding gradually dissolves the pain and suffering.

The main idea is as follows: Pain, suffering, and pleasure become the "seen," mere objects before us, which will vanish or be destroyed like any other transient object in life.

Remember, pain and all emotions exist in the mind. For the "witness position" to work, we must realize that WE ARE NOT THE MIND. We are something beyond it—the Self. That is our real nature.

If we can be a witness to the world and everything in it, can we not also witness the pain within our own mind? When we become the witness, we cease to be the experiencer of experiences.

Another intriguing thought comes to mind as I write this: when we become a witness, don't pleasure and pain lose their individual identities and merge into one?

Just give it a thought!

------ • ● • ------

What Does it Mean to be a Disciple?

In the path of spirituality, there is a school of thought that one must find a teacher (a guru, a preceptor) to reach the goal. The goal is described by many in different ways. For the purpose of this discussion, let us describe the goal as "always being at peace, and being forever free from suffering." The spiritual goal is also referred to as Truth, which is the realization of the true nature of our identity, the world, God, and happiness.

Many believe that one must, first of all, find a guru and become a disciple to that guru. In other words, you become a "disciple" when you find a guru (in person). This is an established belief that many hold very dearly. Therefore, to attain the goal, one must first find "your guru."

Here is something to reflect on. Any action is first preceded by a thought. In fact, the genesis of action is thought. As the famous saying goes, "as we think, so we become."

What is the first thing that arises in the mind before you take any action? The individual wishes to know the Truth or attain the spiritual goal. When the aspiration to know the Truth is born in the mind, you become a "disciple"—a disciple of the Truth.

This is similar to the following situation: When a child is born to a woman, at that very instant, she becomes a mother.

From then on, that aspiration to know the Truth becomes your guide. In fact, the "aspiration or yearning to know the Truth" is your first guru and shall always remain your guru as long as that aspiration is alive. It is that yearning that leads you to an "individual" you call guru, or a book, or any other thing or situation that becomes your teacher or guide.

Here is something we have all experienced: When there is a question, and when it has gained in intensity of yearning and sincerity to know, the answer manifests itself somehow. It could come from anywhere, from anything, from anyone, and at any time.

Let us first become a disciple of the Truth.

Let us keep the flame of yearning to know the Truth alive!

We Have Made Every Person in our Life a Label

We categorize people with labels: *He is my brother, she is my friend, that is my colleague.* Through these relationship names and associations, we confine our perception of others to mere labels. Friend, brother, sister, husband, wife, colleague, neighbour, stranger, guru, disciple—the list is endless.

Labels allow us to navigate relationships conveniently.

Each label evokes a set of emotions and expectations. With a label also comes a series of unwritten conventions, and each relationship seems to follow a prescribed rulebook.

But is this truly necessary?

Yes, it is true that labels are useful. They offer an introduction to who the other person is in "my" context. They point to familiarity and nothing more. But remember, that is not the absolute identity of the person.

The problem is that they remain a label. Both the one who labels and the one who is labelled end up limiting the relationship. They obscure the deeper, truer nature of our connections. Our bonds extend far beyond these conventions and expectations, and no label can encompass their depth.

When we limit someone to "friend" or "brother," doesn't it feel shallow? Inadequate? Even a bit unfair? Such titles cannot capture the full essence of our relationships. They fail to reveal the true nature of another person and limit the way we perceive each other.

To move beyond labels, we must look deeper. This requires a journey within, a dive into the depths of our own hearts. Only by knowing ourselves can we truly begin to understand another. Beneath these surface characteristics, beyond the layers of love, hate, likes, and dislikes, lies something universal. At our deepest core, we are one.

Imagine sitting with someone by the sea, watching the setting sun. Words are unnecessary, as communication transcends speech, gaze, and touch. It is not what we say or do; it is the deep recognition that we are the same at our core. This sameness is what allows us to truly connect, to feel one another in profound ways.

Let us recognize this inherent oneness and go beyond the titles and labels. Beyond the layers of personality and emotion, we are connected to the same Universal One—the source of all. When we embrace this oneness, we transcend our labels and truly see, feel, and experience each other.

Let us recognize that oneness!

Let us realize that oneness!

Let us be that oneness!

———•◆•———

Remember, Self-assertion can be Positive or Negative

While meditating, one may repeat an aphoristic statement like "I am Brahman." Constant repetition is key in meditation practices that use mantras, grounded in the principle "as we think, so we become." Mantras like "I am free," "I am detached," etc., reinforce positive ideas in oneself, guiding one toward embodying them. This practice hinges on self-assertion.

Note that these are positive reinforcements, intended to bring transformative changes to aid one's spiritual pursuit.

But there are also thoughts with a negative outlook.

Here is an example: some people tell themselves and others, "I am a householder." By thinking and speaking this, they imply that householders cannot pursue a spiritual path. The notion of "I am a householder" has almost become derogatory, suggesting that the householder's life is incompatible with spiritual goals.

When people affirm, "I am a householder," they risk believing they cannot attain a spiritual goal. Just as one may repeat "I am free" to feel a sense of freedom, one might say "I am a householder" and subconsciously hinder their own spiritual progress. This primarily stems from the misplaced notion that householders are less qualified for spiritual pursuits.

Reminding oneself of being a householder may reinforce this perceived limitation. Over time, this affirmation can become a subconscious block, convincing one they won't progress on the path to the Supreme.

The word 'spiritual' is often wrongly perceived as antagonistic to 'household life'—a grossly misplaced notion that prevents progress toward the goal.

Remember, the spiritual pursuit is about attaining everlasting peace and freedom from suffering. Why would any human not desire such a state?

There is a need to view household life as a favourable, even ideal, context for spiritual growth—a step that prepares one to scale spiritual heights perhaps faster than any other path. This is, in fact, the truth.

The householder is well-suited to the spiritual path! Embrace this, and a new channel toward the goal opens.

Do Spirituality and Management go Together?

It will be a mistake to blindly extrapolate ideas from spirituality into the domain of management (like resource utilization, change management, planning, etc.). When we talk of spirituality and management, it is important to understand the relevance and scope of each.

The domain of spirituality is aimed at addressing the following questions: What is the nature of the individual? What is the nature of the world we see around us? What is the notion of creator or God? What is the relationship between the creator, the individual and the world? How can one realize their real nature or identity? How to live life so that we are able to cruise through life — with all its trials and tribulations — always remaining in a state of peace and equanimity?

In short, spirituality is aimed at realizing our inmost core, our real nature—the Self.

Management deals with the systems and processes relating to planning, organizing, and managing the resources, including human, financial, physical, etc., to attain the goals of the organization. In other words, management deals with the objects and situations of the world around us.

In spirituality, the goal is liberation or realization of the real nature of the individual or attainment of peace and ever-lasting happiness. In management, the goal is growth and success of the business organization in terms of revenue, profits, or other objective goals.

In spirituality, the focus is the individual, and it involves nothing and nobody else. However, in management, the focus is the organization of human beings.

In spirituality, the means are the inner realm of the human being—mind, intelligence, sense organs, Self. Whereas in management, the resources are raw materials, human resources, finances, vendors, etc. that are external in nature.

In spirituality, the process involves study (or listening), introspection and meditation to realize the Truth, and all these are inward focused practices. Whereas in the case of management there are numerous inter-related systems, processes, procedures, policies, team-work, etc.

Is Spirituality not relevant in the context of management? It is certainly relevant and applicable, but not in the way most people imagine.

Spirituality and its concepts cannot be applied to the management of the business organization, which means that they cannot be applied to systems, processes, procedures, guidelines, policies, etc. of the organization.

Spirituality is relevant only in the context of the individual's inner (subjective) dimension.

———•—◆—•———

Waves Eagerly Meet the Shore, Only to Recede

The effervescent waves on the vast sea,

Each with a different stature and form,

With an eternal longing for the shores,

They rushed toward the golden sands.

Imbued with passion for the pleasing land,

The waves roared and danced with untold delight.

Their upcoming tryst with the earthy shores,

They imagined to be their only call.

Passing through numerous storms and calms,

They finally reached the land afar;

Elation was seen in their frothy form

As they glided across the hardy land.

While this was what they always aspired to,

Now their frothy figure turned flat and still;

For they realized deep within their hearts,

This was just not their final resting place.

As water, they knew that their form was gross;

They had met land that was the very same.

Clearly realizing their mistake there,

They sought to return to the ocean's core.

To find their true nature was now the goal,

Which could not be found in the outer realm.

They receded into their inner depths,

To seek their own infinite, inner calm.

The Goal is Beyond Thought, Speech and Action

This morning after my bath, I went to light the lamp at the small shrine I keep at home. The setting was a bit different today than other days. As I went for the bath I was listening to a few old songs from movies and they had been continuing for a while in the morning. The songs continued to play even as I had returned from my bath.

As I was about to light the lamp, the song 'over the rainbow' was playing. And I was humming along. As I lit the lamp, the humming had continued and the sound filled my heart—of course the room was filled with the sound of the song and the accompanying music.

The act of lighting the lamp, my humming, Judy Garland's voice in the background, the music accompanying it all, the fragrance from the incense sticks, the glow from the lamp, the chillness of the morning, and the morning light in the room—all these seemed to have merged into one. It felt as if there was no difference between what the different senses perceived.

Later, while having my breakfast, I wondered. We are so used to chanting something as a form of prayer, using different thoughts made up of words.

But at that moment earlier today, while lighting the lamp, there were no words. It was a movie song in the background. And the setting was beautiful!

Then I thought—did not words come later in the order of creation; even thoughts came later. But the elements of the cosmos existed before all that—sound (devoid of words), light (without any names), smell (without us having to interpret them).

Sound—I do not know in what form—preceded words. We came up with words and gave them meaning. But the heart today connected with all the elements without words, without conventions, without meaning—as if in their most pure form.

The experience of the elements—without name, without form, without words, without meaning, seemed like the most beautiful prayer. The words seemed inadequate, unable to convey all that my heart felt.

My heart called out these thoughts:

May this heart rise above wishes and wants,

May this heart rise above prayer and words,

May this heart rise above sound and light,

May this heart find its abode in that which is beyond thoughts, sound, speech, and action.

In Reality, Can Sounds Disturb Us?

On this one occasion, I was sitting by the side of a flowing stream, experiencing joy listening to the sound of the gentle flow of the water. After some time, there was this persistent sound coming from a nearby factory, as if it were taking away the joy of listening to the sound of the water flowing.

The gentle flow of water was creating a sublime and soothing sound, while this factory sound was creating an "apparent" disturbance.

But soon I found that the sound from the factory was continuous. The sound of the water flow was being drowned out and dominated by the sound of the machines. While, in terms of decibel levels, the machine sound was higher than that of the water flow, I soon felt that the "disturbance" was in my mind—later it seemed rather obvious too.

After some time, I had returned to my room. Sitting quietly, I began to focus my attention on the sound from the machines that was still reaching me. In my mind, I ignored all other sounds and stayed with only the machine sound. All other sounds receded to the background, and what stayed was the machine sound alone.

Then, something interesting happened. Even that machine sound began fading in my mind. And soon, the sound from the machines was not disturbing at all. It was as if I was meditating on the sound of the machines.

I thought, in this state, even a sound from a temple bell could disturb me because it would distract me from my attention on the sound I had wilfully focused on.

Now, going beyond this, I thought—is any one sound more disturbing than another?

Perhaps, if the source of the sounds is continuously changing, then there is scope for disturbance because the change of sound draws our attention.

Let me go back to the sound of machines that was piercing to the ears. Primarily, it was a different sound—different from the ones I am used to and from the ones I associate with pleasantness. So, it was jarring and disturbing.

But when I stay with that sound alone, over time, the impact of the sound "dissolves" in the mind—and it becomes just another sound.

In other words, my mind dissolves the impact of the sound on itself. So, the response to the external sound is "born" in the mind, is initially identified as "disturbing" in the mind, and the mind itself "dissolves" it within.

At one point, the mind becomes an impersonal and disassociated witness of the sound, and then the sound is rendered weak; rather, it is no longer able to generate any "disturbing" response in my mind.

I am reminded of my childhood days when we would travel to Chennai to be with my grandmother and others. Their home was next to a railway track for the local trains. The tracks were just around fifteen feet away. The local trains would shuttle up and down all day long. During the day, it was fun watching the trains. On the first few nights, one would wake up, startled by the sound of the fast-moving trains. But soon, that problem was gone, and we slept soundly to the sound of the moving trains.

Let us now extend the discussion beyond sound. So far, our point of focus has been the sound and the associated disturbance.

After all, what is sound? It is something my mind pays attention to. It is not merely a physical phenomenon in the outside world. It is what my ears catch, that is registered as sound.

It is what my mind identifies, registers, and connects with, that becomes sound or voice in my mind.

If that is the case, then here again, the whole thing rests on the mind.

Therefore, the discussion we had in the context of "disturbance from sound" holds true for any other stream of inputs that reach my mind. What I was experiencing with the sound of water and sound of machines, I can extend to fear, sorrow, anxiety, and other such emotions or disturbances.

<hr>

Should I Allow Certain Thoughts to Disturb Me?

Sometimes, some thoughts arise in the mind that we are uncomfortable with. They are unwanted, and they disturb us.

Let us take the case of the following thoughts: "an ill-feeling towards someone," "an unpleasant thought," "a deeply fearful thought of a loss," etc.

Some of these thoughts arise suddenly and refuse to go away. No matter what we do, we are unable to wish them away.

What do we do?

Let us take a thought or recollection 'X' that is disturbing. At any point in time, only one thought holds our attention. When we move to thought Y, X is no longer troubling us.

If we can shift our attention from X to another, deliberately, then thought X is no longer disturbing us. Easier said than done.

When X is disturbing us, there is some component of X that has elements to which we are deeply attached. So, how can we get away from thought X when so many things are pulling us there?

Only a greater or nobler "idea" can pull us away from thought X. Also, forceful extrication cannot be an answer, because the opposing force will be as strong. Remember, every action has an equal and opposite reaction.

If we merely change our attention to another thought, it may seem like a solution for the moment. But that earlier thought has just shifted to the background and has not been won over.

Often, we get stuck with thought X because we do not find another thought on which we can place our attention, one that elevates our position regarding X. Sometimes, we just distract ourselves with weaker thoughts, which obviously do not work.

The greater our attachment to the elements of thought X, the greater is the difficulty in getting away.

How do we elevate our thoughts and enrich our thought process instead of just finding "distractions" for temporary relief?

Here is one approach. Enquire into the following: Was that thought something we wished for? It came from somewhere, without permission. We have no ownership or responsibility regarding the same. Why should we hold on to that thought? Why should we feel accountable for it? Why should we feel guilty about it?

Let thoughts come. They came without an invite. Let us treat that thought with indifference. Let us not pay attention to it. Like a guest who was unwelcome or ignored, that thought also vanishes gradually.

The Soulful Voice of a Teardrop

Right from the corner of your eye,

Like a raindrop falling from the sky,

Though you may feel in control, you know,

Down the cheeks I shall ever flow.

Have you ever wondered why,

In moods either low or high,

Whatever your emotions hurl,

I am the same watery pearl.

Behold the rainbow that shines

On the horizon of your subtle mind,

Caused by the light of the soul inside,

As I go down in my usual stride.

I am the same in pain and pleasure;

In both, my source is the same, I'm sure.

So too is the story in your case:

Joy and sorrow share the very same base.

Why do you then grieve, my friend?

For both joy and misery you transcend;

That's the real freedom and growth.

Like me, know you are free from both.

While the mind has its many swings,

You, the Soul, are where all life springs.

While waves are what people behold,

You, dear, are the very calmness untold.

I have seen the depth of your soul,

And there, you are forever whole.

I become a tear of joy or sorrow blind

Only when I cross your biased mind.

My waves are ever the same,

Whether you leap in joy or cry in shame.

You are in a state of eternal rejoice;

I am just a form of your mind's voice.

Whenever you have let me free,

I have only brought relief to thee.

Believe me, what I say is true:

I have and shall never desert you.

It is as if the Idea of Maya Itself is Illusory

In Vedanta, *maya* (illusion, unreality) is a central concept concerning the world, and everyone seems to like this idea.

When I first encountered the term, I often found that people used it in a light-hearted way, saying, "it's all *maya*." Back then, I never heard anyone use the term in a serious context. Things have not changed much, since then. The manner in which it is said, the words carry no seriousness. It is also used to cover up one's limitations.

For example, when someone points out that X is heavily caught up in acquiring wealth, leading to other issues and a loss of peace of mind, X responds by saying, "everything is unreal, what can I do? I am helpless."

It is often used to suggest, "it's all the result of *maya*; don't blame me." Or it is used as a weak excuse to explain suffering. I say "weak" because I have not used many using it in a manner that seems to bring strength and detachment. Quite the contrary, it seems to convey misery.

Maya broadly seems to carry two meanings: an unreal or illusory image, or the power of Brahman (the Supreme Reality) to manifest as this phenomenal universe.

Is this term relevant to the spiritual seeker? In my humble opinion, "NO!"

Why do I say that? As a spiritual seeker, one cannot avoid interactions with the world. As long as we are living in the world, there is no point in invoking the notion of the world's unreality. In that context, interpreting the universe as *maya* does not benefit the seeker in any way. There is no gain in saying, "the world is unreal."

The idea of *maya* will be realized by one who has realized the Truth—"Everything is Brahman (the Supreme Reality)." To the one who has realized the Truth, the world is *maya*. To such a one, it does not matter.

So, in the final analysis, for a seeker, there is no meaning in any elaborate discussion regarding *maya*. It is more important to attain detachment, acceptance, poise, peace, and contentment while interacting with the world.

Let Go of "Thinking" to Solve the Problem

Among the various activities occurring in our minds, the common ones are feeling, remembering, decision-making, problem-solving, and worrying. These are distinguished functionally. However, at the level of the smallest functional unit, it all comes down to a single element: *thought.* A thought may correspond to a complex series of neurological activities in the brain, involving many neurons, but that is not our concern here. Let us stay at the level of "thought."

Let us take the example of problem-solving. The problem at hand might be a simple arithmetic task, like multiplying two numbers. Here, the information we need to solve the problem is already within us; in other words, we know it.

Let us explore this further. Suppose we see the problem written on a piece of paper, such as "26 x 21 = ?". The moment we look at it, a thought arises that signals familiarity with the problem. This recognition itself is a thought. Immediately after, the stored knowledge of how to solve it takes over. It is almost like the brain goes into "auto-pilot" mode.

Looking back, we wonder—what did we actually "do" to solve the problem? It feels as though a specific part of our brain took over and completed the task without deliberate input from us. When we reflect on it, we do not sense any intentional effort on our part actively driving the process.

Now, consider a different case: we know that we "know" how to solve the problem, but for some reason, we cannot recall the solution. What does this indicate? The auto-pilot process seems to stall, and no matter what we do, the recall only happens when it happens. It is as if we have no control over it.

Are we really in control? And this is just with simple problems.

Let us now consider problems that are less straightforward, situations in which we do not have a clear solution but are familiar with the context—let us say, a life situation rather than a science problem.

When we examine the process carefully, what is happening? Various thoughts come up. Some of them may seem to address the situation at hand. Some others, in hindsight, seem foolish. Some may seem very insightful. But they all appear on their own.

But, at times, the harder we try, the more stuck or helpless we feel. However, when we sit quietly, without striving hard to find a solution, we seem to find "smarter" solution(s).

On closer examination, it seems that the effort to find a solution often involves *not* trying to find one, almost like letting go of the act of effort itself. "Attempting to think" seems to become an obstacle.

In fact, our thinking often obstructs us—especially when we start pursuing a particular thought with urgency. Removing "obstacles to knowledge" seems to reveal true knowledge. The less we force thinking, the more nature seems to take over. It is almost as though nature knows how to solve the problem, and we merely become the means by which it unfolds. Yet, when we think we are solving it, we sometimes drift farther from the solution.

Paradoxically, it seems that *not* trying to solve a problem appears to be the way to solve it. It seems rather strange, but the more "I think about it," the more I come to that conclusion. Strange indeed!

— • —

A Closer Look at the Idea of "Watching One's Thoughts"

In the context of spiritual practice, "watching one's thoughts" is a common exercise. What is the underlying idea behind this practice? What secrets does it reveal about our true nature?

Here is a summary of the practice: Sit quietly, away from external disturbances. Close your eyes. You notice the thoughts more distinctly, as against when your eyes were open. Observe them as they come and go, without being drawn into them or attaching to them. Have no opinion about the thoughts; simply witness them. [Variations of this approach may exist.]

What is the purpose of this exercise, which seems like an attempt to "read one's own mind"? This apparently simple act holds immense potential.

After some practice, once you achieve steadiness in observing thoughts without involvement, reflect on the following: Observing a thought implies that you are *not* the thought.

Take, for instance, a feeling of jealousy toward someone. Jealousy arises in the mind as a feeling. Just as you observe your thoughts, you can watch the feeling of jealousy arise, subside, and eventually vanish. This demonstrates that you are a witness to the feeling of jealousy. In the same way, you can be a witness to all other emotions—such as greed, compassion, anger, and fear.

In essence, the mind consists of desires, intentions, doubts, resolutions, non-resolutions, shame, thoughts, fears, and so on.

This means that you are a witness to the mind and everything that transpires within it. In other words, the realization dawns: "I am not the mind. I am that which witnesses the mind."

Through interactions with the world, the mind generates various experiences—some bringing happiness, others pain and suffering. The process of "watching one's thoughts" reveals the following:

You are not the mind, and these experiences are not truly yours.

You are simply the witness to the mind's various experiences.

This witness is the Self, referred to here as "I."

This separation from the mind—being a witness to it—holds the secret to freedom from misery, fear, and suffering.

My Mind is Never an Isolated One

All of spirituality addresses the human mind at an individual level. Though we often discuss the idea of a universal consciousness, we remain closely tied to the concept of the individual mind.

But can we, in reality, explore the mind purely as an isolated entity? We pursue freedom or liberation of the mind, focusing exclusively on our own. Can we truly think of the mind as existing in isolation? Is that even possible?

If we were alone on this planet, would we even need to think about the concept of the mind? Would there be any necessity to transform it? In such a state, our mind—or more precisely, our brain—would likely perform only the bare minimum of mental functions.

Yet, we are not solitary beings. We share this planet with others of our species who possess similar physical and mental characteristics. Our minds function in fundamentally similar ways.

We readily understand terms like love, fear, kindness, greed, joy, and hatred without needing elaborate explanations. This suggests that mental processes are shared across humanity. But is this understanding sufficient?

All these emotions lose their significance the moment another individual is removed from the equation. In other words, 'another individual' is fundamental to the existence of these emotions within us.

When we examine the various ripples and disturbances in our minds, there is invariably another human mind—whether consciously or subconsciously—shaping our mental responses and behaviours. Even when we attempt to address our mind's flaws or mistakes, it is never in isolation. Somewhere, other minds are active, influencing our own mental patterns.

At times, this influence may not be immediately apparent. Take, for example, the suffering caused by intense jealousy. At first, it may seem tied to an inanimate object, such as someone's possession or achievement. But upon closer examination, it becomes clear that the jealousy arises from comparing ourselves to another individual."

The interconnectedness of minds is a subject worthy of exploration. An individual mind does not act in isolation.

This brings us to another concept—the "collective mind." The collective mind is what governs the universe and its progression. It operates at various levels: the family, society, city, and so on.

This is what we experience as 'our life'. The environment we live in and the behaviours we exhibit are shaped by the 'collective mind' based on the context in which the individuals exist. The harmony we strive for is, in fact, harmony within the collective mind.

Harmony within the collective mind leads to peace and the preservation of humankind; disharmony leads to destruction.

———— •◆•• ————

Why So Many Terms to Describe the Spiritual Goal?

Soon after I began exploring spirituality, I was inundated with countless ideas. I first encountered the term "Self-realization" as the goal for a seeker.

Before long, I discovered that there are many other terms used to describe this spiritual goal. Here are some of them: Self-realization, God-realization, oneness of all creation, immortality, *moksha*, *mukti*, *nirvana*, crossing the ocean of worldliness, transcending the cycle of birth and death, oneness of the Individual Self and the Universal Self, oneness of the Self and Brahman, Divine Abode, and liberation while living.

The list goes on. At different times, I encountered various terms, each with its own meaning. Sometimes a single term, like *moksha*, is interpreted differently depending on the context. Early on, I found myself identifying with different goals at different times, leading to a stage of intrigue and wonder: Why so many terms to describe the goal?

Why didn't humanity settle on one statement? Some might say these terms all refer to the same thing. If so, why do we need so many terms?

Oneness is the central idea in all of them—the oneness of the individual self and the universal self, the oneness of Self and Brahman. Then, I was struck by an amusing thought: if union, or rather the realization of oneness, is the goal, then there is ultimately no seeker and no sought. The seeker dissolves into the sought; in fact, the seeker and the sought are one. We begin with the idea of a goal only to realize that there is no seeker and that even the idea of seeking vanishes.

Let me return to the subject of different terms for the spiritual goal.

Over time, another thought emerged. All these terms describing the goal began to seem meaningless. What is truly important for living in this world? I want to be at peace with the world; I want to remain poised in all situations; I wish to be unfazed by life's challenges; I want to be free from suffering, fear, anger, jealousy, and hatred.

This description of the goal resonated with me more. Some might argue that the earlier list of terms describes the means to achieve these states. Fair enough.

Then, at some point, I came across the scriptures describing *mukti* as everlasting happiness or the state of being ever-free from suffering. This description of *mukti*, too, deeply resonated with me.

My Spiritual Pursuit is Not an Independent One

In the spiritual path, we often feel that this is *"my pursuit"* and that I am solely responsible for it. I assume that I can be in whatever state I choose. But in this interconnected world, is it truly so? Can we ever really be on our own? Our state is influenced by those around us.

Consider this scenario: there are individuals P1 to P8 in a particular setting—whether at home, work, or elsewhere. Let us focus on the individual P1. When in such a collective environment, P1's mental state will inevitably be affected by the personalities of P2 to P8 and their interactions. For instance, if P3 dislikes P1 and constantly creates difficulties for P1, P4 is very close to P3, and P6 is indifferent to P1—sooner or later, P1 will feel the effects of this atmosphere created by P2 to P8.

No matter how much P1 tries to remain unaffected, it is difficult to avoid this influence, which often results in stress. Even if P1 believes that a spiritually awakened mind can remain free, P1 may feel helpless. This might be different if P1 were in a higher position or a different role compared to P2 to P8.

For instance, if P1 were the boss of P2 to P8, they might be on a different interactional plane and P1 would be less impacted by the others. But as a peer, it becomes nearly impossible not to be influenced.

So, what do people do in such situations? They might choose to leave that environment, finding a different place. Even scriptures advise us to seek the company of the good and wise and avoid the company of the wicked. Why should this matter if someone has full control over one's own mental state? Why do the scriptures mention it?

(This raises a deeper question: *how do we decide if someone is 'wicked'?*)

Places like *ashrams* (monasteries) often select the types of people allowed to associate or live there, primarily to maintain harmony within the environment.

Consider water boiling in a pan. As heat is applied, the molecules in the water begin to separate. As the heat increases, the agitation intensifies, leading to the separation of particles and eventual vaporization of the water. There is no water left in the pan.

Similarly, the environment we live in must be maintained in a certain way. If the "heat" in the environment rises, it causes agitation, which can lead to people distancing themselves or even leaving.

Thus, the environment must create a setting where love, compassion, and kindness can thrive.

The first and last steps on the spiritual path are the same: *love, compassion, and kindness*—with only these in between!

What Does Going Beyond Grief Mean?

According to the dictionary, grief is defined as "keen mental distress over affliction or loss; sharp sorrow; painful regret." In spirituality, we aim to attain a state of "eternal happiness" accompanied by the absence of sorrow. The Upanishads say, "the one who realizes the Truth goes beyond sorrow."

But what does it mean to go beyond sorrow? This calls for reflection and an experiential understanding of these terms.

Can a human truly go beyond affliction? If there is an individual, there will inevitably be friends, family, and relatives. When pain, suffering, ill health, accidents, disease, or death affect those we hold dear, will there not be grief? Happiness is often spoken of alongside sorrow; if there is a body, there will be pain, disease, and eventually death. Can affliction or sorrow be entirely avoided? There will be discomfort and sadness in response to the sickness and death of loved ones. However, we can strive to be free from misery or suffering.

This requires understanding terms like pain, sadness, sorrow, grief, and suffering. Let us differentiate these broadly into three categories:

1. **The event or occurrence**—These include disease, accidents, loss, separation, conflicts in relationships, death, etc. We have no control over these things that happen.

2. **The "first response" of the mind**—This could manifest as pain, sadness, disappointment, or hurt. This is a natural response for anyone. For example, when we hear of a friend's passing, we cannot help but feel sadness. (You may choose another term to express this "first response.") This response also varies from person to person.

3. **Extended grief or suffering**—Sometimes, we allow that initial response to intensify and persist, which can lead to

prolonged grief, sorrow, or unhappiness. This often stems from excessive attachment and constant brooding over what is associated with the sadness.

We cannot control categories 1 and 2. 1 is what happens, and we have no control there. 2 is a natural and spontaneous response of the mind. But we do have control over category 3. We can prevent our experience from escalating into misery or suffering.

(The terms we have used are not important. Let us understand what we are dealing with, using our own experiences.)

Let us revisit the phrase from the Upanishads: *"going beyond sorrow."* Consider point 2 above: when a loved one passes, can anyone reasonably say, "I should not feel grief at the loss"? To do so would deny an essential aspect of being human. Loss will be felt, though the way it is experienced and named may vary.

When we are connected with another being—whether a plant, animal, person, or even something inanimate—and they encounter pain or suffering, there is bound to be disappointment, sorrow, or pain.

So, what does "going beyond sorrow" mean? Perhaps our language lacks the precision to describe this state. Maybe we need more specific terms for this experience.

Is it truly possible to go beyond grief? Even saints like Ramakrishna Paramahamsa experienced pain and sadness, regardless of its source.

Going beyond grief does not mean being immune to the sadness of loss. It means being free from the delusion that grief should persist as misery. While there is an initial response of disappointment, it does not translate into prolonged grief or suffering.

As humans, we cannot be free from pain, but by realizing the Self, we can remain poised, even while facing that pain.

Let us go beyond the words, and reflect on the essence of what we have discussed.

———•—

The Idea of Renunciation Requires Deeper Reflection

We often come across the word 'to renounce' in scriptures. Its root (in Sanskrit) carries meanings such as to leave, abandon, quit, go away from, give up, and shun. This word is repeated so frequently that it starts echoing in our minds, to the point where we may even forget what it is asking us to abandon.

In spiritual literature, the word 'abandon' is used in the sense of 'giving up,' not as in 'deserting' (such as 'abandoning a friend in need').

Giving up anything is not easy. How often have you thought of discarding a piece of clothing you have not worn in years, only to keep it anyway?

The word appears so often that it leads us to think that the path of spirituality is all about "renouncing" or "giving up" or "leaving." But it is quite the opposite. Spirituality is about embracing everything and everyone without distinction. It is about developing an all-embracing personality, one ready to engage with the entire universe of beings, possibilities, ideas, and concepts, until we become whole and complete.

This expansion leads to the realization of an infinite dimension, which is referred to as Brahman (literally, "expanse," "the universal"). Though we are constantly told to "renounce," careful introspection reveals it is not about renouncing everything but rather about embracing a "readiness to renounce" or "readiness to give up."

We need various things to lead a life, but the problem arises when we become attached to those things, and this attachment leads to suffering. True freedom lies in the readiness to let go, to walk away. That readiness is detachment. This ever-ready state to renounce without hesitation is true freedom—an embracing of the entire universe, balanced with a readiness to let it go joyfully.

Possessions (objects of the world) do not bind us; our attachment to them and our reluctance to let go do. Let us explore this idea further. Imagine you have 100,000 rupees in your pocket. Now picture two situations: in one, you give that money to someone in need; in the other, someone forcibly takes it from you. In both cases, the outcome is the same—you no longer possess the money. So, what causes pain? The latter situation, of course. Why? Because you were not *ready*.

Concepts like controlling the mind, restraining the senses, and practicing detachment are introduced so the mind can be ready to step away from things like money, rewards, fame, people, status, power, relationships, etc. But the idea is not about a physical renunciation of these things. It is not about "possessing nothing."

Let us remember: "We can be bound without possessing anything, and we can be free while possessing an entire city."

Now let us examine this concept from another angle. Suppose we take renunciation literally, aiming to physically renounce everything. To what extent can we carry this idea? Suppose someone says, "Renounce everything." Is that really possible?

It would be nonsensical to think along these lines. Why?

The idea of *sannyasa* (renunciation in Sanskrit) is often interpreted to mean renouncing or leaving "all" worldly possessions—wealth, family, property, profession, and so on. Having renounced "everything", you still hold on to one thing—the "status of being a renouncer", the status or title of a *sannyasin* (a monk, renouncer). And along with that "status" comes ideas, rules, lifestyle changes, etc., which can bind one just as much as anything else. So, what's the point?

By repeatedly emphasizing renunciation, we create myths within spirituality that leave seekers with intimidating or impractical ideals. Many seekers carry the "burden of renunciation," torn between the world they live in and the one they hope to enter someday—a day that never seems to come. Some commentators interpret renunciation as giving up all but the bare essentials. This, too, is difficult for most people.

So, the idea of renunciation is best understood as (1) a readiness to leave, (2) detachment and impartiality toward everything and everyone, (3) a graceful acceptance of loss, and (4) a poised acceptance of each situation.

Viewed in this way, renunciation gains new meaning:

You may have possessions, yet be ready to share with others. You may belong to a family, yet embrace all beings with love and without bias. You may hold personal beliefs in religion or God, yet accept and respect others' beliefs as much as your own. You may engage in work or profession, yet perform all work as a service to humanity. You may live in this world but be in a constant state of readiness to walk away from it.

So, what is to be renounced? And is this concept relevant to our lives? Yes, it is.

Let us renounce our limitations, which prevent us from experiencing life fully. Let us renounce our biases, which prevent us from seeing all beings as one. Let us renounce desire and the feeling of lack, which prevent us from being content. Let us renounce discrimination between fellow beings, which prevents us from seeing the ONE in all.

Now, let us examine the four goals of human life (in Hinduism) known as *purusharthas*: *dharma*, *artha*, *kaama*, and *moksha*. While living a life grounded in dharma, we acquire wealth and resources (*artha*); then fulfil our desires (*kaama*); and finally turn our attention toward the ultimate goal of *moksha* (liberation). Liberation is defined as "everlasting happiness, free from suffering." There are multiple paths to liberation, and renunciation is one of them.

Here is another important point that calls for some reflection: By interpreting renunciation solely as physically giving up everything, we miss the profound concept of 'transcendence.' Transcendence shows us how to be free, even though one is constantly engaged with things, people, events, situations, etc. of this world, rising above success and failure, happiness and sorrow, victory and defeat, etc.

As seekers, we need to reflect on the following: Our spiritual goal is to be content, full, complete. If this is so and we wish to be free in this world, then what is the real meaning and purport of 'renunciation?'

The Path of Solitude to Embrace the Whole

Alone, I entered this wondrous world of existence;
Alone, I experienced the comfort of parental shelter.

Alone, I faced the challenges of youthful sojourn;
Alone, I relish the joyful moments in life.

Alone, I experience the losses and pains of the heart;
Alone, I deal with the trials and tribulations of the world.

Alone, I enjoy the beauty of nature and its bounties;
Alone, I witness the fury of nature in amazement.

Alone, I try to shape my destiny in this world;

Alone, I face the consequences of my actions.

Alone, I sense the pain and suffering of the destitute;

Alone, I feel indignation seeing the ills in society.

Alone, I carry the burden of guilt from my wrongs;

Alone, I surf the tides of my mind.

Alone, I endure the pain this body presents;

Alone, I shall fall, as this mortal body drops to the earth.

Alone am I, among family and friends;

Alone am I, even amidst the multitude.

Alone am I, but never lonely;

Alone am I, but never running away from the world.

Alone, I am the witness to the entire world;

Alone, I am the witness to all the experiences in my mind.

Alone, I realize the real meaning of 'alone';

'Alone'… That is my true nature, my true identity.

Alone am I, in this journey of the mind, called life;

Alone is not emptiness, but the experience of fullness.

Alone, I am the traveller … the path … and the destination;

The truth is … I ALONE AM. I ALONE AM.

Understanding the Cause of Afflictions Helps Us

The scriptures describe three types of afflictions in human life: those arising from the influence of planets or divine agencies, those created by beings, elements, or materials, and those stemming from our body or mind.

Is there a more descriptive way to understand afflictions? Let us explore this in a way that also hints at how we can free ourselves from the impact of these afflictions. Here is an attempt at a classification:

1. Caused by nature (floods, weather, animals, plants)

2. Caused by accidents (man-made mistakes, such as motor accidents)

3. Resulting from disease

4. Resulting from the death of someone

5. Caused by human actions (war, riots, mobs, economic crises)

6. Caused by individuals (murder, rape, theft, fraud)

7. Caused by lack of resources (poverty, hunger)

8. Related to human interactions (enmity, friction in relationships, divorce)

9. Related to one's own mind (jealousy, greed, hatred, fear, anger)

When faced with an affliction, consider the cause of the problem, and reflect on which of these categories it falls into.

Some of these causes are largely beyond our influence, or we have very little influence in preventing them. Why is it helpful to know this? Recognizing what we cannot control, enables us to deal with situations with poise and recover, preventing the affliction from lingering as prolonged misery.

Some afflictions, especially those born from the mind, are entirely within our control. The scriptures guide us on how we can be free from these mental afflictions.

Examine the problems in your life and see how many of them stem from causes within your control. This ongoing reflection will help lessen the impact of afflictions, leading to a clearer understanding of life and its challenges!

Pain is Not Part of Memory, We Recreate it Now

I often wonder what the word 'knowledge' means. I remember reading about the concepts of data, information, knowledge, and wisdom many years ago. What is the relationship between the words 'brain' and 'knowledge'? The brain stores data for us in the form of memory.

Something happened many years ago: X said something to me. I was hurt by it. I never recovered from it.

When I recall it now, I may remember that 'X said something' and that 'I was hurt by it.'

However, what I do not recall are the emotions that were associated with it then. Yes, I remember being hurt, but *not* the specific feelings or emotions. I may remember the *type* of feelings, but not the actual feelings themselves. In other words, I do not have the same experience now.

In the same way, pleasure and joy are not part of memory.

What does this mean?

Emotions are always of the present. Emotions are always here and now. Pain and grief are not part of memory. So, if we live in the present, there is no suffering!

We sometimes hear people say, "I am carrying so much pain from the past." This calls for serious reflection. Can you ever carry the pain from the past? What you carry is the memory of the pain you experienced then. It is not the pain itself, but the memory of the anecdote that had caused the pain.

What you experience from that instance is freshly created pain. You bring that event into the present and recreate the emotions now. The pain you experience is the pain you create now. It is different from the pain you felt then.

That is why we say 'time will heal,' because we do not carry forward pain or any other emotion.

Whether it is from a week ago, a year ago, or a decade ago, in the present moment, we are free—not only from pain but from all kinds of emotions of the past.

In the present, we are free. It is like pure water, uncoloured and unflavoured, ready to be tinged or flavoured by anything you care to add, now.

So, when we suffer from the memory of the past, we are actually putting effort into recreating that instance and its details repeatedly. Having recreated everything in our mind, we make it real to us *now*. And we feel a fresh set of emotions, which are of the present moment—not the same emotions we felt years ago.

In that sense, pain, misery, suffering, etc. are all things we put effort into, to feel them again and again. Why should we exert so much effort?

It is only the present moment that is free from pain of the past. Hence, the importance of living in the present moment.

———•———

Will or Resolve: This is a Very Crucial Faculty

Bhagavad Gita 3.42 says: "The five senses (including vision, hearing, etc.) are considered superior to (subtler than) the body, which is gross; the mind is superior to the senses; and the intellect is superior to the mind. The Self (the witness to the mind and intellect) is superior to (subtler than) the intellect."

Let me focus on one part of this: "the intellect is superior to the mind."

Is it really so? This thought has occupied my mind for some time. Why am I questioning this? Let me try to explain.

In my efforts to improve my fitness, I have been working on moderating my eating habits. I have found that fried foods cause the most harm to my body. My intellect has processed this and determined that, to maintain a healthier lifestyle, I should avoid fried foods. My intellect also gathers supporting information to conclude that fried foods should be excluded from my diet.

So far, so good. The intellect seems to be in control, guiding the mind. In this sense, it does appear superior to the mind.

But when I see a tempting fried dish, all that commitment vanishes in an instant.

What happened to all that work by the intellect? Did it not get overridden by the mind's temptation? In that moment, wasn't the mind dominant? By what logic, then, is the intellect superior to the mind?

Thinking further… What are we missing here? Let us re-examine the process. I mentioned a "commitment" to avoid certain foods. This introduces a new concept: "will" or "resolve."

On closer examination, in the hierarchy of body-senses-mind-intellect-Self, there appears to be a missing link—the will, or resolve.

Two points emerge from this discussion: (1) the intellect does not have complete control over the mind; and (2) there exists an entity called *will* that plays a crucial role in guiding the mind's actions.

It seems to me that this faculty of *will* is the most crucial element in the entire spiritual pursuit—in fact, in all of life. If we can understand this secret, life itself is conquered.

The entire pursuit boils down to this: How can we stay committed to a resolve? How do we ensure we succeed in our resolve?

Think… This is the only challenge to surmount, the only problem to solve, the only quality to possess.

————•————

Have We Ever Tried to Explore the Cause-and-Effect Chain?

Anything we do, we immediately look for a result—and a favourable one at that. Are we able to see all the "outcomes" (plural) for every action performed? We can confidently say "No!"

In our eagerness for favourable results, we see only what appeals to us. Anything else is not even regarded as an "outcome."

Consider the following: we plant a sapling in the vegetable garden. Let us say it is the first of February. After a couple of months, we look at the few vegetables hanging on the plant and feel proud of our effort. We are happy with the outcome and derive satisfaction from doing something useful. Had the plant not produced fruits as we expected, we would have been disappointed and might have abandoned any future gardening plans.

The timeline is as follows: planting the sapling on February 1st, flowering on March 1st, and fruits appearing on April 1st. We call what happened on February 1st "effort" and what happened on April 1st "outcome" or "result." But is it really so? Is everything so linear and simple?

What about February 20th, when the first signs of a flower appeared? Isn't that also an outcome of the effort on February 1st? Thus, every moment on the timeline is an outcome, and every cell that changes in the plant is an outcome.

Now, let us broaden our perspective. So far, we have looked at effort and outcome only from *our* point of view, as the ones who planted the sapling. Is that all that happened in the context of effort and outcome?

What about the sunlight, the earth, the manure, the gardener's care, cleaning, and the contributions of birds and bees? All these are efforts. Without them, our single effort would have been in vain. That is regarding effort.

Now let us consider outcomes. It is not just the act of plucking vegetables from the plant on April 1st that counts as an outcome. That's just one event in the plant's life at that moment. The rest of the ecosystem benefits from the plant all along: bees sit on its flowers, insects and birds interact with it, and the earth gains from the fallen flowers. These are the outcomes we can perceive on the physical plane. But is that all? Certainly not.

Another consideration—the entire discussion so far has been on the physical plane, but life is not confined to the physical realm. Think carefully and deeply.

Consider this scenario: on March 4th, the plant has a few flowers. An individual passing by the garden at 6:00 pm, who had been having a difficult day, felt depressed. At 6:02 pm, he noticed those flowers and felt joy, briefly forgetting his worries, and experiencing a moment of indescribable peace.

What is this? Is it not part of the series of outcomes?

The point is that we look at effort and outcomes in a narrow, linear way. But is life truly like that? Think!

If we truly understand what work or action is and the nature of its progression, then how can we be "attached" to the work we do and to the "fruits of action"? This understanding paves the way to Karma Yoga.

The most important thing is simply to act—perform actions and allow the natural unfolding of events that follow.

When we understand that the "action-and-outcome" chain is really "action-and-watching-the-unfolding," the whole phenomenon becomes a beautiful and wonderful performance, entirely in the hands of nature. It is like watching an expert sculptor at work: we are merely the chisel and hammer in the sculptor's hands.

Viewed this way, our views on success and failure also change.

What is our definition of success and failure? From this perspective, can we truly define success or failure? Our usual narrow perspective on success and failure leads only to more problems and misery.

When we say, "I did it," we rarely understand the implications of that statement. Instead, we make this statement based on a belief that "I have done it." But have we ever examined whether this statement is true? We assumed it to be true and began to believe it.

Take any action—our statement, "I did it," persists because "YOU" are the centre of your world. You have not considered it any other way. Let us take a specific example: "I went to the market and bought a pair of shoes."

Did we ever examine this, before we believed it? Do we actually think, "I went to the market and bought a pair of shoes"? So many factors contributed to that action. Someone probably drove the car or bus; someone built the road; the family may have cooperated, creating favourable conditions; and others at the store played a role. There are also environmental factors (weather, etc.), and other agents (no city strikes, no riots, etc.). The list is long, and we can never be sure we have covered everything.

If that is the case, how can we claim, "I did it"? And not only that—we expect credit and recognition for it. In the workplace, we may feel upset if someone else receives the credit.

What does this indicate? We do not understand causality even in the simplest physical sense. We do not even care to explore it, perhaps because it might make us uncomfortable.

Causality is complex and indescribable. It suffices to say that our claim "I did it" is not true.

Self-mastery is True Surrender

"Surrender!" I am told.

"To whom?" I ask,

And questions pour in relentlessly,

Consuming my imagination.

Does it mean giving up my independence?

Does it mean I simply do as I am told?

Have I become the vanquished?

Will I lose my individuality?

What happens to my identity?

Do I now act on instructions?

Must I give up reflection?

Do I forsake all that I possess?

To surrender is not to submit to a person,

Nor to become a slave to a tradition,

Nor to conform to a doctrine—

It is to rise above all ideologies.

The spiritual quest is a path to freedom.

To entertain a notion of surrender

To something or someone

Is a bondage difficult to destroy.

They say to surrender is "to be free from ego,"

"It is for ego-effacement," they say.

But truly, it is ego alone

That says, "I surrender."

Your act of surrender depends on your identity:

As body and mind, to surrender is to submit.

Realizing the Self, you are one with the Cosmic,

And then, there is nothing left to surrender to.

True surrender is a journey to realize one's true identity,

To be free from all identities,

To abandon any imagined object of surrender,

To liberate oneself from the idea of submission.

To surrender, if at all,

Is to embrace the Universal, the Cosmic—

Or if you choose, the Divine.

It is to unite, or rather, to realize unity with the Universal.

To surrender is to accept things as they are,

To welcome all that comes.

To surrender is to treat light and darkness alike,

To behold a wondrous world forever.

To surrender is self-mastery.

It is a position of strength,

A state of true independence,

A manifestation of freedom.

To surrender is

To be liberated from the sense of doership,

To abandon the stance of the sufferer,

To become a "mighty performer."

To surrender is freedom from all bondage,

To surrender is everlasting peace.

To surrender is the state of fullness.

To surrender is to have *conquered!*

Some Pointers for Cultivating the Position of Non-doership

The idea of non-doership is central to Karma Yoga. What does it mean?

In any action, the following elements are involved: the inner faculties (mind, intellect), the instrument of action (body, limbs), external tools, the environment (conditions), and chance (providence).

Generally, when performing an action, you believe, "I am doing this." But is that assumption correct? It is the mind that conceives the idea. When you think "I am doing," you are mistakenly identifying "I" with the mind. However, the true "I" is not the mind.

Similarly, you say, "I am doing," because you assume that "my body and hands" are performing the task. Yet this claim is also based on the mistaken association of "I" with the body.

In truth, "I" is neither the body, mind, intellect, nor ego. It is the Self, beyond all of these. At the level of the Self, "You are a non-doer."

When you identify with your true nature, the Self, you realize that although various tasks are being performed, you, in fact, remain a non-doer.

How does one realize the state of non-doership in practice? How can we cultivate this shift in thinking and being? Here are some pointers:

1. Constantly engage in introspection about your true nature—the Self, which is distinct from the body, mind, and intellect.

2. Let go of the ego associated with being the performer.

3. Dissociate from both the action and its outcome, remaining detached from both.

4. Recognize the Supreme's role in every action and surrender to that One Presence.

5. See yourself as merely an instrument in the hands of the Divine.

6. Maintain even-mindedness regarding outcomes, be they success or failure.

7. Let actions arise out of the need to serve others, without selfish motives.

8. Perform actions as an offering to the Divine.

9. Even if an action fulfils a personal need, view it as simply meeting an essential requirement, free from selfish motives or expectations of a particular outcome.

10. No action in this world is completed by an individual alone. For instance, when you say, "I am traveling from Delhi to Mumbai," the journey is not possible without the transport services, support from others, and countless other factors that make it feasible. Reflecting on any activity reveals that no action can be accomplished entirely alone. Even this understanding fosters a sense of non-doership, serving as the foundation for deeper realization.

What is Behind Good and Bad Thoughts?

When exploring the nature of thoughts, I noticed that they almost seem to spring up from nowhere. When I examine a good thought and trace it back to where it came from, I do not find anything inherently "good" there. There is just 'nothing' there (though "nothing" may not be the perfect word for it). Similarly, when I look behind a bad thought, there is nothing to suggest that it was bad in origin. What was there before it? I don't think it was something bad that gave rise to the thought. Once again, there was just 'nothing.'

Something that can give rise to both good and bad cannot be intrinsically good or bad. If something were intrinsically good, it would give rise only to good; if it were intrinsically bad, it would give rise only to bad.

Clearly, something that can generate both must be beyond the categories of good and bad. In fact, it cannot carry any specific label or trait by itself—because of the variety it creates.

So, at that level, I am free from notions of good and bad.

The variety comes from the nature of that where the variety manifests; i.e., in the mind.

Another perspective is this: the idea of something as good or bad is highly subjective and relative. Thus, whatever lies beneath, at the very source of thoughts (if we can speak of such a thing in the mind), must be free from any fixed colour or attribute.

This insight points to the possibility of remaining unaffected by whatever thought emerges. Isn't fear just another thought that surfaces in our mind? Why, then, do we let it affect us so deeply? Think about it!

⸻ ⬥ ⸻

'Letting Go' is the Only Effective Way of Controlling Thoughts

Can I control my thoughts? What does control even mean? Can I truly control?

In the realm of thoughts, "control" might actually mean "letting go" or exercising "no control." In other words, to "control" is to practice "no control."

Suppose I say, "O mind, don't think about chocolate." Will the mind comply? Can it even comply? The more we try to avoid a thought, the more we end up thinking about it—since we must keep the very thought in mind to avoid it.

So, the only solution is to let go of the thought, which means letting go of the very objective we are trying to achieve.

Could we generalize this further? Perhaps the only way to solve a problem is to let go of the thought of the problem—essentially, to let go of the pursuit of solving it. [Here, "problem" refers specifically to issues within the mind, not to practical situations in the external world—though even in those cases, this idea can have some relevance.]

* * *

"What is the Purpose of this Universe?"— An Irrelevant Question

We tend to attribute a purpose to everything we do and everything that happens, often imagining a motive behind any action. This may be why so many ask, "Why did God create this universe?" Somehow, I have never been inclined to wonder about that.

Still, a few thoughts come to mind in response. When people start with "Why did…," they assume someone or something created it. Let me stay with that for a moment. If the universe was created with a purpose, that purpose would indeed seem strange. Given the current state of the world, it does not seem to reflect any clear, planned purpose. Some might say there was a purpose initially, but somewhere along the way, things spiralled out of control.

The other possibility is that the universe was created, and from then on, everything unfolded by chance and nature. This view seems plausible to me. That is—perhaps the universe came into existence, and all subsequent developments were governed by natural processes (good, bad, or otherwise).

Certain basic physical, biological, chemical, and societal laws seem to drive change, with many of those changes influenced by the dominant species: humans.

Imagine this complex entity—the universe—coming into existence and changing constantly, every nanosecond. Based on fundamental principles, it will continue to evolve. There is no need to posit a controller to micro-manage every detail of the universe, including us and our lives.

There is a lesson here for humanity. Should we be so concerned with the "purpose" behind every event?

Why can't we follow a similar principle? Do what we do and let go. Let things unfold as they will. They, too, will follow the natural laws, as everything is part of nature. Let us free ourselves from anxieties about outcomes, about the future. Let us be free now!

———•◆•———

Are we Capable of Undirected Love?

Consider the feeling of "love." It is directed—directed at someone. We hold the other person in our thoughts, sometimes even right in front of us. That is usually the case.

This feeling is not limited to just one individual. We may feel it toward quite a few people in our lives. But relatively speaking, it is still only a few.

I often reflect on this, and certain questions come to mind: How do I extend this feeling to more and more people? How do I do this for no reason or motive at all? How do I reach a stage where I love unconditionally? How do I feel love toward those I do not even know? How do I extend it toward those I am "not fond" of? And so on…

Then, suddenly, a thought arose: "Can love be *undirected?*" But then, love, by definition, is directed toward another person. At least, that is how we usually understand it.

I began to wonder: Why couldn't this feeling of "undirected love" be cultivated? If it encompasses all, then it is not directed toward just one or a few.

Here is a thought on undirected love: Consider the sun. We simply say, "the sun shines." We do not have to specify, "the sun is shining on the tree" or "the sun is shining on the river." The object it shines upon does not need to be mentioned. Similarly, I feel the human mind is capable of "undirected love."

What would that state of mind be, capable of "broadcasting" this feeling toward no one in particular? What would that feeling be like? How would such a mind exist?

Why can't we experience a feeling of "love" radiating from the heart toward no one in particular? Practically, this could be visualized as "love toward every being in the universe." What would such a mind be like?

Would it be a state where the opposite feeling—hatred or dislike—completely vanishes from our minds? When there is no hatred or ill-feeling toward anyone, it is a beginning. I feel that the absence of hatred does not necessarily mean love.

How do I cultivate this feeling? How do I move from "no ill-feeling toward others" to "love toward all," and then to "undirected love"?

Somehow, I feel instinctively that there is a possibility of "undirected love," distinct from merely "loving all."

Let my mind move toward that. Let me begin by aspiring for it!

If a feeling of happiness can exist without any associated object, why couldn't a feeling of love exist without a specific direction?

I am enjoying this thought and idea, even if it is not easily comprehensible, and such a state may not be easy to attain.

———•❖•———

Let me Embrace the Self in every Interaction

When I encounter a situation with another person that leaves me feeling discomfort, irritation, anger, or suffering, I often wonder what I should do going forward. I used to think the answer lay in "acceptance"—i.e., accepting the situation. But that did not solve the problem. Then, I thought I should forgive the other individual. Initially, this seemed to help, but that, too, was short-lived. I realized that no single approach consistently solves the problem. It may provide a temporary fix.

What does it mean to "solve the problem"? It is not merely about facing the situation bravely, avoiding anger, or simply being able to accept and forgive the other person. Nor is it just about facing the person with warmth or understanding. I discovered that I needed to go beyond all these approaches. The solution, I found, requires a combination of practices that operate together:

1. **Acceptance**: True acceptance goes beyond accepting the person. It involves recognizing that it is the situation that caused whatever happened; anyone in that situation might have acted similarly. Multiple factors contribute

to an event, yet we often "blame it all on the individual." Acceptance has two aspects: accepting the situation and feeling that the other is worthy of being accepted. Mere acceptance can sometimes foster an egotistical sense that "I am accepting," subtly implying, "I am right, and you are wrong."

2. **Forgiveness**: Thinking "I forgive the other" can lead to a holier-than-thou attitude. Thus, I also seek forgiveness from the other. Regardless of the situation, in varying degrees, both parties contribute to the outcome. I forgive and seek forgiveness wholeheartedly and unconditionally.

3. **Owning the Other (Love)**: This goes beyond mere mental affirmation; it involves embracing the other fully, considering them as dear as the closest person in one's life. In other words, I strive to feel genuine love for them. We are often more forgiving of those we like and less tolerant of those we don't. The key here is to embrace the other with love.

4. **Seeing Nature at Work**: All people, along with their thoughts, behaviours, and actions, are influenced by the *gunas* born of nature. Recognizing this, I can no longer blame the other for what occurred. If the other person appears to be at fault, I respond with compassion, understanding that nature, through the *gunas*, is at work.

[guna: This Sanskrit term translates to quality, attribute, or property. Nature consists of three gunas—sattva, rajas, and tamas. Everything and everyone is a combination of these three gunas, which exist in varying proportions and can change over time. The qualities are: (1) sattva, referring to harmony, goodness, purity, and virtue; (2) rajas, referring to passion, activity, drive, egoism, and movement; and (3) tamas, referring to ignorance, inertia, lethargy, dullness, and delusion.]

5. **I Am the Self**: My response to interactions—pleasure, pain, anger, fear—is only at the level of the mind. I remind myself that these reactions are not my true Self. "I" am the Self, a witness to what transpires in my mind.

6. **Seeing Oneness**: Our true nature is the Self, the same Self that exists in all beings. This realization brings to light our essential unity: we are all one at the core.

Though these approaches may seem similar, each addresses a different aspect of my personality. The goal is to transcend the interaction itself and address the mind's environment. Often, I find that solutions address only the specific transaction at hand, but when another challenging situation arises, my response remains the same, or at best shows only slight improvement.

In conclusion, I realized that these practices need to work together within me. This approach to understanding interactions gradually reinforces the following insights: (a) My true nature is the Self; (b) it is the *gunas* that drive behaviour and actions; and (c) the same Self exists in all beings.

Every interaction in the world acknowledges that whatever occurs does so on the physical or phenomenal plane. But the "I" that I refer to is not the one directly involved in the interaction. Disturbance, anger, irritation, and seeking acceptance, forgiveness and reconciliation are all at the level of the mind.

I need to internalize that the unaffected "I" is my true nature, allowing me to rise above these ongoing challenges.

It is fascinating how our day-to-day interactions hold the keys to deeper truths about ourselves and how these everyday encounters can gradually lead us toward realizing our true nature.

The Relationship between the Human and the Divine

How and why did humans conceive of the Divine? Reflecting on this can lead to a deeper understanding of ourselves and our aspirations in life.

There are two broad notions regarding the Divine, though they are by no means the only possible perspectives. Each individual should feel free to explore this subject, without the limitation of any preconceived notions.

One common view holds that the Divine is a "creator-controller-sustainer-destroyer." This concept of the Divine is modelled on how we see ourselves as physical beings with distinct functions and activities. In this view, the Divine gives and also takes away. This mirrors how we experience the world and our interactions with others around us. The relationship with the Divine, then, is shaped by perceiving it as "superhuman" and assigning it a supreme position, hence why we write "Divine" with a sense of reverence.

For many, this relationship mirrors human interactions, functioning as a kind of "give and take." The Divine is personified, and devotion often translates to exchanges — prayers, offerings, acts of service, surrender, and austerities, all aimed at receiving something in return: wealth, progeny, comfort, health, peace, success, and so on. Though these acts may take noble forms, the underlying intention is often to gain the Divine's favour, with the hope of obtaining something.

The rest of life continues as usual, with this relationship forming another compartment, often separate from daily actions. This transaction (with the Divine) may feel disconnected from other aspects of life, except as a means to make them more comfortable. Presented this way, it may sound crude, but take a moment to think about it without jumping to conclusions. Reflect deeply.

Upon closer examination, this is often the foundation of many religious practices. Yes, this description is perhaps an oversimplification, but my intent here is to encourage reflection on our relationship with our own concept of the Divine, not to impose any specific view.

Now let us consider a second view of the Divine. We possess certain qualities that make us human, qualities shared by all. We may view these as derived from a common source, an inheritance from a Supreme presence. This shared source allows us to cohabit in harmony, as descendants of a common origin.

In this view, the Divine embodies the highest form of human qualities: all-compassionate, all-loving, all-truthful, all-knowing, and so forth. Here, the Divine is seen as the zenith of the qualities we aspire to cultivate. This perspective opens a different path — one that centres on "becoming Divine" ourselves.

If examined closely, this is the essence of spirituality. It is based on personal transformation, offering a natural, subtle path for inner growth.

Now, consider for yourself where you may fit in this exploration. It need not be one view or the other, but let this serve as a direction for your own journey in understanding the Divine.

—•◆•—

The Adventure Within, Beyond the Mind

I long to set out on a wondrous adventure,

To places glimpsed in that dainty old picture.

But I cannot decide on the perfect destination—

Should it be a peak or a sapphire blue ocean?

Undisturbed forests, unsullied waters—
Which of these realms should I choose among quarters?
As my mind wandered, unable to decide,
Only confusion and chaos reigned inside.

My thoughts first roamed far and wide,
Without my body taking a single stride.
I felt vastness and grandeur deep within,
With wondrous beauty and majesty therein.

At last satisfied with this novel find,
I set out to journey the infinite mind—
An adventure requiring no bags or cash,
Unfazed by rain or lightning's flash.

Preparing to embark on this grand passage,
I freed my mind from all unwanted baggage.
I left behind books, work, plans, and wishes,
Clearing the way for a journey without glitches.

As I sailed into the vast mind-ocean,
Thought-waves arose, disturbing my motion.
Diving deeper, I found calmness there,
Enjoying the stillness in my Soul's care.

The winds of anxiety stirred up the swim—
Would this voyage turn hopeless and grim?
But the sail of knowledge kept me in poise,
And in the deep mind-sea, I found quiet joy.

Then, to the mountainous terrain of the inner core,

My adventurous heart began to soar.

Standing on the precipice of inner strife,

Harnessed by virtues, I confronted life.

In scaling the peak of purity,

I drew on the strength of truth and clarity.

Reaching the summit of that majestic height,

I glimpsed visions beyond normal sight.

My mind then took flight in wonder—

Higher than the condor could blunder.

On wings of will and purpose and goal,

I soared aloft as an ecstatic Soul.

What an extraordinary adventure it was—

Unrestricted, yet bound by the mind's own laws.

Humbly, I stand before Nature's wonder,

In awe of such rapture, deep and unbounded.

This sublime odyssey of inner discovery

Surpasses the grandeur of outer scenery.

The pleasures we seek from abundant sights

Fade before our soul's invisible lights.

It is Intriguing to Reflect upon Our Common Universal Nature

At any point during our formative years, did anyone explicitly teach us the quality we call "hate"—or, for that matter, any other quality? Did we independently look up its meaning in the dictionary, or read about it elsewhere and come to understand it? The answer is a clear no!

How is it that qualities or traits like love, hate, dislike, greed, fear, generosity, and trust did not need to be taught to us, nor did we have to learn them from anything or anyone?

What does this imply? It is a fascinating and thought-provoking idea.

Imagine this scenario: you find yourself alone with another person with whom you share no commonalities—no community, race, culture, gender, religion, or even language. Yet, in time, it is easy to imagine that you both would bond with each other. You might find yourselves laughing at something, feeling curious or sad about something, and so on.

This suggests that all human beings inherently possess these traits. We are wired for them. This is the "factory setting" of the mind. These reactions, responses, and feelings are intrinsic to our minds and, thus, fundamental to human nature.

In other words, all human beings share the same qualities. When I say, "I am angry," "I am greedy," or "I feel sad," no one ever questions, "But what do you mean by greedy?" We all understand these emotions. Not only do we understand, but we have experienced each of them.

What does this mean? All these traits are part of every human personality—yours and mine alike. Each of these qualities exists within us. We have all experienced them in one form or another.

Does this mean we are all consumed by hatred, greed, and similar traits? No, that is not what I mean. Those of us who feel we are not "greedy", simply allow other traits to be more dominant, thus keeping "greed" dormant. But we still know what greed is.

So, it is up to us as humans to allow the "higher nature" traits—the positive traits—to be more dominant than the rest.

What does this imply? It is something for each of us to think about and ponder over.

Here are some questions this raises in my mind: How can I condemn or hate someone else for being "hateful"? Can I honestly say I have never known greed or jealousy? Am I so full of positive traits that I do not know what "evil" is?

This demonstrates that, at our very core, we are all the same—not just in the qualities within our minds. The witness to all these functions, feelings, qualities, and emotions in our minds is the same for each of us. It is the same Self in all.

Freedom is not the Freedom to Do Whatever we Want

As we grow up, the idea of freedom begins to enter our thoughts. I am not sure if we used the word itself at a young age, but we knew the feeling well enough. We sensed it when faced with restrictions, feeling the absence of freedom keenly. This was the experience of childhood.

Then came the time when we studied freedom as part of history. As a people, we strove for freedom from foreign rule. This was our next encounter with the word: freedom, in the context of liberation from confinement, oppression, or slavery.

Let us dwell on this for a moment. However much we read history books and stories, do we truly understand what it was like for people who weren't free? We might grasp the idea of bondage intellectually, but do we feel what the oppressed felt?

This experience of freedom is about liberation from something external—from someone or something beyond ourselves. So, we first come to see freedom as release from an external force—a person, a group, or a condition.

In the course of daily life, we often think about freedom from the people around us—whether at home, at work, or in society. In this context, we consider freedom as release from rules, regulations, restrictions, formalities, and disciplines.

But is that truly freedom? Looking closely, in each of these cases, the desire is really for freedom from our own notions and interpretations within our minds. Even if rules and restrictions come from others, it is ultimately our own minds that create the sense of bondage; we bind ourselves with our understanding of ideas originating from others.

Consider an example: we see a sign on the road that says, *"Men at Work. Diversion. Turn left and take Route ABC."* The moment we see it, we feel as if our freedom has been lost, as if someone is imposing a restriction on our movement. This creates a sense of irritation.

Where does this interpretation occur? In our own mind. Where is the lack of freedom felt? In the mind alone. Our mind immediately sees this as an infringement of our freedom. Through the sense organs, our experiences are interpreted by the mind as favourable or unfavourable, leading to feelings like happiness, sorrow, restriction, and fear.

Any curtailment of freedom, any sense of bondage, is felt in the mind alone—and so, freedom, too, is only in the mind. This was succinctly expressed by Antoine de Saint-Exupéry: *"I know but one freedom, and that is the freedom of the mind."*

In our constrained ways of thinking, we often focus on "freedom to do." We fight various battles, both external and internal, believing that freedom is the ability to do what we want, when, where, and how we want—or not to do what we don't want.

But I feel the answer lies in "freedom to be." In this domain, we are in complete control. In this realm, we need no one's permission, and there are no rules or codes of conduct. No one says, "Do this" or "Don't do that."

When my mind is free, external impositions cease to matter. The Greek philosopher Epictetus summed it up beautifully: *"No man is free who is not a master of himself."*

Thus, freedom is complete mastery over the mind.

—•—

A Pure Mind: A Mind That Sees Things as They Are

In the context of religion and spirituality, we often hear the term "purity." What is purity? Over the last few years, I have wondered about this term more and more.

In the context of material things, we have a reasonably clear notion of what purity means. For example, when we talk about gold, water, honey, or milk, we consider purity as the absence of any "impurity."

Take water, for instance: can we practically expect absolute purity, except in laboratory conditions? We have certain views regarding "acceptable levels of impurities" and still call the water "pure."

So, even with material things, purity is, at best, a relative term. Even when products are advertised, producers who claim purity often include disclaimers, indirectly acknowledging the presence of impurities.

Thus, we understand purity as relative rather than absolute. In fact, we have nearly stopped using the term "pure" in the context of material things; perhaps people would hardly believe us if we claimed something was pure.

When it comes to religion or spirituality, however, the focus of purity shifts from matter to the individual—more specifically, to the personality.

What is purity in an individual? We might consider the cleanliness of the body as purity of the body. Purity can also be discussed at the level of speech. Beyond the body and speech, though, lies the mind. In the mind, purity is all about its environment and thoughts.

Pure thoughts make a pure mind. But is it possible to have pure thoughts—thoughts that are "always" good, noble, benevolent, compassionate, kind, etc.?

As far as the mind is concerned, thoughts simply arise. Can I say that my thoughts will be one hundred percent pure? At least for now, I would not say that. Could I reach such a state? I am not even considering that—and perhaps, I do not wish to. I would rather let the mind be what it is, as it is.

What matters to me is creating an environment (in the mind) that, as far as possible, fosters positive thoughts. More importantly, I am concerned with how I respond to the thoughts that arise— whether good, bad, or indifferent.

I am happier with allowing the mind its natural freedom to generate its own thoughts. I do not want to battle with it by rejecting certain thoughts. Instead, I am content with having the courage to face whatever thoughts arise, rather than ignoring or pretending they are not mine.

I want to be sincere in treating my thoughts with respect. I feel it is important to recognize my thoughts, especially the "negative" ones, rather than ignore them.

For example, when we watch a butterfly on a flower, a newborn calf, or an infant's smile, in that instant—however brief—we experience a state free from judgments, free from good or bad thoughts, free from life's troubles, free from desires and hopes—an absolutely free state.

I feel this is a glimpse of what "purity" could mean for the mind. At that moment, we are not even commenting on the beauty or wonder of nature.

Because if we are admiring beauty, it implies we are rejecting what we perceive as the lack of beauty in nature. In that pure state, we have no commentary on nature—no judgments—whatever the duration of that experience.

Scriptures define purity of the mind as "a mind free from desires"—free from expectations and attachment. Only then can we see the world and its phenomena without judgment or bias, just as they are.

———•◆•———

True Surrender Lies in Acceptance

What does it mean to surrender? When we speak of surrender in a 'spiritual' context, what are we truly 'surrendering'? Who is surrendering, and to whom? The concept invites us to examine our identity and our understanding of freedom, control, and acceptance.

First, we might ask, what exactly do we surrender? Does it mean surrendering our freedom, our ability to make decisions, or even our analytical and introspective capacities? Are we letting go of our power over what we do and how we do it?

Who is surrendering? Is it the individual, the personality? Is it the identity tied to our roles as professionals, parents, or spouses? Or is it the mind-intelligence-ego complex—the identification we carry as disciple, pupil, or devotee?

The meaning of surrender depends deeply on who we believe ourselves to be and what we believe we are surrendering.

To whom, then, do we surrender? In the spiritual journey, this act of surrender typically orients us toward either the guru or the divine. In the context of spiritual pursuit, surrender is not about giving up our independence or submitting to servitude. It is not about surrendering our minds or handing over our intelligence. Rather, surrender is a practice of profound acceptance and humility.

So, what does the act of surrender entail? Surrender, in essence, is acceptance—to stop questioning or challenging the flow of events and to acknowledge whatever happens. It is recognizing that all outcomes are guided by natural laws—impersonal, unbiased, and impartial.

In surrender, we are called to act without attachment, to trust that the outcome will follow its natural course. This acceptance frees us from the weight of expectation, leaving us open to the wisdom that flows naturally when we let go.

Are All Practices and Philosophies in Harmony with Each Other?

Consider a subject like physics. It contains numerous ideas, concepts, and theories, all of which are in harmony with each other. For example, our understanding of motion, gravity, and acceleration aligns consistently, whether we discuss riding a bicycle or driving a car. There are no conflicts there.

But in the context of life and systems of philosophy, spirituality, or religion, this is often not the case. If we adopt different philosophies or fragments of philosophies to suit our convenience, we are likely to encounter problems. It is essential that all ideas, concepts, and theories we embrace, are in harmony with each other. If not, conflicts arise. These conflicts prevent us from effectively addressing the life situations we aim to resolve, leading to more suffering.

Why do we experience this conflict or dilemma? Today, we are exposed to countless systems of thought. Different channels, like the Internet, books, and social media, bombard us with varied ideas, making it easy for us to be swayed. We often pick up bits and pieces of different theories, techniques, and concepts, ultimately trying to navigate life based on this fragmented mix of ideas. The net result? Confusion and further conflict.

While we may enjoy intellectually engaging with diverse ideas, we struggle when it comes to practicing or applying them to real-life situations.

The only solution is to empty the mind of all ideas and gradually build an understanding, one piece at a time—importantly, without being overly influenced by the abundance of ideas coming from all directions.

Some who engage in spiritual pursuits take up diverse practices—worship, austerities, rituals, discourses, philosophies, meditation, and so on—thinking these are all serving their goal. But when challenges, trials, and tribulations arise, these ideas often fall apart because the different practices were not in harmony with each other.

Harmony is achieved when all practices are based on the same philosophy or principle and are consistently interpreted to adapt to an individual's personal needs.

Mind—A Little Wingless Parakeet

Atop an old tree lived a white parakeet,

Life, at that height, now seemed incomplete.

Undecided whether or not to take a flight,

She reflected on a future that wasn't so bright.

While there were no nets to hold her there,

Her own web of beliefs was hard to tear.

She convinced herself she could not fly,

Though she had it in her to reach the sky.

She had been told this tree is her home,

But that would not align with her soul's tone.

Though this parakeet was meant to be free,

Somehow, she tied herself to this tree.

While she blamed her fate for her plight,

To fly away she knew was her birthright.

While each dawn was darker than before,

She was unwilling to admit it, for sure.

She knew she did not belong to this place,

And had lost her fondness without a trace.

When it came to the decision to fly away,

She was trapped in her mind's tricky play.

Her only wings were hopes and dreams,

That might give her a new life, it seems.

The parakeet thought she'd fly to her nest,

But that was to remain a dream in her chest.

Freedom was the nature of this little bird,

But caged she was in her own vision blurred.

The world knew her as the bird that sings,

That parakeet had clipped her own wings.

———————

Light as a Metaphor: Discovering the Source of Existence

In the early morning, a faint light begins to fill the room. Observing it, we realize it is natural light. Stepping onto the balcony, we are greeted by the brightness outside, and the world bathed in a gentle glow. Looking toward the east, we notice it glows even brighter than the west.

Now, imagine we had no knowledge of something called "the sun." It is a cloudy day, and through gaps in the clouds, a few rays of light filter through.

As the clouds begin to clear, we notice one part of the sky growing particularly bright. We still do not know whether the source of this light has any particular shape or form. We only see that this part of the sky is getting brighter and brighter, yet we are unable to fully perceive the source of the light.

Soon, as the clouds completely dissipate, an object emerges that is so overwhelmingly bright that we cannot discern its shape. We are left unable to comprehend anything beyond the sheer intensity of its light.

In a way, this diffused light, ever-present and all-encompassing, indicates the presence of its source, the sun. We may never truly see the sun in its complete form—astronomers and cosmologists interpret it for us.

Similarly, the entire world around us—life, both animate and inanimate—is evidence of the Supreme. Although we may not directly perceive the Supreme in an active form, its presence is implicit in everything around us.

Just as the visibility of all things suggests there is a source of light—whether it be the sun or a bulb—the vibrancy and dynamism of the world suggest the presence of Brahman, the ultimate principle that illuminates the entire universe. Here, "illuminates" does not refer to literal light but to the force of existence and consciousness itself.

For us, the very fact that we see a vibrant world around us is indication enough of a supreme entity. At the outset, we may not even call it the Supreme; we might simply call it "X." From there, the journey of spirituality begins, with the exploration of this "X" and a deeper understanding of its nature.

———•—◆—•———

Trapped in a Self-Created Cage of Concepts, Theories, and Ideas

In the beginning, spirituality seems fascinating, inspiring, intriguing—even thrilling. In this excitement, you (the seeker) start exploring different approaches, practices, techniques, and philosophies. Each new encounter feels relevant and revealing. At this stage, you are like a child who has discovered a treasure chest of toys, eager to pick up everything.

The ultimate goal is spoken of in various ways: self-realization, freedom from suffering, liberation, equanimity in happiness and sorrow, even-mindedness in success and failure, and so on. These descriptions lead you to form personal "images" of the spiritual goal, shaped by the many ways it is described in books and by commentators. With the Internet and personal networks, you are met with a flood of viewpoints, interpretations, and techniques, and you find yourself drawn to each one.

Initially, there is a feeling of "progress." It feels good. Your mind seems to find peace with your surroundings and the world. But after some years—or perhaps just months, depending on the individual—a sense of stagnation sets in. The "imagined" goal seems out of reach. The mind is rattled by challenges or even by trivial situations. You start feeling that progress has stalled. This inner conflict is subtle but unsettling.

Imagine this scenario: you had dreamed of owning a luxury car within five years, but it did not happen. You may feel disheartened, but at least you understand why the car is not a reality.

However, in spiritual pursuit, a perceived "lack of progress" is not so easily comprehended. You thought you had understood the mind and gained control over it, yet a single crisis—at work or within the family—leaves you questioning where you truly stand on this journey.

This situation can be deeply unsettling for any seeker. There is a feeling of being lost, and doubt regarding the spiritual pursuit itself creeps in. [This may not happen to every seeker, but it is not uncommon.]

It is important to understand that such experiences are part of many seekers' spiritual journeys. Let us examine some fundamentals here.

Consider this analogy: the lifelong dream of visiting Niagara Falls. From the start, you have a clear idea of what you want—

of where you want to go. You know what "Niagara Falls" is, and this understanding ensures that you will not mistake some small waterfall at Mount Fuji, for the famed Niagara. Nor, having arrived at Niagara, will you confuse it with the Taj Mahal or Disneyland. You understand what reaching Niagara Falls means, and you know what kind of effort it takes to get there. For tangible goals, we usually know both what we want and how to reach it.

Now, returning to the spiritual pursuit: when you began this journey, you formed an image of what that goal was. Perhaps someone or a book mentioned "liberation" or "eternal bliss." Linguistically, these terms make sense to you. They are described in ways that excite you. But you still do not really know what they mean because they lie beyond your direct experience, so you form a certain "image" of them.

The same applies to terms like "Self-realization" and "transcendence." Remember, these are not part of the tangible, objective world. They are beyond even the realm of the mind, and hence they are referred to as "indescribable".

Take the phrase "equanimity in success and failure." There is no ambiguity in the language; you understand what success and failure mean. But what does it actually mean to *be* in that state of equanimity? That is a different matter altogether.

This is the seeker's predicament. The seeker is, in a sense, trapped in a "cage" created by the images attached to terms like self-realization, eternal bliss, liberation, nirvana, samadhi, and immortality. It is a cage built from the very esoteric and impressive words that initially captivated the seeker. Ironically, the seeker often does not even realize that they are trapped.

Think about it: these concepts, ideas, and goals are meant to relieve the seeker, but instead, they become a "web" of ideas that ensnares them. When rightly understood and realized, these concepts can bestow complete freedom; when incorrectly assumed, they become the very cage that binds. What an irony!

Some seekers eventually realize they are trapped. Many continue on, unaware.

The only way out is to break through the cage reinforced by misguided perceptions. As Adi Shankaracharya puts it, to wield "the hammer that destroys delusion." Then, reconstruct the journey and pursuit afresh. It is very much achievable.

How to Make Sense of the Various Terms in Spirituality?

When you encounter a spiritual term like "liberation" (or *moksha* in Sanskrit), the task is not to understand what it means theoretically, nor what a book or a guru says it means. The real question is: What does this term mean to *you* and *your life*? Remember, the spiritual journey is a journey of your mind, and no one else has access to that. Each individual's understanding of spiritual goals is unique, and rightly so—because we are all different.

Begin afresh, with a clear understanding of what that goal means to you. This requires deep, honest, and simple questioning within yourself. Break down these esoteric-sounding goals into practical terms you fully relate to, so that the path ahead becomes clearer, and you understand exactly what you need to do.

Take a simple example: suppose your dream is to own a specific car that has recently gained popularity. You do not stop at identifying the model; you go further, describing the engine type, the seat style, and the fuel efficiency you want. By breaking it down to these details, you make it easier to pursue your dream. Without that clarity, you would struggle to make a final decision.

Similarly, in the spiritual journey, you must understand what you want from your pursuit. Gradually, build that understanding of the state of mind you seek, articulated in clear terms, free of jargon. If you keep using terms like "liberation" without practical clarity, it only misleads you. Instead, you need to understand what liberation, or any goal, truly means in practical terms.

This clarity guides your efforts and shows you which practices align with your goal and current state of mind. It also helps you prioritize.

Otherwise, the tendency is to accumulate countless goals, getting excited about everything: a friend suggests a new technique, a book introduces a beautiful philosophy, or you hear of a successful seeker's journey. When you get drawn to every goal that appeals to you, your mind searches for books, lectures, tips, techniques, practices—each pointing in a different direction.

If you keep adopting each new idea, your attention, energy, and commitment become scattered. Without a proper understanding of the terms and goals, misconceptions begin to set in, and these misconceptions become chains that bind you.

In effect, you become trapped by the impulse to gather ideas from all directions, to grasp at every insight or teaching. This greed is a great obstacle in the spiritual path. Greed is greed, regardless of what it is about—even if it is for spiritual knowledge. Instead, focus on diving within and committing to one thing. Otherwise, this dissipation of energy toward your many imagined goals leads you further from what you truly seek.

To gain focus, set aside the books, forget the other sources for a while, and identify one idea that you want to achieve. If, for example, you say with conviction, "I want to be content in life," that alone can be sufficient. This one clear idea can define your life's path. You do not need external inputs, complex philosophies, or grand terminologies. It is about clarity, conviction, perseverance, and patience.

Clarity emerges when you describe what you want in your own words, not through the words of someone else or scripture. Trust in your own words and conviction.

Once clarity and commitment to your pursuit solidify, the necessary inputs will come—whether from a guru, a book, or other sources. These will arise naturally, not from pursuit, but from alignment with your goal.

As a seeker, remember that you are aiming to liberate yourself from inner bondage. This bondage is not external; it resides within. If bondage is within, where will liberation be found? Within, as well. Ultimately, both bondage and liberation exist within the seeker.

⸺ ⬥ ⸺

Rejoice in the Dance of Life and Death

Death seems everywhere, woven into the fabric of existence. It has no identity apart from life, just as life has none apart from it—they are inseparable, bound as one.

With each passing moment, something dies, and something new is born. We perceive death through the concept of past, present, and future, viewing it as the cycle of time itself. This connection is why both time and death are often referred to as *kaala* (in Sanskrit).

Yet, seeing death merely as time passing blinds us to a deeper truth. The essence of death, I believe, transcends time. We resist the passage of time, reluctant to let go of the present. Perhaps that is why we equate the end of time with the idea of death.

But beyond the idea of time lies the true nature of life and death—a waltz where each is woven into the other. There is nothing morbid in this dance. Death, in fact, celebrates life.

Each falling leaf, each petal drifting to the ground, each moment that fades—these are expressions of death, yet they are equally infused with life. Life and death are entwined, like two threads inseparable in a single weave. There can be no death without life, no life without death. To embrace death is to fully embrace life.

When we see life through the lens of our individual existence, we make death personal. But life and death are not personal; they extend beyond the boundaries of the individual self. To look past the individual is to dissolve the fear of death—it is to see life unending.

How can we address or define death? How can we truly know it? Somewhere deep within, there is an impulse to see death as something personified, yet it resists any fixed identity.

What is death, truly? Why is there awe and fear around it? Why do we regard it as an end? Our unfulfilled desires, our inability to accept impermanence—these shape our ideas of death. To fear losing what we possess, to shun the unknown, these make death a mystery.

But by seeing life as whole and complete, we recognize that death is everywhere, in each moment, completing the cycle of existence.

Without embracing death, we miss life's fullness. Death allows us to appreciate life's diversity; it reminds us that every joy and sorrow, every union and parting, are moments we only understand because we know endings exist.

O Mind, do not ignore the presence of death, constant and unyielding. See its playfulness as it waves to us with every passing second. In each farewell, in every dream launched with expectation, death smiles at us, waiting patiently. When we clutch at life's tangible moments, death stands nearby, ready to greet us.

Death is neither reality nor finality. Birth, too, is not an ultimate truth. Beyond both lies a continuous flow, a reality that transcends the confines of life and death. It is this truth, alive in each moment, that unveils the completeness of life.

We can see the enchanting dance of the Cosmic Presence when we transcend the fear of the phenomenon called "death".

A Balanced Perspective
for Understanding Detachment

In spiritual traditions, detachment is often emphasized as a vital trait for a seeker on the path to self-realization. It is considered an essential "means" to reaching a spiritual goal. Over time, "detachment" has entered common parlance, with similar terms—indifference, dispassion, freedom from desires—often used. Some perceive detachment negatively, as if it implies a lack of caring or indifference, which raises the question: why?

To explain detachment, we sometimes use concepts that are overly negative or even morbid. People often reflect on life's deeper questions only during difficult times—why everything, including life, is transient, or whether every relationship ultimately ends in loss. Perhaps it serves to draw the seeker's attention to the matter at hand.

But genuine detachment is about cultivating a positive indifference, a quality that keeps us unbiased, calm, and steady.

Why should detachment be linked solely to life's transient moments or painful experiences? Should a mother only become detached from her child if the child leaves or if loss seems inevitable? This approach risks embedding a negative view of detachment and spirituality in people's minds.

It is evident that we often ponder questions like "What is the purpose of life?" or "Why me?" only during challenging times, while in moments of happiness, success, or celebration, such questions rarely arise.

A balanced perspective allows us to remain unruffled in every situation, perform our best in all undertakings, and make each relationship rich and rewarding. Isn't this the true purpose of detachment?

Allowing Disappointments to Linger Damages Relationships

We all have our own stories of suffering and, at times, feel that life has been particularly unfair to us. We may even think that others and their families are leading easier lives, which only seems to amplify our sense of hardship.

A crucial point to understand here is that we tend to feel as though life has given us much pain and suffering. But it is worth noting that, while situations arise that cause us pain, suffering itself is something we create.

For instance, if a needle pricks us, we feel pain. This pain is a signal—a warning—to guard against potential harm. Similarly, situations in life where we feel that X has caused us pain can be seen as warnings or signals. They are information, indicators of areas to address. Imagine someone calling to inform us that our car is on fire. The information is simply there to help us act. It may sound overly simple, but approaching situations as information to act on, can be transformative.

Now, let us examine the idea of suffering. There are times in life when multiple demands weigh on us. Say, a family member is unwell and requires our care. Meanwhile, a critical project at work also demands our attention. At the same time, other family members are unavailable to step in. Understandably, this can feel overwhelming.

In these situations, while we may take the necessary actions—caring for the family member and managing work obligations—the internal experience is different. We often find ourselves feeling irritated or even bitter toward other family members for not providing support or toward colleagues who, we feel, added to our stress. This bitterness can grow if left unchecked.

What is happening here? We have handled the immediate needs at home and work, but what remains is the lingering resentment toward others who, we feel, contributed to our stress, or did not step in to help. Even feelings of frustration might arise, such as wondering why the illness or work problem happened now, of all times.

However, if we look closely, we see that the suffering is no longer from the situation itself. It is from the negative emotions that have been allowed to linger—anger, bitterness, and agitation toward others.

While this may not be the case every time, in my own experience I have noticed that it is often true.

Let us give some honest thought to this. When we allow disappointment and agitation toward others to settle in our minds, we risk harming our relationships with them, creating a cycle of unnecessary suffering and estrangement.

It Becomes True Knowledge When it is Integrated and Living Knowledge

Consider the following scenario: you are prone to anger at the slightest provocation and have struggled with it for years. Occasionally, you become aware of this issue and feel you should do something about it. Then, one day, you read a book and experience a sudden flash of insight. You feel, in that moment, as though you have found the answer to your 'anger problem'—you are convinced you have already solved it, at least 80%.

But then, a month later, something at work sets you off, and you flare up again. Suddenly, you realize you have not solved the problem after all. You might even start to doubt the analysis in the book, that once seemed so enlightening.

What happened? Why didn't that insight solve the problem of anger? Let us examine this carefully. While we may not uncover "the secret" to solving such issues, we can at least try to understand where our approach to solving problems might be falling short.

Our personality is complex—an intricate web of traits, worldviews, qualities, and attributes. At any given moment, multiple aspects of our personality interact to influence our reactions and behaviour. The insight about anger we read in that book remained a fragmented piece of knowledge. It did not become integrated with our worldview, personality, and nature. Knowledge only becomes functional—"living knowledge"—when it integrates with all aspects of our nature, personality, and value system.

So, what should we do to achieve this integration? There may not be a clear, one-size-fits-all method to address personality challenges, nor can we expect to find a guaranteed process that will correct every aberration. Instead, we have to develop our own approaches for tackling our issues. Let us first understand where things tend to go wrong.

Consider this example: you are listening to an expert discussing "personality transformation," explaining how to control anger. Assume that this expert has indeed mastered the solution. They speak for about 15 minutes, condensing years of effort and experimentation into three bullet points and a short explanation.

Is it realistic to think we can use this input and immediately conquer a lifelong problem? I am not saying it is impossible—sometimes, change happens in an instant. But more often, significant personal challenges require time and effort. The expert you listened to found their solution after years of struggle; so, let us at least give our own struggles that same patience and persistence.

When someone shares an insight, it is based on their unique personality, worldview, culture, and background. We cannot simply take their words and apply them, unchanged, to our lives. Only through constant introspection and conscious effort can that acquired knowledge become fully integrated into our personality, ultimately bringing about results.

What often happens is that we read or hear something inspiring and feel a surge of motivation in the moment. But without sustained effort, that spark quickly fades. The knowledge remains a fragmented piece in our minds, never becoming an intrinsic part of us. Sometimes, we bookmark a video or save an article to revisit, but that knowledge still sits there, untouched and separate from us.

In our TED-talks culture, we might think that watching a 15-minute presentation gives us true understanding. But these experts have devoted their entire lives to distilling their knowledge, which we then treat like fast food. This expectation is misplaced.

Think about it—really think about it. Knowledge becomes transformative only when it becomes an inseparable part of who we are. Each of us must work out our own answer, our own solution, rather than expecting a ready-made formula.

Meditation is Not the Goal in Spiritual Pursuit

With all the attention "meditation" receives worldwide, people start to believe that "if you are into meditation, you have arrived in the space of spirituality." However, meditation is not the goal; it is just one of the means to attaining the goal of "freedom," where freedom means (1) being content and fulfilled (a complete absence of any lack); (2) remaining unagitated by the world and its objects; (3) being eternally free from suffering; and (4) achieving complete independence from the world for happiness and peace. *(Note: Objects here refer to things, people, work, activities, events, situations, relationships, name, fame, etc.)*

Many assign meditation a very exalted status, thinking that the spiritual pursuit is all about meditation. Yet there are two other essential steps: the first is listening or study, where one is introduced to the principles that govern spirituality. Remember, meditation is based on a set of principles, and there is no universal approach to meditation. Meditation practices vary across different schools of philosophy, so one should be firmly grounded in these fundamentals.

The second step is introspection, where the seeker gains conviction regarding what was understood in step one. Introspection or reflection involves validating our understanding and arriving at a doubt-free conviction through reason and analysis regarding what we have understood.

These two steps are crucial, and without them, success in meditation is unlikely. In meditation, one realizes what has been studied, understood, and established through conviction. Meditation, in simple terms, *internalizes* what one has learned.

Through listening, study, and introspection, we learn about the Self. But the experience (realization) of the Self occurs only through meditation.

Are We in a Position to Comprehend the Purpose of Life?

'Purpose' means the reason for which something exists or is done, made, used, etc. or aim or goal. In other words, it is the intent behind our actions—engaging in pursuits that create meaningful impact, achieve desired results, or give us a sense of pride and purposefulness.

The first important point to note is that we are not in a position to see the 'entire impact' of what we do. This is because we look for results we are familiar with. In many cases, we have no idea whether the results are favourable or unfavourable, as our ability to judge them is in doubt. We tend to look for results or effects in the 'circle' around us—our 'familiar space'—and are not able to understand or see things that happen outside that familiar circle or space.

The second important factor is 'time.' Whatever we do or engage in, we expect to see results within a foreseeable timeframe, on a scale we can comprehend. For most things, we are not even willing to consider results beyond a year. What to say of times beyond our lifetime or a few thousand years.

Why do we feel that anything meaningful or purposeful we do should bear fruit this very instant, now? Think: something I do now may mature only after a few hundred years. Wouldn't that be more meaningful and purposeful? If something were to come into existence in an instant, it may also vanish with the same speed. Anything that is of 'real' use or purpose has to mature over a period of time, which we often are not able to comprehend.

Let us re-evaluate what it means to do something with 'purpose'!

The third important consideration is 'substance'. When we do something, we expect the result to be of a certain kind, of some substance, in some form. Again, are we truly capable of understanding or assessing the outcomes of what we do in terms of substance, shape, or form? For example, a seed we sow today may become fossil fuel at some later time. Should we think only that we are planting a tree to eat its fruits next year?

Thus, our ability to comprehend the results of our actions is questionable in three dimensions—space, time, and substance (*desha*, *kaala*, and *vastu* respectively in Sanskrit).

There is a fourth element: 'causation'. Are we in a position to fully comprehend the cause-and-effect chain in the context of any action?

Based on all these, are we in any position to define the purpose of life? By using only our limited comprehension, we risk making life less purposeful.

Think: Are we capable of comprehending the impact of our very existence in the context of the universe—either now or in the future? Our mind and intelligence are capable of grasping changes or impacts only within the 'scales' that our limited capabilities permit, in the context of space, time, substance, and causation.

In this background, how should we think of leading our lives?

Allow life to unfold. Accept things as they are.

Rejoice in the variety. Rejoice in the mystery.

Welcome changes, as we are not able to see what they mean.

Just do what the situation demands, to the best of our ability.

And above all, leave everything to Nature.

Visualize it like this: We have cast a pair of dice. We do not know when the pair will stop rolling. We do not know what the outcome will be. All we can do is throw!

——•●•——

We Connect the Dots for Our Convenience

As human beings, it is as if we have a compulsion to know the cause of everything that happens in the world. We immediately ask questions like "how?" and "why?"

In fact, we like to know the cause-and-effect chain. In other words, we like to connect the dots.

Often, it is not just about "knowing the truth." We like to connect the dots in a manner that affirms to ourselves what we want to believe.

We are biased in our understanding of cause and effect. Why? Because attachment to objects (things, people, relationships, events, etc.) involved in the cause-and-effect chain drives the way we connect the dots.

Remember, this connecting of dots is not a formal process on paper. It happens in the mind, and the outcome is shaped by the state of our mind.

Often, what we wish to believe decides how we connect the dots.

Consider the following scenario: An accident took place, and someone close to you was hurt in it. In your mind, you feel that "all this happened because you did not go along for help." Now, you connect all preceding events leading to the accident in a way that proves your hypothesis.

Whether what happened was favourable or unfavourable, we connect the dots to reinforce what we want to believe.

Remember, in many cases, this connecting of dots just reinforces suffering.

I am not against finding out the what, how, and why of an event. Trying to find the immediate cause is one thing; but constructing a cause-and-effect chain based on a series of past occurrences is another.

———•◆•———

Do Not Become a Slave to the Very Path That is Meant to Liberate

Aspiring to realize everlasting happiness and complete freedom from suffering, we take up the spiritual pursuit. This path is meant to lead us to "complete freedom"—not just at the destination but throughout the journey itself, which embraces openness, acceptance, and liberation.

Before we embarked on this path, we were already slaves to countless ideas, notions, and assumptions about the world. We were in bondage to the objects of the world, including things, people, work, activities, events, relationships, name, fame, and position. This attachment to these objects was the source of our suffering.

However, as we begin the spiritual journey, we encounter new concepts, theories, philosophies, truisms, and models presented as if cast in stone, with the directive to "surrender" to them. Soon, we risk becoming "slaves" to these very ideas. Texts, commentators, and speakers share insights based on their experiences, but if we cling solely to their words without understanding the essence, we become bound to "our interpretation of their presentations".

We are introduced to beliefs, even exposed to notions of sin as related to transgressions on the path, and we may find ourselves enslaved by these ideas. Initiated into a new set of rules, regulations, rituals, practices, and techniques, we sometimes lose sight of their true spirit, adhering only to the letter. Eventually, we may discover we have become enslaved by the very idea of "seeker-hood," trapped in a cage of rigid do's and don'ts.

We may have initially approached this path seeking freedom from various bondages, but soon we find ourselves in the fetters of new concepts and often do not realize we have traded one form of slavery for another. Spirituality is not about blind conformity to set concepts, rules, or regulations or adhering strictly to certain "schools of thought."

Only when we realize we are seekers of freedom, not slaves, do we truly begin our journey to liberation.

Bondage to anything is still bondage. Being a slave to anything is still slavery. Let us remain free in our outlook as seekers of freedom. Let us be free.

⬥

My Thoughts Are Not Mine

My thoughts—animated and unbound, as they soared in the sky of my soul.

They held aspirations, like a butterfly breaking free of its chrysalis;

They had enthusiasm, like a boy stepping into his youth;

They had direction, like an arrow that had left the bow;

They brimmed with love, like a mother for her child;

They pulsed with life, like waves dancing in the ocean;

But alas!

As I reached for them, wanting to feel, to know, to claim—

These thoughts became selfish, for I wanted to possess them;

They became stingy, for they had more of "I" in them;

They were constricted, because I wanted to control them;

They were binding, for I wanted to hold them;

They became lifeless, because I craved to experience them;

They were weakened, for I wanted to indulge in them.

O Lord,

Grant me the grace to be a witness,

To ride the waves of thought upon the ocean of the mind;

Grant me the sail of love and detachment,

To drift freely and naturally through this sea of life;

Grant me the wisdom to realize these thoughts are not mine,

For they are but a spark of the cosmic!

⚊⚫⚊

Why Do We Bother to Use the Word "Spiritual"?

I remember the initial months and years of my journey in spiritual pursuit. Conditioned by what I often heard from those around me, I too began labelling things as "spiritual" and "not spiritual." Here, *things* refer to objects, people, activities, events, and even professions.

Even the spheres of life became compartmentalized and labelled as either conducive to spiritual pursuit or not.

Then, the magnitude of this mistake dawned on me.

If you examine it in simple terms, *eternal peace of mind* is the goal of this pursuit. We want this peace of mind at all times—not just when we are at home, at work, or elsewhere. More importantly, it is the same mind that is active in all places and interactions, and we seek poise, peace, and happiness in that same mind.

Above all, it is the same Self (Consciousness) that pervades everything.

Therefore, "everything" is spiritual; or "nothing" is spiritual. How, then, can I compartmentalize life? In fact, any attempt to use the label *spiritual* may become an impediment to progress in this journey toward everlasting peace.

What makes life 'spiritual' is the pursuit of attaining ultimate freedom. What matters is the aim and the journey toward this attainment. Leading a spiritual life does not prescribe a particular way of living but instead highlights the guiding purpose of one's life. Being a businessman, a householder, a commander in the army, or a moneylender does not negate a spiritual life; similarly, wearing ochre robes does not necessarily make life spiritual. The term 'spiritual' qualifies the goal or guiding purpose in our lives, rather than dictating how we live day-to-day.

Self-enquiry is Not the Same as Self-transformation

The journey of self-improvement (or self-transformation) is very different from that of Self-enquiry. Self-transformation is aimed at the mind. Qualities like compassion, generosity, freedom from anger, freedom from envy, kindness, etc., all pertain to the mind. We may feel that we lack certain qualities in our behaviour, conduct, or interactions with the world around us. This prompts us to embark on the path of self-improvement, where the focus is on becoming "better" or "more effective" in the worldly sense. Here, the "self" refers to 'one's own' and not to the "Self" (Consciousness).

Now let us turn to Self-enquiry. Self-enquiry is the process or practice of investigating one's real nature, the Self. The Self is not the body, mind, intellect, or ego; it is beyond all these and is the witness of the mind, intelligence, etc. and their functions. The purpose of Self-enquiry is ultimately to lead one to the realization of the Self.

We can see that self-improvement and Self-enquiry are very different and operate in two distinct domains. The domain of the first is the mind and culminates in the mind. The second begins in the mind, goes beyond it, and culminates in the Self.

As long as we are focused on self-improvement, we remain within the realm of the mind, making the idea of Self-enquiry and the journey toward Self-realization distant. To realize the Self, one must go beyond the mind. As long as we remain attached to the mind and its qualities, emotions, etc., the Self will remain elusive.

We can even say that self-improvement and Self-enquiry are mutually exclusive.

However, as one embarks on the journey of Self-enquiry, in the initial stages, there is considerable focus on gaining control of the mind. For instance, cultivating detachment, freedom from hatred, and renunciation of desires are all at the level of the mind. But here, the focus is not on becoming a "better person." It is to gain mastery over the mind.

Let us consider an example: wanting to control anger in the context of worldly interactions. When we approach this, the investigation occurs only within the context of the mind, the ego, and the objects of the world—all of which are non-Self. The moment we think of any object of the world, or the mind and its functions, we are in the realm of non-Self. This is an obstacle on the path to realizing the Self.

When we think, "I am not calm" or "I am angry," the mind is superimposed on the Self. The absence of calmness or the presence of anger is at the level of the mind. This superimposition arises from ignorance and delusion.

The "process" of self-improvement or self-transformation always involves the notion of time. When we think, "I will be free from anger," a time factor enters. The Self, however, is free from the constraints of the three periods of time—past, present, and future.

Again, we see that self-improvement and Self-enquiry are incompatible.

An important insight regarding Self-realization is stated in the *Bhagavad Gita* (3.33): "Even one who has realized the Self acts in accordance with one's own nature. All beings are constantly under the influence of their own nature. What can restraint at the level of the mind do?"

Even for one who has realized the Self, certain deeper tendencies of the mind may still be active. This reinforces the idea that self-improvement and Self-realization do not necessarily go together.

I hope you take time to reflect deeply on the subject of Self-enquiry and Self-transformation and avoid any hasty conclusions.

Reflect Deeply on the Idea of Omniscience

How can anyone make an assurance or promise that goes against the laws of Nature? How can anyone claim an act that defies nature's laws? Spirituality, by its very definition, transcends the physical and operates outside the domain of nature and its laws. The very term *spiritual* pertains to the Self. Any individual who claims to be in the realm of the spiritual, cannot make claims or promises that violate nature's laws, nor can they assert magical or mystical actions and outcomes. In true spirituality, such claims are false.

Anyone within the spiritual realm cannot assert that a jasmine can bloom on a rose plant. Imagining or presenting such an act would only serve to mislead those sincerely seeking Truth. If everything in the phenomenal universe is an illusion, then anything deemed miraculous or mystical is also an illusion. Anything within the phenomenal universe is inherently far from the notion of Supreme Reality. Remember: to dwell on mystical ideas or illusions as Truth is a distraction or deviation from the path.

Anything that manifests in the universe must operate under the laws of nature. To claim that a mango tree will bear a pumpkin or that one can change the natural course of the human body, not only violates nature but also misrepresents the essence of spirituality. Spiritual understanding does not imply a departure from natural order; anything that happens to any being on this planet is subject to nature's laws and is thus within the realm of scientific observation and analysis.

The concepts of being all-knowing, all-powerful, and all-pervading apply only to the Supreme Reality, or Brahman, and not to any particular manifestation within the universe. 'All-knowing', in this context, does not imply possessing complete knowledge of the phenomenal universe or the thoughts and minds of others.

The Upanishadic statement "One who knows Brahman becomes Brahman" is often misinterpreted. Every manifestation is inherently confined by the boundaries and limitations of its own nature.

The Sound of Those Bells and Chants

It was the early hours of just another dawn,

Far away, the sun shone like an earthen lamp;

Longing was my part of the waking earth,

And embraced the first of the coming light.

Soaking in the peace of the sublime morn,

I prepared my mind for the day to come;

That was not my first daybreak though,

I relished the moment when time stood still.

Then came the sound of a temple bell,

Soothing as it was in the early calm;

From another direction came Vedic chants,

They caressed every bit of my aspiring self.

As I bathed in the sound of an uplifting chime,

I heard the melody of a church bell toll;

As I was about to reflect on that stirring note,

Came the low chants from a distant mosque.

Harmonic notes from two distinct bells,

Met without prejudice in the all-pervading sky;

Though coming from a temple and chapel afar,

They were but a symphony within my heart.

The two notes merged in my being then,

And resonated the presence of an unseen One;

How can I call this divine, but mundane that,

If I cannot separate the two, deep in my heart.

The sounds are distinct, science may say,

But they are one for my vibrant mind;

Frequency of the two is unique to the ears,

Still as one, they symbolize the Eternal Lord.

Chants from a temple and those from a mosque,

Dissolved as do waves in the ocean we call the sky;

While the sound of the bell came from a metal inert,

The chants did arise from an animated soul.

If those bells or chants, coming from any faith,

Are not distinguished in the cavern of my soul;

Then, violating the very Nature's universal laws,

How can I discriminate at the level of the form?

The Allure of the Unattained

In life, we are often captivated by things we do not possess. We are attracted by what others have, which somehow appear to be better than what we own. Observing what others possess, we may feel that we lack something essential (a feeling often labelled as FOMO—the fear of missing out), and soon we are overtaken by the thought, "If only I had that."

This yearning arises because there is always something 'out there' that seems more appealing. Visiting someone's home, for example, something about an item catches our eye, and we instantly enter comparison mode. 'That table is better than ours,' we think, which only leads to dissatisfaction and discontent.

What we are drawn to might be another religion, philosophy, lifestyle, car, neighbourhood, or something else entirely. We tend to feel that whatever lies "out there" is better than what we have.

Constantly seeking what is "out there" (another belief, path, or lifestyle) makes us think that fulfilment is always just beyond reach. Even in spirituality or religion, others' practices may seem more appealing, effective, and complete.

At the root of all this is a lack of contentment. When we are always drawn to what's beyond our current grasp and cannot be satisfied with what we already have, the search never ends.

We must learn to see things as they are, without projecting them into desires. See things in absolute terms, as they are, without translating them into something we want. Avoid the habit of comparison.

———•◆•———

Do Organizations Really Help in Guiding Spiritual Pursuits of Seekers?

The question before us: Can an organization (with its structure, hierarchy, objectives, finances, people, real estate, branches, support functions, etc.) help in furthering a seeker's journey toward a spiritual goal?

Let us first examine the journey of an individual who, having attained their own spiritual goal, creates an organization aimed at guiding large numbers of seekers. Broadly, this process unfolds as follows:

In some cases, an individual's personal experience(s) on the path to freedom may inspire them to share that experience with others. This leads to the idea of creating an organization or institution with a vision of propagating "Truth" or their interpretation of what Truth is. A statement of objectives is established to govern the organization's functioning. To fulfil these objectives, the organization identifies a set of activities to engage in. An organization carrying out its objectives requires resources, in terms of money, materials, real estate, and corresponding functions to manage them. Like any organization, there is a felt need to expand its reach to more people and places. Anyone familiar with organizations will note that an organization "has to grow to sustain itself." Thus, the constant need to expand, diversify, and enhance its reach becomes the primary focus. Soon, the organization's own growth, sustenance, and survival take precedence over everything else.

Now, let us turn our attention to the individual seeker's need.

The pursuit of liberation, often referred to as a "spiritual pursuit," is deeply personal and individual. Not only is it personal, but it is also a "personalized" journey, shaped by the unique characteristics and personality of the seeker. Based on their requirements and need for guidance, a seeker often forms a personal relationship and bond with a guru, who serves as a guide in personalizing the teachings of the scriptures and providing inputs to forge ahead in the spiritual pursuit.

The seeker must ask themselves: "What is my spiritual goal? What do I need to do to reach that goal? Do I need an organization to get there?"

Even if an individual chooses to go with an organization, the critical focus should be on their own personal goal and what is needed to achieve it. Organizations bring with them their own rules, regulations, culture, philosophy, interpretations of scriptures, and other frameworks. Additionally, there are also the organization's needs for structure, function, survival, and growth.

This poses a dilemma for the individual seeker, who is now faced with the following: (1) their own spiritual pursuit; (2) the organization's expectations of them within the context of the spiritual pursuit; (3) the organization's need for the individual's contribution to its growth and sustenance; and (4) the individual's professional and family commitments.

The question before the individual seeker: "I am deeply committed to my goal of everlasting freedom, contentment, and peace. This commitment brought me to this path and eventually to this organization. Am I truly doing justice to my spiritual pursuit? Am I able to sustain my focus and commitment to this goal? Am I making the necessary progress on this path?"

Here I am reminded of what J Krishnamurti said: "You may remember the story of how the devil and a friend of his were walking down the street when they saw ahead of them a man stoop down and pick up something from the ground, look at it, and put it away in his pocket. The friend said to the devil, "What did that man pick up?" "He picked up a piece of Truth," said the devil. "That is a very bad business for you, then," said his friend. "Oh, not at all," the devil replied, "I am going to let him organize it."

We are Responsible for the Fragmented World

It is a strange and amusing irony of mankind:

The first operation we learn is to bring together, to *add*,

But the last of the four is what we retain—*divide*,

And we live it through every moment of our lives.

With every passing moment of growing up,

This is the idea we, unfortunately, develop;

It gains root in every aspect of our personality,

Going against the very essence of equality.

Even within the confines of the family environment,

We learn to differentiate between "us" and "them."

It is communicated in no uncertain terms:

We praise what is ours, and others we condemn.

Man divided the earth into geographical boundaries;

This, he thought, gave him a national identity.

It resulted in nothing but division among men—

Alas! Based on this, we built walls—us versus them.

In search of God, man conceived religion

As a torch to lead us to the union with the Divine.

While it was to bring out the noblest in man—

Alas! Based on this, we built walls—us versus them.

Nature, based on environmental conditions,

Adapted our bodies and features to surroundings;

Thus, we developed bodily traits and colours of skin—

Alas! Based on this, we built walls—us versus them.

The services we render brought in the next divide:

A doctor is superior to a mason, and a mason over a maid;

While all this was meant to be in service of the Lord—

Alas! Based on this, we built walls—us versus them.

A natural urge to express thoughts and feelings

Gave man the rich tool of language for communication;

But languages and dialects emerged in hundreds—

Alas! Based on this, we built walls—us versus them.

Then came the sharing of resources gifted by Nature,

Perhaps due to some sheer act of randomness;

Some possessed more, and others relatively less—

Alas! Based on this, we built walls—us versus them.

Every aspect of life becomes a reason to divide:

Education, profession, and even social pride;

Even the beliefs we espouse and the teams we back—

Alas! Based on this, we built walls—us versus them.

Nature Herself was thoughtful in her design;

She created solar systems, planets, and galaxies.

Perhaps knowing that man would divide and fight,

She placed some in galaxies we cannot even sight.

The idea of division arose from the need to share,

But it has become the means to discriminate;

Diversity from the brush in the hands of the Lord—

Unable to see beauty, man picked up the sword.

The divisions we see and create all around us

Are nothing but a reflection of what is inside us;

Every act of discrimination is one of isolation,

Only constricting us, leading to desolation.

—◆—

There is Nothing Miraculous About Miracles

What is a miracle? Everyone seems quite enamoured of it, especially within the spheres of religion and spirituality. I began by consulting the dictionary, which defines a miracle as "an effect or extraordinary event in the physical world that surpasses all known human or natural powers and is ascribed to a supernatural cause." It also says, "such an effect considered a work of God."

But let us move away from the dictionary meaning for a moment. From a practical perspective, we generally use the word "miracle" in two ways: (1) When we use it outside a spiritual or religious context, we simply express wonder or marvel. We are not attributing a supernatural cause; we just see something as unusual, rare, or unexplainable, at least not easily. (2) When, either explicitly or implicitly, we attribute a supernatural cause—God or some divine force.

In the first instance, something remarkable happens, and we might exclaim, "That was miraculous!" suggesting an event outside the usual. This is understandable.

However, here is something I find puzzling: why do some people feel they need to see miracles to accept the presence of God, or to validate someone as a spiritual teacher or religious guide?

Is a miracle truly necessary or sufficient for the existence of God or for someone to be considered a spiritual master? And why do we need to interpret it from the observer's point of view?

Why do we, in general, feel this urge to perceive things as miracles to gain comfort or solace? When we label some coincidence as a miracle, it often leads to reverence, sometimes even worship, to the extent that we suppress our own intelligence and rationality.

The need to experience the miraculous has also led some spiritual teachers, and those associated with them, to present even ordinary events in ways that evoke awe and wonder in their followers, provoking exclamations of "What a miracle!" They feel compelled to attribute something supernatural to even the mundane.

Hence, we encounter so many stories intended to evoke a jaw-dropping effect on listeners or readers.

Why this urge to believe in something only if it carries miraculous interpretations? Because of this, we are continually fed such stories.

Are we moving away from the simplicity of life? Miracles lie within the ordinary, simple moments of our lives.

The everyday occurrences we experience are no less miraculous. From waking to falling asleep, every moment could be seen as a miracle, if we allowed ourselves to see it that way.

The very acts of waking, sleeping, and dreaming, or the lack thereof—aren't these all wondrous in themselves? The sunrise, the blooming of flowers, the grass beneath our feet, the process of digestion, our being alive, the rhythms of health and illness—all of these are as wondrous as anything else.

But we often refuse to see them this way. These miracles have lost their value, perhaps because of their predictability and frequency.

Imagine a believer in God who sees God every day, presenting as an ordinary person, handing over a bouquet of flowers. Soon, they would likely begin to doubt it was God.

We fall into the trap of our imagination, our own ideas of what a miracle is, and what God is. We each have our own definitions of miracles, often very different from the next person's. Even an ardent devotee often feels the need for ongoing reinforcements through "miracles" to keep faith alive.

If, for any reason, events cease to happen in the way we define as miraculous, we may even question the status of that divinity.

Remember, the assessment of any event or effect as a miracle is just our interpretation, our conclusion, or opinion.

If I encounter my friend at a distant medical store buying the same medicine, why must I call that a miracle? That is precisely why the word 'coincidence' exists in the dictionary.

Why don't we simply appreciate everything in the world for what it is, as a beautiful creation of Nature?

Why should we feel compelled to knit a complex web of divine or supernatural causes to appreciate it or rejoice in it?

In the simplicity of it all lies the wonder.

In simplicity lies the miracle.

We often get so lost in attributing some supernatural cause to events that we fail to enjoy them as they are, to see the beauty in their simplicity.

And often, we attribute miracles to a higher power—God—when we don't even fully believe or feel that presence. To me, that is the real wonder.

If we believe that anything can be miraculous and have a supernatural cause, then we must accept that everything in this world is a miracle. But we do not often feel this way. We tend to be selective in our judgment. Isn't that a contradiction?

If a miracle—an event caused by something supernatural—is possible, then everything in this universe is a miracle. There can be no argument.

If we are selective, it reveals our uncertainty about anything supernatural or divine.

Either everything is a miracle, or we must agree that there is nothing called a miracle—everything is merely coincidence.

In religion and spirituality, this logic holds firmly. There is no ambiguity. If we doubt the concept of miracles in a spiritual or religious sense, and cannot be convinced that "everything is a miracle," then our spiritual journey has reached an end.

When we exclaim that something is a miracle, it is often a natural and spontaneous reaction, not a rational response.

It is the heart that calls something a miracle, often immediately before the mind begins to explain it. The more we analyse, the less miraculous it seems. We become convinced, without reason, that it was indeed a miracle.

In trying to reason with an unreasonable mind, explain an unexplainable event, apply logic to an illogical occurrence, and demystify the mysteries of Nature, we fail and conclude: *it is a Miracle of Nature!*

The miracle of a human being is nothing but the miracle of Nature!

When we consider anything a miracle, let it be our recognition of Nature's wonder, our gratitude, and our appreciation of the infinite mystery of existence.

Once an event has taken place, we can think about it and often identify a clear cause. In that sense, it ceases to be a miracle.

Some questions that arise for me: Can we predict a miracle? Does Nature perform miracles? What message does a miracle convey to us?

We are a living miracle!

The greatest mystery, after all, is LIFE ITSELF!

In Not Knowing is Living

Do I have to know everything, for in not knowing is acceptance;

Do I have to know anything, for in not knowing is being;

Do I have to have a goal, for in not knowing is the mystery;

Do I have to have all answers, for in not knowing is the wonder;

Do I have to have any questions, for in not knowing is curiosity;

Do I have to know what I want, for in not knowing is discovery;

Do I have to be in control, for in not knowing is surrender;

Do I have to have a purpose, for in not knowing is freedom;

Do I have to have a direction, for in not knowing is adventure;

Do I have to have a plan, for in not knowing is spontaneity;

Do I have to have a routine, for in not knowing is flow;

Do I have to have an engagement, for in not knowing is presence.

In not knowing is contentment!

In not knowing is completeness!

In not knowing is fulfilment!

In not knowing is peace!

------ ·●· ------

Are We Losing Our Ability to Wonder?

With the advancement of science and technology, what will happen to imagination and wonder? Humanity seeks answers to everything. For every phenomenon we encounter, we want a "scientific" explanation. For every mystery or seemingly unexplainable occurrence, we try to provide an answer. The answer is often incomplete, yet we treat this "work in progress" as the final answer, and we stop wondering. We like to believe that we have solved the mystery.

I hope humanity does not reach a stage where every phenomenon is fully explained by science. It is the mysteries and unsolved aspects of the universe that keep humanity moving forward. On a personal level, too, mystery and wonder should remain.

We seldom spend time with nature; we mostly see digital images of it, if at all. But we do not experience it directly. Imagery of the sea, stars, mountains, waves, sun, and moon is increasingly left to AI and other scientific developments.

Let us now turn inward. The mysteries of our inner realm are as wondrous and enigmatic as the vast external universe. Yet, when it comes to our inner world, we seem to believe we have all the answers. I do not believe that. The mystery will remain.

The mystery should remain.

———•———

Lessons I learnt in my Spiritual Quest... Learning Continues

In my spiritual quest for peace and fulfilment, there have been numerous lessons that have profoundly influenced the way I think and live. To claim that these are the only lessons would be incorrect; ...for, the journey continues. Here are some of the lessons that come to mind, from the last two decades of this journey: [*The term 'object', used below, refers to things, people, work, activities, events, situations, name, fame, position, relationships, etc.*

Objects of the world are not, and can never be, a source

of true happiness. They can only give fleeting pleasures.

Answers to situations leading to happiness and suffering

do not lie in the world. They are to be found deep within.

Journey of life is not about living in this world until death;

it is an inner journey, with all experiences in the mind.

All actions are of the mind alone, and not of the body.

The fruits are incidental. The real outcome is in the mind.

Happiness is not in acquiring and preserving objects.
True happiness lies in being free from desires for them.

Misery, suffering are not caused by objects of the world.
They are the result of desires, preferences, and prejudices.

Freedom is not doing what (when, how) one wants to do.
It is about letting go of the compulsion of wanting to do.

Pains, problems, and challenges in life are inevitable.
But the suffering we experience is the mind's creation.

Everything, without exception, is transient in this world.
I am just a witness to all that which is coming and going.

Nothing can be added to you, that can cause happiness.
Nothing can be taken away from you, and cause misery.

Attachment gives a false sense of possession, ownership.
That false sense of security is but a seed for suffering.

Realizing that I am forever happy, content, full, fearless,
despite the world, is the true state of peace and freedom

Freedom is not in giving up wealth, position, and people.
Living with them, it is in giving up attachment to these.

Success is being free from notions of success and failure.
It is being unagitated, poised, accepting of every outcome.

Doing what we do with expectations, is misery, bondage.
Accepting whatever presents itself by chance, is freedom.

No one here can give you a badge of honour or success.
None can insult or defeat you, or give a label of failure.

If afraid of losing your possessions, then nothing is yours.
When not afraid of losing them, the world belongs to you.

Any distinction like spiritual and material is meaningless.
They strike at the very foundation of oneness in the world.

Self-knowledge is not for moving away from the world.
It is for living a full, vibrant life, amidst this very world.

The Self-pursuit is not about reading, listening, meditating.
It is applying the knowledge in all that we do in life, daily.

My true identity is not defined by what I do, or by labels.
It is what "I AM", naturally. It is identity-less, like water.

Idea, discipline, technique, or mantra, you are exposed to,
receive, hold, and apply it lightly, as you would a flower.

We have freewill with regards to effort in our inner realm.
It does not apply to world phenomena. Nature rules there.

Introspection is not an analysis of the mind and the objects.
It is gaining conviction about what lies beyond the mind.

Meditation is not about thinking over the idea of the Self.
Thinking, you remain only in the mind, far from the Self.

Quest for the Self is not objective, like pursuit of wealth;
Here, what you are pursuing is the same as what you are.

Pursuit of bliss of the Self is not a chase after external objects.

Giving up all pursuits and objects, what remains is the Self.

You do not need to have the answers to everything in life.

Rejoice in the mystery. Embracing the unknown is freedom.

Reason helps you understand the truth beyond any doubt.

Meditation helps you realize the truth that's beyond reason.

In a creative pursuit, the spark comes on 'giving up' effort.

In pursuit of the Self too, give up "effortfulness". Be light.

The "knowledge" in Self-knowledge is not a cognitive one.

Like in love, the direct path to the Self transcends reason.

Zillions of words cannot describe the taste of sugar to you.

You will know it, when you taste it. So is Truth. It's simple.

------◆------

Bhagavad Gita is Not a Text on Management or Administration

Management involves the systems and processes for planning, organizing, and managing resources—human, financial, physical, etc.—to achieve the goals of an organization, whether in business or otherwise. In other words, management focuses on the objects and situations in the world around us.

Spirituality, however, is about guiding the human being toward the goal of liberation or freedom, and attaining peace and everlasting happiness, which entails realizing one's true nature. It is not about exploring the world or its phenomena. In the realm of spirituality, the world itself is often considered an illusion.

What, then, is the Bhagavad Gita? The Bhagavad Gita is a spiritual text aimed at supporting the quest for liberation. It is presented as a dialogue between Arjuna, a warrior, and Krishna, who serves as his charioteer in the battle. When Arjuna is struck by grief at the thought of fighting his friends and relatives, he turns to Krishna for enlightenment and freedom from his sorrow. Krishna's response guides Arjuna toward the spiritual goal of liberation.

Although Arjuna and Krishna are in the midst of a battlefield, their dialogue is not about battle strategies. The fact that they are warriors does not make their conversation about statecraft, administration, or management. The significance of their discussion taking place in a battlefield setting suggests that freedom from suffering and true peace can be attained while fully engaged in the world—as part of family, work, society, and all our interactions.

If the Bhagavad Gita were only about management or administration, it would be relevant solely to those fields. Yet people from all walks of life read it and benefit from its teachings. The Gita itself states, at the end of each chapter, that it is *Brahmavidya*—knowledge of the Self. There is no ambiguity in this purpose.

To present the dialogue as merely addressing business management or organizational issues would be misleading. The Bhagavad Gita is not a book of values or Dharma alone, nor is it a guide on management, administration, or war strategies. It is not a manual on religious doctrine either. It is a text for attaining *moksha*—liberation.

That said, it is deeply rooted in Hindu philosophy, incorporating many ideas, concepts, and themes of Sanatana Dharma.

———— • ● • ————

Non-violence: Is it Only Physical in Nature?

Ahimsa (non-violence, non-hurtingness) is commonly understood as abstaining from causing injury to another, whether by speech or action. These are the tangible forms we usually identify with.

Let us consider it on the level of thoughts. Any action (or speech) originates as a thought. Scriptures say that "what is done by the mind is what is action, and not that which is done by the body." It is thoughts that take the form of speech or action.

So, however much we avoid (or disguise) it, a "violent thought" will reveal itself in speech or action sooner or later and will result in harm to another.

As seekers trying to understand our own minds, here is a point to reflect on: When we have a thought that is "violent" or full of "ill-will" toward another, who is the first person to be hurt?

It is our own mind!

Therefore, let us reflect on the idea of non-violence from a fresh perspective.

Distinction Between Questioning and Enquiring

Here are some familiar questions: "Why should I believe in God?", "Why should I explore the realm of spirituality now?", "Why should I accept the idea of the Self?" and so on.

While the two words—questioning and enquiring—literally mean the same thing, "questioning" often carries a tone of challenging, dismissing, or refusing to accept. And this is often the tone of the questions above.

What is called for instead is "questioning with the intent to know", which is what enquiry or investigation is all about.

Let us not get hung up on the nomenclature and focus instead on the intent of the two words (questioning and enquiry).

The entire pursuit of knowledge in Sanatana Dharma (Hinduism) is based on enquiry. Sanatana Dharma uses "enquiry" as a path. Many of the Upanishads, which reveal the knowledge of Vedanta, are presented as dialogues. The *Bhagavad Gita* too is presented as a dialogue, with Arjuna enquiring into the secret of freedom.

This is why the spiritual pursuit in Vedanta begins with an enquiry into the Self, often called Self-enquiry.

Enquiry begins with a "yearning to know," marked by sincerity. It typically stems from a personal experience that triggers a question. Such a question is not an academic one—it is "personal." Arjuna was struck by grief on the battlefield, which led to the dialogue of the *Bhagavad Gita*.

The *Mundaka Upanishad* begins with an enquiry: "Knowing what, does everything in this world become known?" or "Knowing what, is there nothing more to be known?"

Only when a question arises from a sincere intent to know does it lead the seeker toward the goal. Otherwise, the question remains academic, and any exploration may, at best, stay academic.

Remember, the intent of the spiritual pursuit is to attain "freedom," and for that, the enquiry must begin with the individual seeker. Each seeker will be guided forward by their own "personal" enquiry. [Freedom refers to forever being free from suffering, or everlasting peace.]

What is the Meaning of "Abiding in the Self"?

What is this thing we call the mind? It is that which produces thoughts, emotions, feelings, ideas, and more. We often perceive the mind as a producer, but does it have an identity beyond that?

Try to locate the mind, spot the mind, or feel the mind. When you set out to do this, you realize there is no tangible entity called "the mind."

The mind is described by countless attributes. How, then, can we place something so attribute-laden in the Self, which is entirely free of attributes?

The thoughts, emotions, and ideas that arise do not define us. They hold no permanent positions or identities. When we free the mind from these layers, the Self shines in its original, unconditioned nature.

To "abide," "rest," or "establish" the mind in the Self—what does this mean? Though these words suggest action, implying a physical placement of one upon the other, they also seem to assume that mind and Self are distinct entities. In truth, the mind is simply an expression of the Self. If you identify yourself with the experiencing mind, you cannot realize your true nature as the Self.

Realization comes by moving away from the limiting adjuncts of body and mind, by dis-identifying with them. When you recognize your identity as the Self alone, the concept of "mind" dissolves. Here, the world is understood as unreal, and the mind loses its identity, leaving only the Self.

When the mind stops seeking happiness in worldly objects, desires disappear. In the absence of desires, the mind ceases to experience the limitations of the body and senses. The veils of the mind are lifted, revealing only the Self. What remains is the Self alone.

When we crave the world and its objects, we confirm an inner sense of lack, one we try to fulfil through external means.

But if there is a sense of lack, how can we experience the fullness, the Self? The Self is whole and complete; only by relinquishing the feeling of lack can we experience this fullness. In this sense, desires and Self-abidance cannot coexist.

———◆———

Another Perspective Regarding the "Purpose of Life"

If we are trying to define the purpose of life, we need to be clear about what life is. The way we look at life will help us understand the purpose of life. This is an important point.

If you define life as the time between birth and death, and having a good time, then the purpose of life is all about acquiring as many things as possible to make us happy and delay death. The idea of the purpose of life is shaped by how we choose to look at life itself.

Reflect on the following. You are looking at a rose. If you see it as something full of fragrance, you may think of creating perfume from it. If you see it as a thing of beauty, you may want to use it to decorate your home. If you see it as something divine, you may use it as an offering at the altar. And so on.

Depending on how you look at a rose, you will want to deal with it accordingly, to derive happiness from it. Remember, the moment you define it, its use is sealed. To delight in the flower without any end to the joy, we have to hold the flower without defining it.

Once you arrive at a purpose, then living becomes all about chasing that purpose. It does not matter what you chase; you are still chasing. You become a slave to that purpose.

No matter how lofty the purpose is in your eyes, the moment you become a slave to it, you are blinded to the beauties, mysteries, and spontaneity of life.

If you want a purpose at all, let it be one that sets you free. The purpose should be elevating and enriching, larger than life itself!

The World Around Us is Nothing but Brahman

We often find ourselves standing in front of a deity in a temple. It is a stone idol, after all. But when we stand there, we see beyond the stone image, recognizing it as a representation of the formless God. We have the awareness not to see it as merely a stone idol; we attribute the powerful presence of the Cosmic Supreme to it.

In Advaita Vedanta, we understand that the world itself is nothing but Brahman. In other words, everything is Brahman—the Supreme Reality.

Just as we do in our temple experience, let us bring this awareness of the Supreme Reality every time we look at or interact with the world.

Our Life is itself a Pilgrimage

To interpret all the inexplicable,

Man conceived of a God infallible;

As he evolved from a primitive state,

He longed for a vision of the Great.

In his imagination, though limited,
God as human had qualities unlimited;
Thus was defined his life's goal:
To be the ideal human or the divine soul.

In this link between man and his maker,
Man sought to emulate his master;
In veneration of his Creator,
He excelled himself to be even greater.

This mere attempt to imitate Him
Gave man a pursuit and an aim;
This journey to human perfection
Is perhaps what we call devotion.

As a devotee draws near the object,
The heart expands, striving to be perfect;
There comes a point in this quest
When the path matters, not the conquest.

To some, love for God is deep and pure;
In surrender, their minds and hearts mature.
They are symbols of unsurpassed romance,
Immersed in bliss and always in a trance.

In our voyage to attain the ideal chosen,
The goal and its means are but one notion;
What we call the ultimate union
Is just an attainment of that perfection.

To reach utopia is but a passage;

Our destiny is to take that voyage.

This is religion of the purest kind—

Life is the only pilgrimage for mankind.

I often marvel at the humble devotee:

Is he truly one because of his Almighty?

Or is the Lord Almighty a holy God

Because of His devout and sincere ward?

Can I Not See Everything That Happens as Auspicious?

The term 'auspicious' is used very often in the context of religion and spirituality. What does it mean? The dictionary says "promising success; propitious, favourable." It is from the Latin 'auspici(um)'—auspic + -ous. *Auspicium*—bird watching, divination from the flight of birds. It refers to a divination or prognostication, originally from observing birds.

Basically, we are looking for signs in nature which give an indication of events to come, more related to nature than anything else. Anyway, the word has come to find a place in our day-to-day vocabulary.

Let us explore the term in the domain of spirituality. Why should anyone wish to use this word 'auspicious' in the context of spiritual pursuit?

Some of the foundational principles in spiritual pursuit are: Accept everything that comes; rise above likes and dislikes, favourable and unfavourable; nothing is intrinsically good or bad; everything happens to enrich my life.

If these are the tenets I, as a seeker, live by, where is the question of auspicious or inauspicious? The whole idea seems erroneous, absurd.

Going further with the thought process, how can I imagine that doing anything, saying anything, or thinking anything can cause something auspicious or inauspicious to anyone—especially to another person?

Suppose I do, say, or think anything; that begins with a thought in my mind. Whatever the thought is (i.e., the nature of the thought)—that stays with me. That thought in my mind will stay as a thought in my memory. Whatever effect that memory brings to me—by being pleasant or unpleasant—will be in my mind.

That thought cannot result in something auspicious or inauspicious to another. Only my action can bring favour or disfavour to another, and that too in the external or physical or objective sense alone.

Think of another scenario. I disobey another, or do not follow their instructions. In other words, I do not do what convention demands. How can that be inauspicious? It will be inauspicious only if I choose to allow that thought process to gain ground in my mind. Only the lingering of that thought can cause discomfort to me.

So, everything depends on what I feel or how I choose to look at it. Suppose my outlook is—"all that happens is good or favourable," then everything in my life is "auspicious." It is my choice!

If I have no harmful thoughts towards another, why should there be any fear of being affected by anyone else's thoughts, speech, or actions? The fear only comes in when, in my mind, I harbour evil or harmful thoughts towards another. Even then, my thoughts will affect me alone and thus my peace of mind. They cannot and will not affect another.

If anything favourable or unfavourable happens (i.e., the occurrence of an event), it is by the laws of "cause and effect" and not by anything mystical. If anything happens that does not have apparent causes (the likelihood of that happening has a probability of zero), let us be very clear that it is only illusory and not real.

In short, my "good" thoughts keep my mind at peace. My harmful thoughts only hurt the environment of my mind and cannot influence another's life in any way whatsoever. And by that same logic, another's thoughts and words cannot become auspicious or inauspicious to me! We can safely include actions of others too!

Then why at all do we need the term auspicious? Yes, that probably is a very relevant question.

Regarding the idea of auspiciousness, let me be guided by the following principles to advance my spiritual quest:

- Let me act with a mindset focused on the welfare, well-being, and success of others.

- In the phenomenal world, governed by nature's principles of cause and effect, actions can yield favourable or unfavourable outcomes that may impact others. In the realm of the mind, however, "unfavourable" thoughts primarily affect the mind that generates them.

- In the realm of the mind, let me perceive everything as inherently "auspicious."

- Let this world, and all that transpires within it, serve to enrich me.

- Let me accept everything that arises, without labelling it as auspicious or inauspicious.

The Core of Spirituality: Be Free from the Objects

In everything we do in this world, we are the centre of the universe. In other words, "I am the one seeing this world, and there is the seen world." "I am doing things, and there are things that get done by me," and so on. So, in every situation, there is "I am the actor," and there is something that is "acted upon" (the object).

The fundamental notion we entertain as humans is that, at any point in time, we are doing something. And when we do something, there is something that gets done; something that is acted upon. Even in language, we do not have a concept of a sentence without a verb. And when we do something, there is an object associated with it.

So, what is the problem with that, you may wonder. The problem is that all our focus is on the "object" and not the "action."

Is there a problem with that? Let us explore further.

Rather than enjoying our action, our attention shifts from our action to the object. Any hindrance or obstacle in attaining that object causes misery, sorrow, grief, etc.

For example, when painting, our attention shifts to the painting itself, instead of enjoying the process of painting. Examine every action; the situation is the same. If the painting does not come out the way we want it, we do not experience any joy from the act of painting.

In the case of "love," the act of love is directed at someone. Even in the dictionary, it is defined as "a profoundly tender, passionate affection for another person." There is another person involved in "love."

Love is directed at someone, and the object of love becomes more important than love itself. That is, the attention is not on the feeling of love our mind generates but on the person it is directed towards. As a result, any unfavourable change in that person impacts the love we feel.

The same is the case with other qualities like compassion, empathy, generosity, etc. Even honesty seems directed. We are honest toward some, and we feel that "I can't be dishonest to you." We even say, "Will I ever lie to you?" This seems to suggest that our honesty depends on "who is at the other end" of our honesty.

What is the problem in all these cases? We are losing out on the joys that we can derive from all the action because we are completely captivated by the object that we act upon. And one can see that this is a sure recipe for sorrow.

This seems to suggest that we are looking at honesty, love, compassion, generosity, etc., as "transactions" or "something we do," as opposed to "being" honest, loving, compassionate, generous, etc., irrespective of who is at the receiving end.

The question to ask ourselves is: "How do I move from 'doing' to 'being'?" Because with doing, there is an object attached.

When we talk of even practices like mindfulness, concentration, attention, or meditation, we have an object: we are mindful of something; we concentrate upon something; we are attentive to something; and we meditate upon something.

The way to joy and contentment is in being with the act, not with the object of action.

Directed love is limited; undirected love is true love. Being honest irrespective of the person is true honesty. In the case of fear, we are fearful of something or somebody. If there is no other, there is no fear.

Even in the case of happiness, we want an object to derive happiness from. We are unable to imagine happiness without an object. The "object" could be a thing, person, work, event, fame, position, power, wealth, etc.

Here is something interesting: even anger, jealousy, hate, greed are all directed—directed at something or somebody.

Look at the moon or the sun. We think that the sun's rays are lighting up the earth. Think again. The sun shines, and any object that comes its way is illuminated. Similarly, the moon sheds its cool rays on anything that comes its way. Thus, we are able to say, "the sun shines." Period! The sun does not shine on the earth alone.

Spirituality is the journey from "seeing life as a series of transactions directed toward objects of the world" to simply "being." In other words, moving from DIRECTEDNESS to NON-DIRECTEDNESS.

With everything being directed at some object or the other, we are reinforcing the notion of duality.

Let us eliminate the object in all our actions.

Let us be happy, without dependence on objects.

Let us be loving, shifting from expressing love toward some.

Let us be compassionate, being compassionate toward all.

The duality ceases in our mental model. The objects of the world cease to exist.

This is Advaita!

Meditation is Not a Sensory Experience

In Vedanta, meditation is associated with the goal of realizing our true identity, the Self, which is beyond the senses, mind, intellect, and ego. Thus, it is beyond sensory perception and emotional experience, which are in the domain of the mind.

This means we can't say, "I had a vision of light" or "I felt a sensation" during meditation. Also, we can't say it was a pleasurable experience, because pleasure and happiness are experiences within the mind.

If meditation is aimed at realizing the Self, how can we attempt to "experience" meditation the way we experience objects or mental states?

What is the way out then?

When we let go of sensory perceptions and free ourselves from the desire (for the mind) to experience something, we go beyond the senses and mind, and what remains is the Self. There is nothing to be done.

The only "experiences" we are familiar with are those in the mind. In that realm, we know pleasure, joy, sorrow, greed, jealousy, anger, fear, and so on. But we are not familiar with any experience beyond the mind. If we do not get any sensory or mental experience, we think we have not had any "experience" at all, because we relate only to the familiar notion of experience.

So, what do we do then?

We have to stop seeking any experience. Just meditate. Do not judge the meditation afterward. Simply stay with it repeatedly. If we continue to derive some experience, then we are still not in the realm of the Self. We are still at the level of mind and intellect.

In this sense, there is nothing to be achieved. If we seek to achieve, we remain in the realm of action, desire, effort, and outcome—whether favourable or unfavourable.

We can't use the word "experience" in the context of meditation. We have to let go of any attempt to experience.

I Am a Kite with No Strings Attached

Like eagles ready for a hunt, I soared high in the sky;
Adorned with hues aplenty, I ceaselessly longed to fly.
Aiming to touch the stars, swelling with childish pride;
Aspiring to have it all, I felt like an eager bride.

Wishing for more from life, my desires began to rise;
Now overcome with greed, I fell for my deeper cries.
"Great height is the finale," thus reasoned my mind;
Never once did I think, I was simply going blind.

After reaching my peak, I thought this was bliss;
But after cruising a while, I sensed something amiss.
What I thought was freedom was a momentary breeze;
What I took for peace was but transient ease.

With reason clouded, I searched for some light;
I looked for answers that would change my plight.
Still lost in thought, I felt a gentle pull;
Alas, "I am still bound"—a reminder in full.

With a tug, my answers came, as clouds seemed to clear;

I felt light as a feather, with the sun's rays near.

Surrendering to the wind, with humility, I let myself be flown;

This acceptance of my place brought joy unknown.

My threads are held by an unseen cosmic hand,

Dancing to them, I thought, was a symphony grand.

Though I may believe it's a cosmic line,

It is still a bondage, though divine.

Letting go of the string of life was delight, epiphany;

I realized at last, eternal drift is my destiny.

"Be free from all strings" was the clear final call—

"No strings attached" is my nature, after all.

Let the Mind go Beyond "I" and "Mine", in the Service of All

We often hear the following terms: attention, concentration, focus, mindfulness, meditation. When we say attention, we are trying to direct the mind to an object. We often hear statements like, "pay attention to the food you are eating; pay attention to the beauties of nature as you walk," etc. To do this, one tries hard to direct the mind toward the object under consideration.

Let us step back a little. There are two aspects to paying attention: (1) directing the mind to an object; (2) not allowing the mind to follow something that is not the object.

We try very hard at (1), but seldom do we stop to think that (2) is key to (1).

Our mind is constantly wandering off to various things in the past and future. That is why we feel distracted, tired, and mentally fatigued. If we prevent the mind from wandering off in multiple directions, then it is naturally in a state of attention.

We easily allow the mind to shift from one thought to another. The challenge is: how do we prevent the mind from wandering off in multiple directions? The mind seems to be in its natural state when it is wandering. In other words, "wanderingness" seems to be the mind's true nature; or, we could say that noise or clutter in the mind comes very naturally to us.

What is the definition of this noise? What causes it? Our doubts, fears, apprehensions, wants, desires, ambitions, likes, dislikes, hatreds, passions, cravings, needs, threats, etc.—these are constantly popping up and clouding the mind.

All of these, individually or in combinations, prevent the mind from staying calm and peaceful. In the presence of these forces, how can the mind be calm? How can attention be possible in such a mind?

Even if we attempt to focus on a single thought, as we do in meditation, it does not work because these negative forces are constantly active, making focus on a single object or thought nearly impossible.

Therefore, the focus must be on eliminating or at least reducing the wanderingness of the mind.

Suppose we say, "I will stay with the thought, I am the Brahman." Even to stay with that ennobling thought, we must be free from all distracting thoughts.

How do we do that? That is the crucial question.

This is perhaps a very important aspect of spiritual pursuit and holds the key to our progress toward the spiritual goal.

While we understand that all those tendencies—likes, dislikes, fears, wants, and so on—are outgoing thoughts, they are all centred around oneself. When the mind is wandering with these various thoughts and tendencies, they are all focused on one entity: "me." They all relate to "I" and "mine."

Thus, the answer lies in making the mind go outward. What? But aren't they already outward? This seems very counter-intuitive.

The answer is to let the thoughts be always on the welfare of others (not 'I' and 'mine'). From the beginning, make the mind other-centred, not selfish, or self-centred. This gradually takes us toward the goal of recognizing and then realizing the same Self in all beings.

———— •◆•• ————

Re-examine Your Position Regarding the Notion of Faith

Some people dismiss the concept of faith, saying, "I don't go by faith; I believe in reason and logic." Some even consider faith inferior to reason itself. However, faith is fundamental to our lives, beginning in the earliest days when we accept what we are told without question. As children, we believe what our families and elders say without contention or doubt. Over time, these beliefs, when reinforced, become a kind of living truth, deeply woven into our perception of reality.

As we grow and enter school or college, our understanding expands, and new beliefs emerge. We are taught that the sun rises in the east, and we accept it without question. Later, we learn that the sun does not truly "rise"—the earth's rotation creates this illusion. We recalibrate our understanding and simply move on, without conflict.

In science, we begin with Newton's laws and move to Einstein's theories, then perhaps to quantum mechanics. When we first learned Newton's laws, we did not demand proof before accepting them; we took them on faith.

Each new understanding doesn't negate the previous one; rather, it expands our perspective. Why, then, do we often become rigid when it comes to certain beliefs? Faith is not about being rigid; it is a starting point, a bridge to exploration and understanding.

Even science operates on this principle. Research begins with a hypothesis or conjecture and can take years of work to eventually prove or disprove. Consider Fermat's Last Theorem. In 1637, mathematician Pierre de Fermat wrote this conjecture in the margin of one of his books, saying the proof was too large to fit there. Generations of mathematicians tackled this problem with faith in Fermat's claim. Despite countless attempts, they did not abandon the problem as impossible. For over 350 years, this faith endured, and in 1994, Andrew Wiles finally provided a proof. Wasn't it faith in Fermat's words that spurred mathematicians to pursue this proof?

Faith is the beginning, not the conclusion. In spirituality, scriptures suggest that there is "something" beyond the mind, called the "Self." Faith in this concept provides the sincerity and conviction to pursue it until realization. This journey is personal and culminates in direct realization of the Truth.

The world is where it is today because people have believed in something greater than themselves and pursued it without doubt. Faith is not merely belief without reason; it is a foundation. Faith is accepting the contributions of those before us. Otherwise, we'd constantly be "reinventing the wheel."

From a Self-centred Mind to an All-Embracing Mind

At the beginning of my spiritual pursuit, I was focussed greatly on newly acquired routines, thoughts, activities, disciplines, and thought processes. They all revolved around "me," with the intent of bringing about a personal transformation that will eventually lead me to my spiritual goal.

Over time, I found myself becoming less flexible, less accepting, less accommodating, less inclusive, and less welcoming. This was not because I intended to be that way, but because my attention was constantly on myself.

However, it was important to recognize that becoming self-centred can never lead to a state of ego-effacement. If anything, it will lead to the opposite.

There was a need to make the mind supple, surrendering, kind, warm, and accommodating. With the mind in such a state, it becomes ever-free, ever-welcoming, ever-kind, all-embracing, and all-inclusive—which is nothing less than the all-embracing Brahman!

With this attitude or orientation, the scriptures say, "you verily become That (the all-embracing One)." The mind goes outward, but now with a different orientation.

Let me embrace the welfare of others; let me recognize that Truth is all-pervading, not just within oneself; let me open to everyone and everything.

Let this lead me to the vastness of my mind; let me experience the limitless through that vastness! Let me expand my mind, making it so vast that it becomes the all-encompassing Presence! Let me experience stillness in that vastness! Let me experience silence in that vastness! Let me BE that vastness!

Therefore, in my spiritual quest, should I not, without fail, include the idea of the "others' welfare" as a core mindset?

The term *Brahman* (Supreme Reality), which I seek to realize, by definition, means "big." How can I hope to attain that bigness, realize that bigness, become that bigness, if I am becoming increasingly constricted, self-centred, etc.?

I may try to justify many of my behaviours, thoughts, actions, etc., within the context of spiritual practices, but unless my thoughts, speech, and actions bring solace, comfort, warmth, peace, and fearlessness to others, I will be far from the spiritual goal. Without empathy, kindness, and compassion towards all others around me, I cannot make progress on this path to Brahmanhood.

The moment I harbour constricting thoughts toward others, I fail. My compassion, kindness, inclusiveness, love, and affection for others cannot be based on their personality, character, attitude, or behaviour. My attitude towards others must be *in spite of* their attitude. Unconditional!

Remember, I speak of my true nature as "unconditionally happy," "unconditionally peaceful," "unconditionally all-embracing," "unconditionally compassionate."

There cannot be a compromise. The key word is *unconditional.*

Let me be forgiving, unconditionally.

Let me be loving, unconditionally.

Let me be all-embracing, unconditionally.

Let me be compassionate and kind, unconditionally.

———•◆•———

Why Do we Say, "I Had a Good Time, I Learnt a Lot"?

How often have we said, "I had a great time; it was very useful," or "I learned a lot," or "I enjoy my work; I am always learning," or "It was great meeting you; I learned a lot." Everything seems to be about learning, purpose, and takeaway. Why? Why do we assess enjoyment by what we gain from it? Why not learn to enjoy an event, an interaction, or an association simply for its own sake—even if there is no learning involved? Why this obsession with learning and returns?

Do we even reflect on what we mean by "learning"? That is a topic for another discussion.

We have reached a point where, if we do not learn something or if an activity or interaction does not serve a purpose, we do not enjoy it—and we may even avoid it. Every activity seems worthwhile only if there is a tangible purpose or agenda. How often do we meet someone without thinking of an agenda? Even to say, "I should meet him, at least, once in six months," is an agenda.

If learning is an important measure, we may feel that meeting one person teaches us more than meeting another. We then tend to prefer one over the other, choosing activities or people based on perceived value. Why is it important to reflect on this?

Consider the following scenario: You meet a friend after a long time. After some conversation, you mentally tune out because there is nothing new you are learning. Sitting there, you wonder, "Why am I even here?" Soon, while you are physically present with your friend, your mind has drifted away.

When we engage in something with a motive, we tend to drift constantly into thoughts about that motive. Whether it is meeting someone or doing something, our mind keeps evaluating the returns of the engagement. Over time, with this mindset, even meeting friends and family becomes about "why."

Gradually, we start seeking "learning" as a means to "enjoy." The more deeply we go into this, the more we depend on learning—or on our idea of what learning is—to find happiness.

But remember, the very purpose of the spiritual pursuit is to "be happy" without depending on the world or its objects.

In the context of meeting someone with an agenda, we are never truly present. Happiness exists only in the present moment, when the mind is not caught up in evaluation.

Here are some points to introspect upon, from the perspective of spiritual pursuit:

How often do I enjoy work for the sake of doing good work, rather than for any reward it brings? How often do I enjoy an interaction for the love of the other person and the joy of their presence, rather than for how "useful" I find it?

Our mind's judgments—like "learned," "useful," or "not useful"— are very limiting.

There is joy when we open ourselves to the universe. There is joy when we open ourselves to infinite possibilities, without judging them as good or bad, useful or not useful.

Why Me? Accepting That We Will Never Have All the Answers

Throughout life, we encounter countless questions. Often, these questions concern the world around us, and many of them can now be answered with a quick search online. Some questions about the world might still lack clear answers, yet we accept this and do not lose sleep over them.

But there are other, deeper questions—questions that relate directly to our lives and the things that happen to us. One of the most significant among them is: "Why me?" In other words, "Why did this happen to me?"

The more we push for answers to this question, the more stress it creates, leading to suffering.

Consider this scenario: *It was a stormy, rainy day with heavy traffic. Suddenly, a tree fell, but it struck only my friend's car. Why did it have to happen to him?*

Notice something interesting here: we usually only ask "Why me?" when something unfavourable happens. When everything goes our way, we rarely stop to ask the same question.

Take a moment to consider—when you ask "Why me?" and someone offers an answer, are you truly prepared for it?

Such questions rarely have "real" answers. Someone may give us a response, but does it really feel like *the* answer?

In many cases, it might be better not to have an answer, as the truth could be unacceptable to us. There are two kinds of answers. One is a straightforward explanation of natural phenomena that caused the event. The other is simply "chance," and no answer here will likely satisfy us.

We will face countless questions like this throughout life. Will we have answers to all of them? Definitely not.

Questions are like clouds in the sky. Every now and then, clouds enhance the beauty of the sun. A sky with no clouds can be difficult to face all the time.

Living is not about having or finding all the answers; it is about being at home with the questions and the unknowns. The mysteries of nature should never cease—that is what makes life so wonderful.

Let us accept that Nature is impersonal. God is impersonal.

------ • ● • ------

Learn to Sit Quietly Without Doing Anything

From childhood, we often hear, "What are you doing just sitting there doing nothing?" or "How can you be so idle?" These words condition us to believe that sitting quietly in one place, doing nothing, is wrong or wasteful.

Of course, there are times when we might be physically inactive, yet the mind is still racing. Others cannot see this mental activity, but it is there. This urge to stay constantly engaged—to always *do* something, *achieve* something, *become* something, or *avoid* something—reflects the desires driving us all the time.

But this conditioning and the desires behind it become obstacles in the spiritual pursuit.

It is essential to understand that the Self's true nature is one of "inaction." In other words, at the level of the Self, we are inactive; the Self is a non-doer. Engaging in activity while staying grounded in the awareness of the non-doing Self is the essence of Karma Yoga.

Let us cultivate the ability to sit quietly without doing anything—or at least to release the compulsion to be active merely for activity's sake.

------ • ● • ------

Recognize the Creative Power Within

You are a painter—be in no doubt,

No less than the Rembrandts of the world,

Always painting on the canvas called life,

With the colours of imagination and creativity,

With the water and oil of your vision of the world,

Using the easel—the world—around you.

Equipped with these, you have complete freedom

To paint, going beyond conventions, rules, norms;

For true creativity will be in harmony with the world.

The process demands authenticity of intent

Coupled with the spontaneity of expression,

Not limited by your expectations of achievement.

Then, in each moment, you shall create a masterpiece,

For it is from the very same cosmic source

From which the entire creation has been unleashed.

If you dig deep into your true identity, you will realize

You have no sense of ownership regarding the painting,

For you were merely a brush in the hands of the Supreme.

The act of painting, and the painting itself,

Are your offerings at the altar of the Supreme.

It is your acknowledgment of the infinite creative power within.

You are unaffected, for you are unattached;

The world may stand in awe of your creation—

You are as much a witness to the painting as the world is.

Enjoy being the witness to the process of painting,

Enjoy the unfolding that is like the blossoming of a flower.

Enjoy being surprised by what you are creating.

Do not assess your creation

By the yardstick of time that you are familiar with;

Do not evaluate it in the crucible of prevailing notions of success.

Allow your creation to lose its individuality,

And merge into the universe of timeless creativity,

To unite with the very source where it came from.

Being the brush in the hands of the Supreme,

You become one with the Supreme;

You transcend the notions of success and failure.

Enquiry Into the Nature of Suffering Holds the Secret

We experience misery, anger, fear, and suffering, and we naturally want it to end. It makes sense to seek freedom from these states—no one wants to remain in such distress.

Yet trying to defeat these feelings by fighting them is ultimately futile. When we confront suffering directly, we create conflict, and conflict only strengthens what we are trying to eliminate. Ironically, the more we struggle against our suffering, the more power we give it. This ongoing battle drains our energy, and each "victory" merely brings temporary relief, often leaving us feeling worn down and depleted.

Eventually, we may reach a point where we ignore the suffering rather than fight it. In truth, letting go of the battle and ceasing to resist brings freedom from the suffering.

That is where lies genuine detachment, and this detachment is where true freedom lies. When we no longer engage in a struggle, the suffering no longer controls us. While the situation itself may not vanish, our connection to it fades, bringing a profound inner peace.

For some, suffering feels all too real. But reflect on what we mean by "real" in this context. Upon closer examination, suffering often reveals itself as transient, shifting and dissolving with time, and this ephemerality lessens its hold on us.

Consider this carefully. Do not look outside yourself or into the past to find solutions to suffering. Avoid examining who said what or why events unfolded as they did. Don't dwell on how you might avoid similar experiences in the future. These efforts only anchor you to suffering.

Instead, reflect inwardly. Ask yourself: Where does suffering reside? What exactly is it that we call suffering? When you say "I am suffering", who or what is that "I"? What is the nature of the experience we identify as suffering?

In these questions lies the path to freedom from suffering.

***

Seeing Names and Forms Prevents Us from Seeing Beyond

Imagine yourself at a music concert. The vocalist is surrounded by a violinist and two percussionists.

You are sitting in the first row. To enjoy the concert, you must free yourself from distractions—the artists' mannerisms, their attire, their silent interactions, and other gestures.

When your attention drifts to these details—the dress worn by each artist, their mannerisms, and so on—you stop truly listening to the music in those moments. You fail to enjoy the subtleties in the performance.

Similarly, in spirituality, we get distracted by names and forms, and this prevents us from perceiving what lies beyond the names and forms. We fail to recognize the substratum of the entire world.

Grace is Nothing But our Own Inner Abundance

We often seek the grace of God, the grace of a guru, or the grace of something we deeply believe in. But what, in reality, is grace? Is it something that comes from outside to enter our lives? Is it a gift bestowed upon us by another? This perspective restricts us and undervalues our true nature.

In essence, grace is not an external gift; it is the abundance within us. It is the boundless potential that we already are.

Grace is the humility within us that opens us up to the universe, allowing all of existence to flow through us. This receptivity to grace is our choice; it is our own power. Do not relinquish that power to an external agency.

Often, we attribute self-realization or spiritual awakening to the grace of the Divine, the grace of the Supreme. But consider: this "grace" is actually our own readiness, our own surrender. Grace is the profound humility that enables the fullness of experience to flow into us.

Imagine wanting to experience the vastness of nature. To truly experience it, we must fully submit to it, opening ourselves completely. When we do, the experience is ours. If we do not, then even if we stand before a great ocean, we may perceive it with our senses yet feel none of its immensity.

Grace, then, is not an external favour bestowed upon us by higher powers. We cannot expect it to manifest on demand. Rather, grace is our own readiness and humility to become a vessel, to welcome whatever comes with openness and gratitude. In this state, we no longer expect favours from external entities, be they divine or otherwise.

True grace is the natural state of oneness with the Cosmic.

------●------

Pondering Over "What is the Purpose of Life?"

"What is the meaning of life?"—I remember pondering over this question for some time. I wondered, *"What is the meaning of a rainbow or a tree?"* The question never appealed to me, so I decided to set it aside forever. Though I used to hear others around me raise this question, I never developed any interest in it.

"What is the purpose of life?" is another popular question, but this too never caught my attention. On some occasions, this question had been directed to me by someone else, prompting me to think about it. In exploring the idea of *"purpose,"* here are some thoughts that crossed my mind. I am not trying to provide any answers here. I am just sharing my thoughts that came up when I ask myself that question.

Can there be a generic answer to this question? It depends on who is asking the question and the situation in which they are asking it.

When I am groping in the dark, *purpose* takes on the meaning of aim, goal, ambition, or aspiration. It provides a certain direction to begin with—that's all. It just defines a starting point. Once a starting point is defined, we need to let go of the idea of purpose.

If there is a particular activity, we ask, *"Why are we doing this?"* So, we may have a purpose for a specific activity. If you are walking from here to a destination, you may ask, *"Where am I headed, and why?"*

But what if there is no reason for doing things, and yet we still do them? What motivates such actions? I concluded that *"you definitely can"* do things without defining a purpose.

When we explore the purpose of life, we attribute a certain meaning to the word *purpose*. Essentially, we ask, *"Why?"*

Consider this scenario: *"Let me go to the garden for a walk,"* says a thought. The immediate question that comes to mind is *"What is the purpose?"* or *"Why?"* You going for the walk depends on the "strength" of that purpose and your commitment to it. Suppose a response arises: *"To listen to the birds and see the trees."* This may not feel motivating enough. But suppose you recall your last medical test results; you may decide to go for that walk.

Even if you go on that walk, you might not notice the newly-bloomed flowers, the blue sky, the falling leaves, or the sound of birds. Instead, you see only those things that connect to your purpose of avoiding that medical bill.

We often approach life in this way. In doing so, we miss out on *"the blooming flowers, the blue sky, falling leaves, chirruping birds, and countless other wonders."*

The following questions come to mind: *To life itself, can I attribute a purpose? Do I need a purpose? Will the purpose of the different activities in life add up to life's purpose?* I found no convincing answers for assigning a *"purpose"* to my journey through life.

Of course, each individual has to evaluate this idea of purpose through their own lens, and should not draw conclusions based solely on what is said here—these are merely my thoughts.

The following thought seemed more powerful than wanting a purpose: by attributing a purpose to life, I take away the beauty, joy, and wonder of life. At every step, I start evaluating how my actions contribute to my life's purpose. In everything I do, then, the question arises: *Does this fulfil my overall purpose?* If it does not, then the action feels meaningless. Does it make sense to approach the wonder of life in such a clinical manner?

The joy of life lies in embracing whatever comes our way, in embracing each moment as it presents itself. I concluded that for life to be fulfilling, one does not need a purpose; in fact, one should not have a purpose. The idea of purpose stifles the spontaneity of life.

A person struggling to find direction may begin by asking, *"What is the purpose of this life?"* That enquiry may offer insights to some.

But what if you do not wish to do anything? What if you refuse to be driven by purpose? Then, without a doubt, this discussion is irrelevant to you!

The truest answer arises when we realize, *"I do not have or need a purpose."* Yes, it sounds counterintuitive or even contradictory. But within this contradiction lies its mystery, within its mystery lies its wonder, and within its wonder lies its joy.

By focusing our attention on a fixed goal or destination, do we not miss the joy of the journey?

This means accepting whatever comes our way. If we do not accept what comes, then we are simply going through motions to reach a goal. How routine and mundane we make life! In greeting everything that comes, we find harmony. Life becomes about welcoming and embracing each moment.

Life becomes a discovery. Life becomes the journey, not the destination. Life becomes the act, not the goal. Life becomes a symphony of nature.

The next obvious question may be, *"How do I know what to do at any point in time?"* What determines my next step?

At any moment, we are in a particular state, defined by our current state of mind. Left to itself, the current state of mind leads us to the next step based on the circumstances. The state we are in is the potential for the next moment. Submitting or surrendering fully to each moment will naturally guide us to the next step or action. This moment holds the answer to the next, and surrendering to it earnestly provides that answer.

With this approach, there is no question of working to a plan. There is no concern for time. There is no anxiety.

All I have to do is take the next step. Anyway, I can only take one step at a time. Having taken one step, that state then shows me the next, and so on. Eternity seems encapsulated in the moment. Time becomes irrelevant. Isn't time, after all, a relative notion? Why worry about time in the context of life and living?

Some say, *"This day, this moment, is all you have."* But what is a *moment* but a mere notion? What is my lifetime in the context of eternity?

Should I let my living be dictated by a ticking clock or a calendar on the wall?

Let each moment present itself with all its splendour, glory, and mystery. Let this moment take me through the present situation. Let this moment be both the cause and the secret of the next. Let this experience be like a cloud drifting away to reveal the full moon. In this moment, I dissolve the very idea of *"purpose."*

Not thinking of a purpose doesn't mean I am surrendering to destiny. I am simply allowing the harmony of nature to unfold, unhindered by my intentions. Is everything not part of nature's higher equilibrium?

In conclusion, let the following thoughts be my guiding light:

Let every moment illuminate the journey,

Let me submit myself, without expectation or anxiety, to nature's laws,

Let me welcome and embrace each moment,

Let me live each moment fully and with all my heart,

Let me not look back or regret the last step.

For in this mystery and splendour lies the beauty of life, the harmony of nature, and the fulfilment of my very being, my existence, my life.

Life itself is the *meaning and purpose* of nature; I do not need to have one.

— • ● • —

Re-examine Your Stance Regarding Gender

Spiritual pursuit is an inward journey culminating in the inmost core of our being. Specifically, it is the pursuit of realizing our true identity, the Self.

One point is beyond doubt: spirituality does not concern itself with the body. Any difference between genders exists only at the level of the body.

The mind is the seat of all our experiences, meaning all our experiences occur in the mind. When it comes to gender, we know from experience that there is no difference in the nature of experiences. There is no distinction between genders at the level of the mind, regarding emotions, feelings, and qualities. Happiness, sorrow, fear, pain, greed, and jealousy are also the same across all genders.

The *Bhagavad Gita* states that the mind is subtler than the senses; intelligence is subtler than the mind; and the Self is subtler than both. From the perspective of intelligence, there is also no difference. In the context of the Self, which is subtler than both mind and intelligence, where is the question of any difference between genders?

Remember, in all pursuits—whether in religion or spirituality—the mind and intelligence are the only instruments for understanding, introspection, austerity, rituals, devotion, meditation, etc. Where, then, is there room for discrimination based on gender?

Some may argue that there are distinctions between genders in terms of mind and intelligence. Even if this were so, we must remember that spirituality is about realizing Consciousness (the Self), which transcends both mind and intelligence—and the Self itself is beyond gender.

Any discrimination based on gender calls for serious introspection and correction.

Why say "This is Scientific" in the Context of Spirituality?

"Science and spirituality," "spirituality and management," and similar topics have become popular subjects for debate, discussion, and discourse. But why should we bring these two words together?

Why use terms like "and" or "vs." to start the conversation? The term "scientific" is often considered superior by many, and I have often wondered why.

At one level, both science and spirituality are knowledge pursuits. Both have attempted to explain and/or answer questions about human life and existence. Science and its various branches aim to explain the external phenomena of this universe, while spirituality relates to the inner realm of human experience.

Science is applicable universally, providing consistent explanations for phenomena across all human beings in the universe. Spirituality, however, is intensely personal. Each individual may hold their own understanding of spirituality and feel its validity without needing external validation.

Spirituality seeks to answer fundamental questions about human existence, rather than those related to matter or external forces. It aims to explore and explain the path to happiness and freedom for the individual. While science has recently begun exploring the brain areas associated with pleasure and happiness, this does not equate to a comprehensive understanding of spiritual experience.

In science, humans are the observers (or experimenters), and external phenomena are the "observed" and the subject of investigation. In spirituality, however, the individual seeks to realize their own true nature. As one delves deeper into spirituality, the observer and the observed become one.

Today, science attempts to study brain activity related to happiness, pain, peace, meditation, and so on, but this does not mean that science addresses the subtler aspects of spirituality. People need to reexamine statements like "science has proof that meditation works."

While reason and logic can play an essential role in understanding and introspection in the realm of spiritual pursuit, they ultimately fall short in realizing the Self. The Self is subtler than the mind and intelligence and transcends them. Meditation, in this context, is a profoundly subtle process in which the meditator, the object of meditation, and the process itself become one.

The next time you say, "I am scientific" when exploring the subject of the Self, pause to reflect on your stance.

Conversations of a Rose and the Eternal Honeybee

I hear your humming presence,

But I don't feel your tender heart.

Do stay a little longer, my dear,

And talk to me before you depart.

You see so many blossoms here,

Yet you seek me out to drink.

You gather sweet nectar from me

But vanish before I can even blink.

I dream of the yonder meadows,

Fields, brooks, and ponds of lilies.

Be my eyes as a flight of fancy

So, I can put my heart at ease.

Describe the gardens you see,

And the flowers you often kiss.

For me to picture in my mind
All those delights I always miss.

You may be drawn by my scent here,
Or enchanted by my red and glee.
Will you not stay a little longer,
And honour my humble plea?

I am not in the best of my colours
With too many folds in my skin.
Stay, and do not leave me, honey!
And tell me where all you have been.

In the warm embrace of my petals
I shall give all the honey I can shed.
Not sure if there will be a morrow
For I may slip into this flowery bed.

Exploring the Interconnectedness of All

The term "Universal Self" or "Universal Consciousness" is often used in discussions on spirituality. Let us stay with the word "universal" for now. I continue to think about this word, and every time it brings up wonderful and interesting ideas.

In the early days of this journey, the question that occupied my imagination was: "What does it mean in a practical sense?" The word "universal" in the context of spirituality seems to suggest "all-pervasiveness." Then it came to mind that the idea of "all-pervasiveness" is also very abstract. In the physical realm or the phenomenal universe, how do we comprehend something that is all-pervading? What is the nature of "that" which is present everywhere at the same time? How do we grasp such an idea?

Is there an alternative to this concept, instead of seeing something as being present everywhere at the same time? A physical object with such a property is inconceivable. How do we then resolve this deadlock?

Then I thought, why not explore the idea of "connectedness" or "interconnectedness" instead of "universality"?

'Connection' in a physical sense is easy to understand. For example, the beads are connected by a thread to make a garland. And now, there is a new kind of connection—wireless. How do we comprehend subtler aspects of connection?

What is connectedness in the context of human beings?

1. **Physical Level:** While Sanatana Dharma discusses the grossness in terms of the five elements (earth, water, fire, air, ether), if we examine it in terms of chemistry, we have hydrogen, helium, oxygen, carbon, and nitrogen in abundance in the Milky Way galaxy. At the level of the human body, we have oxygen, carbon, hydrogen, nitrogen. We are all made of the same elements.

2. **Mind Level:** At the subtle level of the mind too, we are all the same—we experience the same feelings, emotions, fears, etc. We can relate to all human experiences. So, at the level of the mind, we share the same substratum, providing a common frame of reference for our feelings and emotions.

3. **Intelligence Level:** Here too, humans share the same foundation. The functions, responses, and operations of intelligence are the same across individuals. Collaboration

between humans is possible because of this common substratum of intelligence that we all possess.

4. **Environment:** We share the same environment. We need the same conditions for a healthy life. Take people from opposite corners of the globe—they require the same conditions to survive, physically and otherwise.

5. **Deeper Questions:** We, as humans, share the same questions regarding life and our existence. How are we born? What is the purpose of this life? Why am I born? What is death? What happens to me after I die? What makes me happy? Why do I avoid grief? Is there a creator of this universe and everything in it? The deeper mysteries of life and death bind us as human beings.

6. **Our Needs:** Another important aspect common to all humans is 'our needs'. We all seek the same things in life— food, clothing, shelter, wealth, security, peace, happiness, and so on. At both the physical and mental levels, our needs are the same.

7. **Pain and Suffering:** When we hear of someone's grief, our hearts go out to them. We naturally reach out. If something tragic happens to someone unknown to us, we cannot set it aside without feeling for them. Why does this happen? It is because of a connectedness we share at the level of pain and suffering. The challenges we face are common to all.

Now, having examined these seven levels that bind us as humans, is there any doubt regarding our connectedness? This deep connectedness seems to indicate one thing—the "common substratum" of us all is the same.

What is this common substratum? Thus has the term "universal" entered the spiritual discourse. Some may use terms like "universal consciousness" or "universal mind." The word "universal" simply points to the pervasiveness of THAT SUBSTRATUM.

Once we see life in this holistic way, it is easy to see where the path to welfare or well-being lies.

My well-being lies in the well-being of all. My happiness lies in the happiness of all. My fearlessness lies in the fearlessness of all. I cannot see myself as a separate, individual human being. My existence, my being, is inextricably tied to the existence and being of all.

Treat Disturbing Thoughts Like a Knock at the Door

Occasionally, a disturbing thought (or thoughts) springs up in the mind. This thought may cause anxiety, guilt, fear, hatred, etc., and we are disturbed by it. Sometimes, this thought that caused a disturbance does not leave as easily as it came. However much we try to draw our attention to something else, it refuses to go away.

Sometimes, we momentarily distract ourselves with other thoughts or actions. But that thought often comes back, sometimes with greater intensity. What is the solution?

Reflect on the following situation: you are relaxing at home. There is a knock on the door. You look through the peephole and find that the person at the door is someone you do not like very much. In that instant, you pause and are no longer relaxed. You think, "Why is he here? I did not invite him. What does he want? My quiet day is ruined." Many thoughts run through your mind. After a brief hesitation, you finally open the door.

Now think about what just happened.

That hesitation at the door and resistance to open it reinforces your dislike. It is the resistance that causes trouble. It reinforces that "dislike for that person," and it stays in your mind, even if it recedes to the background for the time being. There are times you remember such a visit from an "unwelcome" guest even after many years. Why?

If only we were to open the door without hesitation, the situation might have been different. Remember, anyone who comes, comes only to go. He is not coming to live with you or to evict you from your home. Any guest comes only to leave.

If you had opened the door without resistance in your mind, this encounter might have ended with a cup of tea with the guest. And soon you would have forgotten about it. But because you hesitated and resisted, you gave that instance almost a permanent place in your mind.

In the same manner, any thought comes only to vanish. Do not pay too much attention to any thought. Allow them to come and go as they please. You did not invite them; they still came. And without your indulgence or permission, they will simply leave. Any resistance causes them to stay on and cement their place in your mind.

—◆—

Re-examine the Statement "I am Spiritual, not Religious"

I often hear people say, "I am spiritual, not religious." It is usually said, in a defensive manner, by those who do not wish to subscribe to conventional religion.

Each person says this based on their understanding of what "spiritual" and "religious" mean. But perhaps, these terms are not as binary as they appear.

Religion is not just about "God," nor is there a single way to interpret the notion of "God."

It might be helpful to start by enquiring, "What is religion?" and "What is spirituality?" without trying to pick one as more convenient or favourable. This is not meant as criticism of the statement itself but as a prompt for deeper reflection.

Some may avoid rituals, temples, or pilgrimages and assume that this makes them "spiritual" rather than "religious." And that's perfectly fine—everyone is entitled to their own perspective. However, this distinction may sometimes arise from a misconception about what each of these terms entail.

Spirituality is not a single philosophy with a uniform approach across the world. In Hinduism, spirituality is grounded in the Upanishads. Even Vedanta (the central philosophy of the Upanishads) is not one monolithic school but includes various philosophies and their interpretations.

Remember, religion in Hinduism is rooted in the Vedas, and the spiritual texts are extensions of these.

Both religion and spirituality engage with the mind. They each have their practices and "rituals," though the forms may differ. Saying "I am spiritual, not religious" simply because one avoids traditional rituals may miss the point, as religion encompasses far more than just rituals, and spirituality is not entirely free from them either.

Every spiritual or religious path requires faith—faith in an underlying philosophy, faith in the texts, and faith in the pursuit itself. Spirituality, especially in Hinduism, often relies on faith in the wisdom of the Upanishads, which are part of the Vedas.

And importantly, both religion and spirituality ultimately aim to realize a Supreme, even if their definitions of this Supreme differ.

Sometimes, those who identify with the spiritual pursuit look upon religion as something inferior to spirituality. They may feel that spirituality is more elevated or refined, perhaps dismissing religion as too "basic" or ritualistic.

However, dismissing religion in favour of spirituality may not bring clarity, as unresolved questions about religious practices can still linger. In Hinduism, the Upanishads are considered the essence of the Vedas, embodying the culminating wisdom of these texts, and bridging both religious and spiritual pursuits.

In re-examining this statement, perhaps we can see that the "spiritual vs. religious" dichotomy does not fully capture the richness and diversity of either path.

------ ● ------

Free Will vs Destiny—The Eternal Debate

This is probably one of the favourite topics in spirituality and religion. Sooner or later, everyone arrives at the question, "Do I have free will?"

Somehow, I have never been bothered by this question. I do not claim to be in some higher state of evolution—I just do not think about it, that is all. Until recently, I had not formed an opinion on it. But, prompted by some questions presented to me, I began thinking about this subject.

What is free will, literally? It is free and independent choice in any situation on the part of the individual, unaffected by external forces or divine intervention.

The opposite view is that everything is pre-ordained or pre-determined, so that humans have no control over situations—a 'fatalistic' view.

Let us now examine the idea of free will closely.

We human beings are an *interdependent* lot. Can I simply will something and expect that it will happen? I am not alone in this world. Even if there were only two human beings in the whole universe, it is unreasonable to expect that what 'I' will, will always happen. (If two people with free will desire the same thing, in whose favour will the result be?) So, absolute free will is simply not possible! This is beyond doubt or debate.

This means there is only limited free will, which implies I do have a role to play in my life.

While I do not have absolute free will to determine outcomes, I do have free choice in every situation. The outcome of my choice, however, may not be in my control. The human being is, in fact, blessed with the freedom to make choices.

If we did not have "limited" free will, human life would become meaningless. It is precisely this element of choice that makes life beautiful, wonderful, intriguing, challenging, and adventurous.

Without limited free will, we would simply sit in one place and say, "Whatever is supposed to happen will happen, so why should I do anything?"

If limited free will were impossible, the entire pursuit of spirituality would be negated, and self-transformation toward the goal of "freedom" would be fictional.

Scriptures are very clear on the importance of self-effort. They stress that it is up to each human being to desire freedom, and only self-effort can achieve it. In fact, texts like the *Yoga-Vasistha* dismiss the notion of fate, encouraging seekers to rely on self-effort in attaining their spiritual goals.

A common example is that of a cow tied to a tree with a long rope. The rope gives the cow freedom to graze within a limited area around the tree, defined by the length of the rope. The cow is free within this circle, where the radius is the length of the rope.

However, sometimes the cow, out of ignorance, circles around the tree, shortening the rope's length. Over time, it feels it has no freedom to move, a limitation that is self-imposed. But the maximum distance it can reach is still defined by the full length of the rope.

Similarly, we humans often think we have no freedom (free will), due to our ignorance. We may never fully understand the length of the "rope"—yet it is actually quite long. However, we often operate within a very small radius. The only difference is that the rope is created by our own mind.

Does this imply something called 'limited destiny'? Now, we are getting trapped in play of words and their meanings.

But one thing we do know for sure—nature's laws are fixed. There is no surprise from nature.

Can we not simply say that life is an unending flow of events and situations—some pleasant, some unpleasant, some favourable, some unfavourable? If something goes against us, it simply means the flow went that way. That is all. Why say it was "pre-ordained" to go that way?

——•—◆—•——

Let us Not Misunderstand the Idea of Knowing in "Knowledge Pursuit"

From childhood, we hear ideas like, "You have to learn," "You must know," "Only if you know, you can progress in life," and "Only if you know, you will be worth something."

363

Thus, we grow up believing, "I must know everything" and "I will become something worthwhile only by knowing everything."

These messages fuel a lifelong drive to know more and learn more, and we begin to feel that we lack something simply because "we don't know." This feeling breeds insecurity, and the desire to know more becomes an endless pursuit.

We want to know all that happens in the world, everything about people we know, and even about people we don't. The fear of not knowing anything, no matter how trivial, drives us.

Ignorance is treated like a sin, knowledge like virtue, and the fear of being left out, of dying without knowing certain things, looms large. We are afraid of being labelled "ig-KNOW-rant."

Insecurity creeps in, accompanied by fear—the fear of not knowing what a friend or colleague knows, the fear of missing out on a training program. We constantly feel the need to know: if we hear something happened, we need to know what it was; if two people meet, we want to know what they spoke about; if there is an event, we have to know the details. We want to know everything about anything we hear, see, or encounter.

If someone tells us something, we not only want to know the information but also how they came to know it, and maybe even what they do not know. If something is shared with us, we wonder why we didn't know it first. And often, if we hear something new, we resist admitting that we didn't know it before.

We create our own interpretation of knowing, feeling confident that once we "know," we truly understand. This gives rise to an arrogance of knowledge—an impulse to let others know that we know, and sometimes even to make sure to let others know that they know less.

There is a universal mantra that "knowledge is power." We feel we must know more than others, must constantly engage in knowing more, and must assess others by what they know. We seek those who seem to know more and, if we believe they "know a lot", we put them on a pedestal.

Schooling is about knowing more. College continues this cycle. Even at the workplace, "knowing more" is often the only driver. When our memory fails to support this, we grow anxious.

Knowledge and knowing, it seems, have become the greatest bondage in the world.

But this entire drama of knowing, of endlessly pursuing knowledge, must eventually end in silence.

Even in the spiritual path, referred to as "knowledge pursuit", it is often all about "to know." But is that the true purpose? Seeking the title of "Knower" was never meant to be the aim of spiritual pursuit.

Yes, learning is valuable, and knowing is important. But let us not stretch this obsession. What will you truly gain from knowing so much? Do not spend so much time and energy acquiring knowledge, that you forget to live your life in full.

------ • ● • ------

A Closer Look at Purushartha and Ashrama in Conjunction

Sanatana Dharma (Hinduism) describes the four-fold objectives of human pursuit, known as *purushartha*. These are *dharma, artha, kaama,* and *moksha*. While leading a life based on *dharma,* one acquires the necessary wealth and resources (*artha*), fulfils svarious desires for enjoyment (*kaama*), and turns attention to the goal of attaining liberation (*moksha*).

It is important to note that the objective of human life is four-fold, not four separate aims. All these four pursuits run in parallel. Every human being requires resources to live and the experiences those resources provide. Different people may focus on these pursuits in varying degrees. The pursuit of resources and enjoyments must be anchored in *dharma* and *moksha*.

While dharma ensures that our pursuits and life itself are based on values, *moksha* anchors us in a higher dimension. *Moksha* is freedom from dependence on worldly objects for happiness, as well as freedom from suffering. Dharma fosters harmony in social life, while *moksha* offers the vision to elevate our lives by realizing our true nature, ultimately freeing us from all bondages that arise in worldly existence. Without dharma and *moksha*, our lives would resemble those of animals. Dharma provides the moral and ethical compass, while *moksha* provides the spiritual compass. Thus, *purushartha* offers a holistic view to living.

Ashrama defines the stages of human life. The four stages of human life are *brahmacharya*, *gaarhasthya*, *vanaprastha*, and *sannyasa*. *Brahmacharya* refers to the stage of being a student (accompanied by chastity). *Gaarhasthya* is the stage of being a householder, engaged in the pursuit of *artha* and *kaama*, managing a family. *Vanaprastha* marks the commencement of disengagement from household life, and *sannyasa* signifies the renunciation of worldly possessions.

Regardless of the life stage or *ashrama*, the four-fold *purushartha* remains functional. Even one who has "renounced" everything still requires minimal resources to live.

Many consider *vanaprastha* and *sannyasa* optional. Reflect on this once more—they are not merely external attainments. Each human being must gradually slow down in terms of acquisitions, possessions, professions, enjoyments, desires, and aspirations. This slowing down is facilitated by the mindset of *vanaprastha*. Ultimately, complete renunciation of attachment to all things is essential for the higher pursuit of *moksha*. Freedom from attachment to worldly objects is crucial, and *sannyasa* represents this renunciation at the mental level.

This framework of four *purusharthas* and four *ashramas* is harmoniously interlinked.

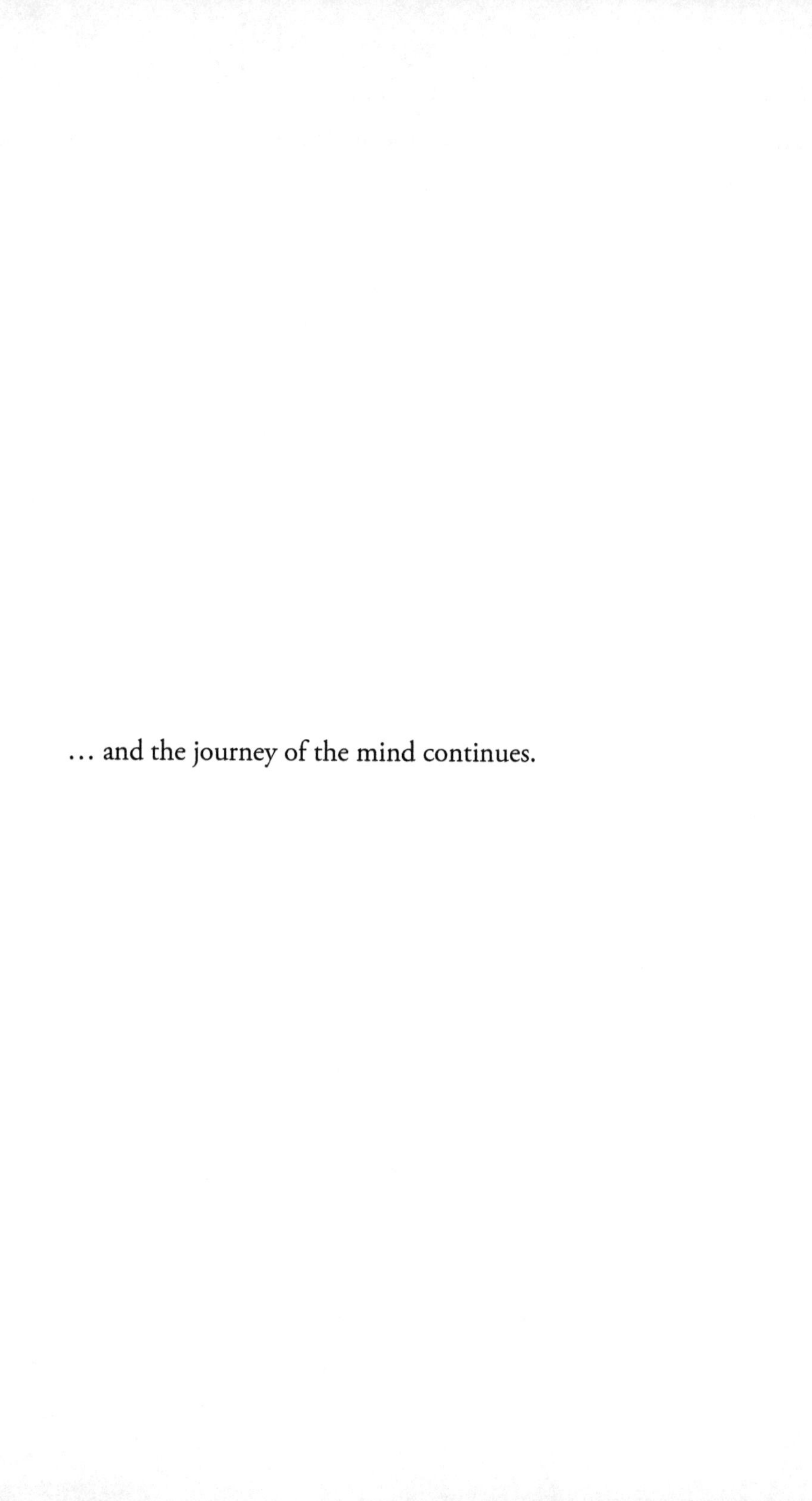

… and the journey of the mind continues.

Other Books by the Author

1. **The Voice of Advaita Vedanta: Insights into Non-Duality**, Published by Atlantic Publishers & Distributors, 2024

2. **Bhaja Govindam—Essence of Vedanta for Peace and Happiness**, Published by Notion Press, 2021

3. **Garland of Pearls of Wisdom**—A commentary on Prashnottara-ratna-maalika by Adi Shankaracharya, Published by Notion Press, 2022

4. **Vishnusahasranama Stotram**—A translation of the commentary on the Thousand Names of Lord Vishnu by Adi Shankaracharya, Published by Chaukhamba Sanskrit Pratishthan, 2021

5. **Good Values, Great Business**, co-authored along with T.D. Chandrasekhar, Published by SAGE Publications India Pvt Ltd., 2019